PENGUIN BOOKS
OTP PLEASE!

Vandana Vasudevan has written extensively for mainstream newspapers and has been a columnist for several years for *Mint* and *DNA*. She studied in the Indian Institute of Management Ahmedabad, and has worked in the corporate sector for many years. She shifted career tracks and became a development sector professional, consulting for various national and international organizations after obtaining a PhD in urban development from the University of Grenoble, France. Besides *OTP Please!*, she is also the author of *Urban Villager: Life in an Indian Satellite Town* and *Tough Customer*.

Despite these serious pursuits, she is a fun person, paranoid of being boring and hence always strives to be interesting and entertaining.

OTP Please!

Online Buyers, Sellers and Gig Workers in South Asia

VANDANA VASUDEVAN

PENGUIN BOOKS

An imprint of Penguin Random House

PENGUIN BOOKS

Penguin Books is an imprint of the Penguin Random House group of companies whose addresses can be found at global.penguinrandomhouse.com

Published by Penguin Random House India Pvt. Ltd
4th Floor, Capital Tower 1, MG Road,
Gurugram 122 002, Haryana, India

First published in Penguin Books by Penguin Random House India 2025

ISBN 9780143463399

Typeset in Minion Pro by Manipal Technologies Limited, Manipal
Printed at Replika Press Pvt. Ltd, India

www.penguin.co.in

To all the workers,
online buyers and sellers who shared their
experiences with generosity, warmth and trust

CONTENTS

WHY AND HOW I WROTE
THIS BOOK

Through the pandemic years, cooped up at home like the rest of the world, I spent much time on my balcony. We had moved to Hyderabad in early 2020, weeks before the first lockdown, and set up home in a residential gated community, which, in the manner of all such dwellings in India, was enclosed in its own world and fortified against the outside by a posse of security guards. There wasn't much happening within the community during those Covid years. Those who would have gone to office and school were on Zoom, the basketball courts were empty and the children's play area was silent. But there was always a lot of activity at the main gate, where guards filtered the incoming traffic. I noticed that most vehicles crowding the gate were not cars, but two-wheelers driven by young men in different-coloured T-shirts, each with a big box balanced on the rear seat, usually of the same hue as their T-shirt. They were delivery men, yes, always men, zipping in and out of the complex, supplying a biryani to someone in one tower, dropping off a dress to another or bread and milk elsewhere. They seemed always to be coming or going, whether early morning or midnight.

I was curious to know who these worker ants of the e-commerce explosion were. What were they doing before people started buying online, and what did they feel about this new livelihood that did not exist even a few years ago? Did they feel connected to the glamour of the startup industry they belonged to? What were their lives like? How did they view their future? Three years later, as I write this in mid-2024, traffic at the main gate has only increased as e-commerce has become endemic to daily life in urban India.

To embark on the project, I read a few newspaper articles about 'gig workers', as they are called. The word 'gig' is an American term coined in the 1920s by jazz musicians who carried their instruments with them and performed at different bars and cafes whenever they were hired. It came to be used for jobs that lasted for a short time and for which payment was made on a piecemeal basis.

I started hanging around in my complex and speaking to some delivery workers, waving them down for a chat before they zipped out of the gates. I heard their stories; some were content, many were unhappy. A prominent union leader in Hyderabad who had been raising his voice about the exploitation of Ola-Uber drivers told me about activists in Delhi, who in turn pointed me to Jaipur because Rajasthan had become the first state to enact legislation for the protection and welfare of platform-based gig workers in July 2023.[1] In the same month, I went to Kerala to understand how this new form of work manifested in a left-oriented state that is hyper-aware of worker rights. In September 2023, Janpahal, an NGO in Delhi representing informal workers, wanted to survey gig workers to understand their lives and issues. I partnered with them as the researcher and author of the final report, which was titled 'The Rights Survey'.[2] Analysing the data over those few months gave me a ringside view of gig work because the survey touched over 5000 workers from more than thirty cities nationwide.

As a picture of workers' roles in the e-commerce ecosystem began to form in my mind, I felt the story was incomplete. Workers didn't exist in a vacuum. They were pressed into service because customers wanted stuff. And wanted it fast, at their doorstep. Who were these customers who were compulsively buying online? What were their motivations for eating fried chicken at odd hours? Why did they avoid going to the neighbourhood *kirana* store to buy toothpaste? Were there hidden costs to the possibility of instant gratification and ease of living? How did 'Let's Swiggy it' or 'Dunzo it' become part of their vocabulary?

At the other end were the sellers of goods—restaurants and online retailers. Were local restaurants, whose *chotus* used to deliver earlier to nearby houses, happier with online delivery? How were they dealing with the new boss in their life—the food delivery app represented by the gig worker waiting impatiently to pick up the order? How was business for a small-time seller of pickles buried on page 50 of the Amazon search page for 'pickles'?

Tying all these moving parts together in a constrictor knot—the most intricate knot to untie—was the app, or the 'platform' as it is called, with its formidable tech, inscrutable algorithm, gigantic repository of data and powerful hold on all the other stakeholders.

As a development-sector researcher, I know that South Asia is studied as a single unit in many contexts, given the shared colonial history and sociocultural similarities leading to common development challenges. So, I read media reports to understand how the e-commerce narrative was unfolding in the Indian subcontinent. The beginnings of a new economic era driven by digital development were already being felt across the South Asian region, though the levels of business maturity and market size differed in each country. I thought it might be both relevant and exciting to widen the ambit and include neighbouring countries in my study. Through the marvel of WhatsApp and LinkedIn, connections resembling a neural network were formed, and I managed to reach the people I wanted to speak to in Pakistan, Bangladesh, Sri Lanka and Nepal. I also visited the last two countries for a first-hand glimpse of technology's impact on daily urban life. Though in Pakistan, Nepal, Bangladesh and Sri Lanka, app-based customers are restricted to the thin middle-class segment in the metros, it is dynamic, and consumers' zeal for using them is comparable to that of their Indian counterparts. For example, online food delivery in Nepal is a vibrant space with more platforms than India—Food Mandu, Bhojdeals and BhokLagyo, to name some of the prominent ones. Foodpanda functions in all four main cities in Pakistan—Lahore, Karachi, Islamabad and Peshawar. In Bangladesh, Foodpanda competes with the home-grown platform Pathao, which is a prominent player in Nepal as well.

After a year-long investigation and hearing hundreds of voices across the region, it is apparent that a socio-economic shift is underway in how we buy, eat, move, work and sell owing to technological advancements. The experiences of consumers, workers and sellers in different countries were so similar that categorizing them country-wise did not make sense. Their narratives have hence been seamlessly woven together across borders.

Although a varied bouquet of apps governs modern life, here I have focused on online retail, food delivery, quick commerce (rapid delivery of household goods bought online), transport or ride-hailing (cabs, autos and motorbikes) and domestic services (beautician, carpenter, etc.) as these are the most popular in daily life, used by people of various demographics and social classes.

I spent many days thinking about the structure and sequencing of this book. Initially, I wanted to divide it into three sections—Customers, Workers and Sellers—and discuss the role of the technology platform within these. But I was uncomfortable with that compartmentalization once I fleshed out the whole tale. What was starkly visible was that specific overarching themes ran through all the sections. Take, for example, the feeling of anxiety. An Ola driver becomes anxious when he realizes the passenger in the rear seat is drunk, but likewise, a woman panics when the Uber driver takes a route not shown on the map. A homemaker in Lahore is relieved that Foodpanda delivers groceries to her doorstep, saving her the trouble of donning a burqa and going to the grocery shop. At the same time, a beautician in Hyderabad, India, working for Urban Company, appreciates the flexible timings that gig work offers, allowing her to take a siesta in the afternoons if she wants. Both experience a sense of freedom despite their different contexts.

The book is, therefore, organized according to the emotions and experiences that are overwhelmingly common to all the actors in the app-based economy of the region. These are:

1. Pleasure
2. Guilt
3. Gratitude
4. Anger
5. Freedom
6. Oppression
7. Anxiety
8. Isolation
9. Courage

By connecting diverse stories and perspectives, I have attempted to explore how these emotions manifest across the different actors on this stage. Each emotion is covered in a separate chapter, concluding with a discussion on how policy, tech companies and we as customers can help balance privilege, power and precarity within this new world that we inhabit.

At the end is an appendix that provides a numerical overview of the digital economy by giving the value of the market, and the number of customers and workers in each country.

However, this is an evolving and inchoate industry, so this story is still taking shape. Sort of like saying, '*Picture abhi baaki hai, mere dost.*' As regulators become more alert about the lacunae in the way digital platforms do business, the platforms, on their part, make course corrections. For example, Swiggy has introduced a seal of hygiene for restaurants it partners with. After a rap on the knuckles by the National Human Rights Commission for labour rights violations in Amazon's Manesar warehouse, the company admitted to these lapses and attempted to take some conciliatory steps. India's fast-growing quick commerce market is heating up as Amazon plans to step in with Tez and join competitors like Zomato's Blinkit, Swiggy Instamart, Zepto and BigBasket. Apart from groceries, in December 2024, Blinkit Bistro and Zepto Café are also promising ten-minute food deliveries! When I was writing about the innovative digital businesses of Bangladesh, there was no political upheaval there. In August 2024, the country descended into chaos and violence in the wake of a regime change. I now wonder if Tania in Dhaka, who wore her hair short and rode a motorbike while working for an all-women transport service, will continue to be the same person amidst the prospect of greater radicalization of Bangladeshi state and society.[3] Sri Lanka elected a new government into power, headed by a left-leaning president. These changes will doubtless affect the growth of new economy businesses, worker rights and disposable income of customers in ways that will only be evident with time.

Despite the dynamic nature of the subject, what seems certain is that we are at a watershed moment in modern human history. Behind the simple acts of ordering food or booking a cab is a slow transformation of how we live, work, buy and sell. The manner in which this tech-driven change is unfolding, in a part of the world that is still largely poor and traditional, makes it extremely interesting to observe, write and, hopefully, read. It is this transition that I aim to capture in this book.

SETTING, CAST AND STORYLINE

The Setting

Online Retail

Autumn in India is the festive season that begins with Ganesh Chaturthi in early September, continues to the nine days of Navaratri usually in October and culminates in Diwali three weeks later. However, in recent years, a new entrant has upstaged these traditional festivals and occupied a prime position in the hearts of the largest population in the world. It is called the Great Indian Festival (GIF), a massive sale conducted during this time by Amazon, the emperor of e-commerce. A wry joke on social media is that this was the only festival that united a culturally diverse country like India. The humour is rooted in some astonishing facts. In 2023, Amazon India clocked a record 1.1 billion customer visits to its website during the GIF.[1] Packages were transported to every pin code in the country, from the remote mountains of Leh to the district of Champhai near the Myanmar-India border to Agatti Island in the Lakshadweep archipelago.[2] Amazon bragged that a customer bought one of its devices, such as an Alexa-enabled smart speaker or a Kindle e-reader, every ten seconds during the GIF.[3] In 2022, Amazon declared on its website: 'The total number of pens bought this festive season could write for enough distance to cover two round-trip journeys to the moon.'[4]

After the liberalization of the Indian economy in the 1990s, economists were fond of declaring, 'Consumerism is the new God.' Online consumerism is now more than that. It is the Supreme Being of the entire multiverse to whom customers helplessly genuflect. Indians are expected to continue buying online at the same pace or even faster, making the Indian consumer internet economy worth one trillion US dollars (that's one and twelve zeros) by 2030.[5]

While Amazon and Walmart-owned Flipkart rule India, Pakistan, Nepal, Bangladesh and Sri Lanka have an equivalent in Daraz. Started in 2012 in Karachi, Pakistan, Daraz has a fascinating history. The company's founder is a Swede, Bjarke Mikkelsen, who served as its CEO for a decade until January 2024, overseeing its acquisition by Alibaba Group in 2018. Though it began in online retail fashion, it is now an e-commerce, logistics and payment infrastructure giant selling upwards of 10 million products and making around 2 million deliveries every month in all the countries it operates in.[6]

Food Delivery

The visual of numerous food delivery workers racing through city streets, frenetically delivering food packets, is ironic in a region that has historically witnessed some of the worst famines in the world.

Today, food, it appears, is available in abundance, at least in the urban areas of South Asia—from inexpensive, industrially produced packaged products and street food to innovative gourmet restaurants that leave visitors from the West astonished.

Riding on this cornucopia is online food delivery, which has made food accessible and commonplace. Easy availability increased disposable incomes, and an intrepid exploration of new flavours are together driving rapid growth of online food delivery.

Online food delivery is ubiquitous even on regular days, but on New Year's Eve and during sporting events such as the Cricket World Cup, the orders reach dizzying levels with astonishing amounts spent on a single day.

'We've delivered almost as many orders on New Year's Eve 2023 as on NYE 2015, 2016, 2017, 2018, 2019, 2020 combined. Excited about the future!' exulted Zomato's founder Deepinder Goyal.[7]

During the India–Pakistan Asia Cup clash in Sri Lanka's Kandy in September 2023, a Bengaluru resident ordered sixty-two biryanis on Swiggy, prompting the pleasantly bewildered company to write on X (formerly Twitter), 'Someone from Bengaluru just ordered 62 units of biryanis?? Who are you? Where exactly are you? Are you hosting a #INDvsPAK match watch party?? Can I come?'[8]

On New Year's Eve 2025, Swiggy Instamart recorded its heftiest order of Rs 70,325 from a user in central Goa. Swiggy claimed that its delivery partners collectively travelled 6,519,841 kilometres—8x the distance to and from Earth to the Moon.[9]

When I began researching the South Asian digital economy for this book in mid-2023, there was nothing significant in Bhutan. But since consumer apps proliferate like bacteria in a nutrient-rich environment, by the time I finished a year later, Bhutan had a clutch of food delivery apps like ZheyGo, MyChharo and Food Chow.

Quick Commerce

In the Mahabharata, when the Pandavas lived in exile in the forest, their wife Draupadi ensured sufficient food for the family and the sages, who often accompanied them, using a divine vessel called the *akshayapatra*. Food placed in this would multiply to ensure everyone ate well, but only until Draupadi, who customarily would be the last one to eat, finished her meal. On one occasion, Sage Durvasa, known for his fiery temper, came to their forest camp after Draupadi had finished eating and the vessel could no longer work its magic. Draupadi panicked like the women of the house still do when unexpected guests arrive. She had run out of groceries, and there was nothing to cook with. Only divine intervention from Lord Krishna could solve her predicament.

Several thousand years later, people have digital intervention in the form of quick commerce. Groceries are delivered to your doorstep minutes after you have pressed a few keys on your phone. Three-fourths of the items bought online by Indian consumers are groceries.[10] Of that, 13 per cent are bought on quick commerce apps such as BlinkIt, Zepto and Swiggy Instamart, where speedy delivery is the core of the app's promise. Even a single bunch of coriander can be purchased for a delivery charge. In the early days of Blinkit, it appeared as though someone was eavesdropping on private conversations. Barely would one have placed the order that the delivery boy would appear at the gate asking to be let in.

Swiggy initially thought Instamart customers were those under thirty-five,[11] but they eventually found that their users cut across age groups. It included those who could not head to a supermarket or a corner grocery store because they didn't have the time, faced mobility issues or wanted to use that time to relax and unwind.

Ride-Hailing

In the summer of 2015, my family and I were preparing to leave Grenoble, a town in eastern France where we had been living for two years, and return to India. Around two weeks before our departure, we were having lunch with Mani, my husband's colleague, who was visiting from Delhi. We were dining al fresco at Place Grenette, a square in the city centre whose perimeter was lined with restaurants. The schools had closed in June, and the place was abuzz with summer revellers buying sorbets and children riding on the carousel.

'You know, we have Uber now in Delhi,' Mani informed us.

He excitedly described how, like in America, anyone could offer a ride and make a few bucks and enthusiastically exclaimed, 'The cars are great! You can even book a Mercedes!'

Our eyes shone. Indians were travelling the same way as someone in California was. How cool was that! All the more reason to return home.

Ride-hailing came to India when Ola began in 2010 and Uber arrived from San Francisco in 2013,[12] epitomising tech-based, futuristic transport. Careem, a category leader in Gulf countries, and Uber arrived in Pakistan in 2015. A fierce battle ensued in which Careem emerged as a clear leader and became synonymous with ride-hailing. In 2019, Uber acquired Careem worldwide. While both continued to operate as independent brands, Uber exited Pakistan's major cities in 2022 and encouraged users to transition to its subsidiary company, Careem.[13] However, a couple of years later, Careem has been pushed to third place by new entrants such as Yango and inDrive.[14]

Bangladesh's Pathao is also the leader in Nepal, while PickMe and Uber are the app-based cab services in Sri Lanka. inDrive is the newest provocateur to these names in India, Nepal and Pakistan. inDrive is an app developed in

2012 in Yakutsk, Siberia, but its unique feature of haggling for rates has seen it expand to forty-five countries.

The gradual inclusion of autos and bike taxis in the ride-hailing platform democratized the experience by expanding its reach and appeal to those who could not afford it when cabs were the only options.

Now, passengers span the gamut from urban youth needing a drop to college to a father from a rural area visiting his son in the city, who has never used an app. He calls his son and says, 'I am in depot number 12 in the bus station; please book the cab.' The cab is booked and tracked until it approaches the father, the OTP shared before signing off with, 'Baba, please get into the white car with the number XXXX, which stopped before you. Call me when you reach.' Some commute every day from the office to home on bikes and autos. Stay-at-home moms travel in off-peak hours for domestic errands. Groups of wedding guests going from the venue to the hotel several times hire a rental cab for eight hours. In South Asian cities notorious for their poor walkability and insufficient public transport, ride-hailing is the equivalent of standing up and getting counted despite frequent head-butting with regulators and drivers of traditional autos and taxis.

Home Services

Pakistan has Ghar Par, a platform that provides beauty services at home in five cities in the country and employs hundreds of women. 'Beauty is very much ingrained in our culture,' said co-founder Arooj Ismail, in an interview with the fashion magazine *Marie Claire* in 2020. 'Even if you look at the lowest socioeconomic class, they may get a face polisher done.'[15]

Next door in India, Urban Company aggregates beauticians, plumbers, carpenters, painters and cleaners. A few apps even send domestic maids as temporary fillers if a customer's help is on leave or a chef who will spawn within an hour if guests show up suddenly.

The Cast

The world of digital commerce consists of four stakeholders.

Customers: That's us, the online buyers armed with smartphones and addicted to convenience, enjoying a higher standard of living than what we grew up with. According to the World Bank, 73 per cent of the region's population was below forty in 2023.[16] They are 'digital natives', a mix of millennials (those born between 1981 and 1996), who were the first to experience the rise of the internet and mobile technology during their formative years and Gen Z (born between 1997 and 2012), who grew up with smartphones, social media and ubiquitous internet access as part of their everyday lives.

The platform: The technology provider whose app is the intermediary between buyer and seller (e.g. Amazon, Uber, Foodpanda, Pathao, etc.).

When Aishwarya Rai and Sushmita Sen won international beauty pageants in 1994, every teen wanted to jump into the fray, and soon enough, local-level pageants like Miss Dombivli and Miss Karnal came up. When Arundhati Roy won the Booker Prize in 1997 and Jhumpa Lahiri won the Pulitzer in 2000, everyone and her niece wrote a book. Now, everyone and their cat is either a startup founder or has a LinkedIn profile that reads: 'Helping build x platform'. Tech startups have become the zeitgeist of our age, proliferating since the second decade of this century. They have wreaked havoc on old transport, food and retail business models, to name a few. They are aggregators who are asset-light. Owning nothing, they make demand meet supply and charge everyone a commission. Tech has glamorized one of the oldest professions known to humankind—that of a *dalal* or a middleman.

India is on a startup high, aided by government policies and the active participation of venture capital firms. As of January 2025, there are over 1,57,000 startups in India, making it the third-largest startup ecosystem globally. Bangladesh has 2500 startups with innovative solutions, such as the popular online educational platform 10 Minute School.[17] Around 720 startups have been established in Pakistan since 2010, of which 67 per cent are still active.[18] Nepal's digital commerce ecosystem is constantly buzzing with new applications, especially in food and grocery delivery.

Two concurrent developments have helped us become the planet of the apps. First, smartphones have joined the list of needs rather than wants. In India, a billion people are expected to possess one by the time we enter the next decade. In 2014, 30 per cent of the population of South Asia was out of reach of a mobile network. Ten years later, only 8 per cent are.[19]

The second is that paying for anything has become effortless. In contemporary urban India, a street vendor selling bananas will flash a QR code at the customer, who will scan it and move twenty rupees from her bank account to the vendor's. Such payments happen more than 400 million times a day across the country.[20] The State Bank of Pakistan is testing Raast, a digital payment system like India's UPI. Sri Lanka's government is urging customers and shops to use LANKAQR, a national standard for digital payments. Nepal has several phone payment apps.

Sellers: These are the online merchants on platforms like Daraz, Amazon and restaurants. These entities were going about their lives offline, managing a shop or eatery. But as more customers started buying online, they scrambled onto the platform expecting a wider reach and a boom in business.

Workers: They are the delivery channel for the product or service the seller sells to the customer via the platform. Just as digitization transformed how the urban middle and upper classes behaved as consumers, it also had an unprecedented effect in the world of labour, creating new types of jobs and working arrangements. From the first Uber ride in May

2010 in San Francisco, the 'Uberization' of the world's economy had begun; people could do a 'gig' whenever they wanted and enter and exit a profession seemingly at will—for example, wait tables in the mornings and morph into a cab driver in the evenings. When the pandemic hit, job losses accumulated in the formal economy, and a wave of people joined the gig economy to survive.

Storyline

Privilege

For their devotion to online buying, customers are amply rewarded. They are the prevailing gods of the e-commerce ecosystem. Sitting in the comfort of a home or office, a customer summons both needs and wants to her doorstep. She can return a product, no questions asked. One worker will come to pick it up, and someone else will arrive promptly with a replacement. Sometimes, one wonders what one did to deserve such pampering.

A stand-up comic on YouTube, Sapan Verma, says in one of his acts: 'My wife and I are addicted to online shopping. At any given point in time, something is always coming to our house or going away from our house. Something is always in transit! Jeff Bezos has hired one Amazon delivery agent just for my house.'[21] He recounts ordering a broom for Rs 120 from Amazon and paying through his credit card. 'The bank loaned me Rs 120 to buy a *jhaadoo*. It gets worse. That particular brand was not there in the Amazon warehouse in Mumbai. So it came sitting in a flight all the way from the Bangalore warehouse! This is too much privilege! I feel that at some point, Amazon should give an error message saying, "No. Go down and buy it." he finishes, to raucous laughter.

A viewer commenting on this video shares how he ordered a bottle of Hajmola Anardana (a tangy digestive tablet) from Amazon for Rs 50 to notch up the bill to Rs 1000 to avail of a discount running at that time. Amazon decided to send the Hajmola separately. The small fifty-rupee bottle came in an outsized cardboard box, covered with thermocol safety layers, delivered from another state after travelling 600 kilometres. The packaging was probably costlier than the item it contained, writes the customer, laughing emojis expressing the absurdity of it all.

That's how important the customer is to the company. Nothing is too silly to send with the highest care. No distance is too far to traverse, and no worker is too harassed to be deployed in service of the customer.

The more the world went online, the more the customer benefited. Online ordering liberated them from dealing with inhospitable streets and the working class. Ride-hailing's key feature of point-to-point pick and drop removes the need to walk. The days of loud bargaining with the auto driver are history as fares are pre-fixed. Payment can be made automatically and, hence, wordlessly. When a cab ride is booked, the balance of information, and hence of power, is tilted towards the customer as we know everything about the driver and the ride before the car even arrives at our door—the driver's name, vehicle make and colour, star ratings, number of rides taken, expected time of arrival to the customer's location, the cost of the ride and where the vehicle is at that moment. As the GPS picks it up, one does not have to type an address for the cab to arrive. On the other hand, the driver knows nothing about the passenger, not even the destination he is headed to, until we give the OTP.

The attention showered by the platform on customers is fully and passionately reciprocated.

In 2024, three biryanis were ordered per second on the Zomato app, which saw a 50 per cent hike in orders from the previous year.[22] In 2023, Hanees, a Mumbai resident, tantalized his tastebuds through 3580 orders over 365 days, averaging more than nine orders per day.[23] In 2022, a Pune resident ordered food worth INR 28 lakh (the cost of a two-bedroom flat in some cities) through Zomato, which bestowed on him the title of 'foodie of the year'.[24]

Guilt follows self-indulgence quickly, with consumers complaining of getting fatter and spending too much, but unable to stop themselves, as it has become ingrained behaviour.

Isolation is endemic to an app-centric life. When everything comes home, there is no crossing paths with others in the community. The social capital fostered through casual interaction is lost.

My parents used to live in Mahim, Mumbai, in the last few years of my dad's life; every evening, they would take a walk in the neighbourhood, sometimes buying fruits from street vendors. After my father passed away, we moved to our house in Andheri, another part of Mumbai. About five years later, one day, my mother got out of the car at Mahim to buy coffee powder from the shop they used to patronize. As she walked towards the shop, someone called to her. It was a vendor my parents used to buy fruits from often. He recognized my mother and asked where my father was and why they had stopped coming. When she brought him up to speed with all that had happened, he expressed his regret at my father's passing and recalled how he would chat with him.

It was an instance that reflected how a person can own the city, and the city can own them through simple human connections. In a busy metropolis like Mumbai, which is always portrayed as fast-paced and businesslike, a migrant fruit seller recognized an old customer, and the two exchanged notes. It was a moment when my mother would have felt like she belonged to Mumbai, amidst all the chaos and traffic, and despite her husband's absence, this was still her city. Dozens of Blinkit delivery boys have come to our doorstep in the past few years. We don't know anyone's name; we've never spoken with them. Sometimes, we don't even see their faces when the payment is already made online because they leave the packet outside the door and run to the next delivery.

Power

Legal scholar Cass Sunstein and Nobel-winning economist Richard Thaler, in their 2008 bestseller *Nudge: Improving*

Decisions About Health, Wealth and Happiness,[25] proposed a set of policies under the broad term 'nudge', through which governments could help people make better decisions about health, wealth and happiness without coercion. For example, making the plate size smaller to reduce calorie intake in canteens or reminding people about the consequences of smoking by showing horrific pictures of cancer. Nudges have been used in commercial establishments even before the term was used to describe the tactic. Supermarkets keep impulse-buying items like chewing gum right next to the cashier to subtly coax customers to pick some and add it to the bill. Nudge marketing is an entire science that companies use to psychologically play with the customer, such that they can exercise their freedom of choice even while having their choice partially manipulated.

In online commerce, nudge marketing gets turbocharged because there is an array of ways to influence buying compared to marketing weaponry in the physical world. In a store, you need to fight temptation only for a few minutes until the billing is done. When you are online, there are a dozen apps on your phone, each sending reminder emails, notifications and pop-ups, apart from steering you in a particular direction when you open the app. 'Only one left in stock!' is a scarcity nudge to create FOMO anxiety in the buyer not to leave the page. 'Limited time deal!' is a trigger to fast action. The default option for a product that stares at us right on top of the page is there by design. It reassures the customer that she doesn't have to take the cognitive load of deciding; it's already done. I order an ice cream tub on a hot day through a food delivery app. A couple of days later, I receive a message. 'Vandana, it's time for a refill of your ice cream . . . Do you want to try a different flavour this time . . .' It feels like someone is cooing in my ear, and soon enough, I reach for the phone, my resolve melting like ice cream in the summer.

The platform's power is not its ability to fulfil your order. It is in knowing what you ordered. This time and every time in the past. It also knows when you placed the order and how much you spent on each purchase. Data analytical tools and artificial intelligence are applied to the information to understand the customer's preferences and patterns of ordering. At one level, I am mildly flattered that someone is monitoring the mundane bits of my dull life, deploying tech and calculating that it's time I had another ice cream. But the truth is that I am being gently steered by AI for profit.[*]

The entire edifice stands on groundbreaking technology, which is the source of its power. Take the food delivery app Swiggy as an example. Swiggy's ex-CTO Dale Vaz explained in an interview in 2019 that the company's data management system processes 40 billion messages per day from customers, drivers and restaurants. 'We are crunching all this data and building the machine learning (ML) models . . . A typical order is assigned to a delivery executive within minutes and delivered within an hour at

---

[*] The power of modern technology companies to nudge consumers in the digital age for commercial purposes is analysed in detail by Shoshana Zuboff in her bestselling book *The Age of Surveillance Capitalism* (2019),

the most (much less usually). The system must respond to abrupt swings in orders and dips in available delivery executives, as well as rain and traffic, while still adhering to the promise made to the customer. Since large-scale on-demand food delivery is a new concept worldwide, there are no tried and tested solutions for this.'[26] Helping the company transform itself into an 'AI-first' company are multiple PhDs from international universities and senior scientists from places like IBM and GE Research.

The platform wields power but also empowers. Working moms pressed for time, young professionals alone in a new city and tired executives desiring a midnight treat—a variety of demographics have experienced the power of the app to help them experience **freedom** and **pleasure**. Ride-hailing apps liberate women by giving them access to places that they may never have managed to visit using South Asia's poor public transport. The spatial ambit has increased for physically challenged people who feel confident to step out now that they can book a cab.

Customers, in turn, wield power when, with a finger flick, they assign a rating to a worker, unmindful of its ramifications. Ratings are far from innocuous numbers to boost customers' confidence that the company cares about the quality of service. Behind the game-like facade of stars or emojis, ratings are the ammunition the company collects from customers to contain, investigate, discipline and reprimand workers.

A customer's complaint and poor rating had rendered Savita, a beautician working for Urban Company in Jaipur, gig-less for months. 'Clients give any rating they want to, depending on their mood. If they have fought at home, they'll give us a poor rating, no matter how well we might have done our job,' is her bitter observation.

She adds, 'As long as everyone gives us five stars, it's fine. But if someone rates us one lower than that, we can immediately tell. Suddenly, the average rating on the app will drop. If we get a single one-star rating, the company blocks our ID, and we can't get any more work. We are forced to sit at home. How do I pay the children's fees and the rent? My husband is a carpet maker. He's ageing now, can't work as much, so I was the main bread earner.'

The app also exercises power on the men whizzing along on their two-wheelers, the human link who, despite all the digital dazzle, are imperative to the equation.

Precarity

The rise of the platform economy has provided job opportunities to millions of workers who were grateful for its existence, mainly because they had lost their old livelihoods in the wake of the economic catastrophe that Covid unleashed.

Workers' **gratitude** has now mutated into simmering **anger** as their finances have dwindled because of rising commissions charged by the aggregator, costlier fuel and a growing awareness that platforms may be trampling on their rights as workers.

The **oppression** built into the gig-work model has become evident, at least to Indian workers. The idea of being 'independent', the carrot about gig work, has slowly proved to be a smokescreen. They have no leeway in deciding their schedule, routes and the price being charged, as all these are controlled by an algorithm in the background. As the protagonist in actor–film-maker Nandita Das's movie *Zwigato*, about a food delivery worker's life, puts it, '*Malik yahan bhi hai, bas dikhta nahi hai.* (Like in a normal job, there is a boss here too. Just that he is invisible.)'

South Asian cities are chaotic places to drive in, ridden with unruly traffic and air pollution. Extreme weather conditions are alarmingly frequent. Yet, gig workers are in a choiceless situation of being out on the streets to earn their daily wages. As a veteran union leader likes to say often, '*Roz kuan khodna hai, roz paani peena hai.* (You must dig a well every day to find water to drink).'

The gig work format is the next most significant overhaul in the world of work after factories were set up in the late eighteenth century. Inherent to the model is high spatial and temporal uncertainty. The cab driver or delivery worker cannot predict where he is going next. Each destination is a surprise when the phone pings. The 'flexibility' is illusory as workers follow a punishing schedule to earn the income they need. The gig worker can never control time. It has him in its vice-like grip. He thinks he will deliver food for a few months and move abroad. But that visa never comes, the employment agent defaults, or a war breaks out in some faraway land. Three years pass, maybe five. Something that started as a 'gig' is now permanent. Permanent gig work is an oxymoron, a contradiction in terms that should not be possible but is a glaring reality.

Small Amazon sellers have faced the brunt of a faceless behemoth that pays them whimsically. 'Next to the formula for Coca-Cola, the deductions that Amazon makes before paying sellers are the best-kept secret,' said a frustrated seller in Bangalore. While well-established restaurants have the muscle power to negotiate low commission rates with the food delivery companies, smaller and newer ones reel under hefty commission rates and discounts they must offer to remain competitive. Small is not beautiful in the app-based economy. To be small is to be powerless and under pressure from customers on the one hand and the platform on the other.

Anxiety is also a constant companion of those working inside cavernous warehouses and 'dark stores' as part of the machinery to please the customer. Inside the cavernous warehouses or 'fulfilment centres' of Amazon, some workers pack, others scan returned items and put them in different bins, hands and fingers working constantly. There is an hourly target, and at the end of the hour, a rating is given based on the achievement of that target. Unmet targets attract feedback from the management up to three times, after which the worker is dismissed and blocked from working for Amazon.

And finally, there are leaders among workers who display **courage** by galvanizing their colleagues and making them aware of their rights in this new format of work and homegrown platforms that aim to provide a level playing field to sellers of all sizes. Through their actions, they strive for a better balance of power, privilege and precarity.

A few notes for clarity:

- Workers have been referred to in the masculine as 'him' as there are barely any female workers. This is a constant reminder of the gender imbalance in location-based gig work.
- 'Workers', 'gig workers' and 'app-based workers' are interchangeable terms.
- 'Delivery workers', 'delivery agents' or 'riders' are those who come to the customer's location and deliver a packet of food or whatever has been purchased online.
- 'Ride-hailing companies' are app-based transport companies, whether the vehicle is a car or a bike.
- 'Drivers' are cab or bike drivers for app-based transport companies like Uber, while 'passengers' are the customers who book these vehicles.
- 'Platforms', 'aggregators' and 'tech companies' all refer to the same entity.
- Names of people have been changed wherever people have wanted to remain anonymous. An asterisk denotes that a pseudonym has been used. I have also changed the names wherever I felt the information shared could impact the person adversely, even if the speaker did not ask for it. All conversations were audio recorded with the speaker's permission.

PLEASURE

Food delivery is not a twenty-first-century invention.

In 1889, when the Naples-based Pizzeria di Pietro e Basta Così created a new style of pizza, the savvy head chef wanted to make sure the royals could try it. So, when King Umberto I and Queen Margherita came to the city, he hand-delivered his creations, making them perhaps the first pizza delivery customers.[1] A Chinese restaurant in Los Angeles was the earliest known reference to the kind of delivery service we know today. Back in 1922, Kin-Chu café asked customers to make a phone call and have hot dishes delivered to their doorstep as late as 1 a.m.[2]

In December 1995, two graduates from Stanford Business School began Waiter.com (formerly known as World Wide Waiter), considered the first online restaurant delivery service, delivering meals to corporate offices in Silicon Valley.[3] Closer home, as early as the nineteenth century, Mumbai's *dabbawalla* system began to deliver lunch to workers so they did not have to leave their workplaces. Eventually, they became the subject of a Harvard case study and achieved Six Sigma certification for their operational efficiency. Domino Pizza introduced the thirty-minute delivery guarantee in the 1960s in the US and brought that same assurance to India in the 1990s, braving criticism for encouraging dangerous driving. Before food delivery became e-commerce, local restaurants would send their chottus to deliver food within a range of about a kilometre at no charge.

Thus, food delivery has existed in various forms for centuries, but it was the pandemic that made the act of delivering food to the buyer's doorstep an estimated $365 billion industry globally.[4]

Staying at home during Covid-19 normalized ordering food and groceries on the phone. Something meant to be a temporary convenience at a particular time of crisis found so much popular appeal that it became the norm. Like Daylight Saving Time, which was first implemented during the two world wars as a temporary measure to conserve energy by maximizing daylight. After the wars, some countries discontinued the practice. Still, many others found that people appreciated the longer evenings and the energy savings, and now almost all of the US and Europe change their clocks according to the season.

Who are these buyers? What primal instincts motivate them to reach for their phones to forage for food and groceries?

Gen Z

Generation Z, the demographic cohort born between the mid-1990s and early 2010s, is at the forefront of this transformative change. As 'digital natives' who have grown up with electronic gadgets ever since they were toddlers, Gen Z is reshaping how we have eaten for centuries in this part of the world. Exploration, curiosity and the desire for new experiences have been part of the elixir of youth since antiquity. But digital technology, with its virtually endless availability of new content that stimulates the senses, has dramatically reshaped novelty-seeking behaviour.

Online food delivery caters to the traits that define Gen Z—quick, convenient, tech-based solutions for all of life's troubles, from mental health to hunger and curiosity and openness to explore everything the world has to offer, whether it is cuisines or foreign dramas on OTT. Real-time updates on order status and accurate delivery time estimates are now baseline expectations. Gen Z customers have kept food aggregators and restaurants on their toes by unambiguously demanding what they need. Sample these instructions from American customers, quoted in the Uber Eats Cravings report of 2023:[5]

> *'Put it in a box instead of a circular container. I refuse to eat any food if presented in a circular container. Please don't ruin my meal for me.'*
>
> *'I have braces, and it is difficult for me to chew. Please, please chop my salad and all ingredients into small pieces.'*
>
> *'Please drench the whole bowl in white sauce with a spiral of red sauce!!!! Thank you so much!!!! Just do what I ask.'*

Qurat-ul-Ain Ali, Karachi

In Karachi, Qurat-ul-Ain Ali, twenty-nine, comes home from work at one of Pakistan's reputed business schools. She opens the Foodpanda app on her phone and orders a chicken biryani, though her mother has cooked dinner. Dining out no longer needs a special occasion—just a strong enough craving for non-home-cooked food.

I met Qurat-ul-Ain one Saturday afternoon on a Zoom call. There is a bit of cross-border confusion because I log on at 3 p.m. IST and find no one there. She thought the meeting was at 3 p.m. Pakistan time, half an hour behind IST. We laughed about this and proceeded to have a two-hour conversation in a mix of Urdu and English about changing lifestyles in Karachi, women's mobility in Pakistan, and how growing Islamization affects daily life, including the style in which ladies stitch their salwar kameez. ('Indian fit' is the tighter one, while the default Pakistani version is more modest and looser!)

'Home food is repetitive, and so is the food in the cafeteria—same old stuff. But Foodpanda gives me access to so much variety; there is chowmein, sandwiches, all kinds of things,' she tells me. Her four siblings also order online, particularly her brother, who is in the last year of school but works for Upwork and Fiverr, online marketplaces where freelancers can find gigs. Since he does his freelance work late at night, he often orders at 2 a.m. or 3 a.m. through Foodpanda, from McDonald's, KFC or Pizza Hut, who deliver at that hour. Sometimes, he uses a local app called GoLootLo, which only offers restaurant discounts.

Anaya, Colombo

Twenty-four-year-old Anaya is a well-to-do Sri Lankan girl who studied at Delhi University and returned to Colombo during the pandemic. She is now working her first job in a research outfit. Lunch is rice and curry, eaten with coworkers and obtained through Pick Me foods. In the evening, when she's back home from work, she gets something small through Uber Eats, referred to as 'short eats' in Sri Lanka. This could be juice, coffee or pancakes.

'Something tiny to reward myself,' she laughs.

'Just a juice or a coffee, with the delivery charge, doesn't it become costly?'

'It does, but it's convenient,' she says and then comes up with a rationale. 'If I take a *tuk* (auto rickshaw) and get it myself, it would be double the amount. So, might as well pay him to bring it.'

'But . . . what about just making coffee at home?'

'Sorry?'

I must have sounded to her like a voice from the ancient past.

I repeat the question. Why couldn't she brew some coffee at home?

'Oh, that's just the toxic hustle culture of our generation. No time to make coffee at home,' she says, giggling again. Her two female colleagues laugh in consent.

'I guess the one from outside tastes better . . . it's probably special, hazelnut flavour or whatever, right?' I say awkwardly.

'Yeah, this is me rewarding myself, so getting it from Uber Eats is much better. Can't compare that quality to what we make at home.'

There is a name for what Anaya is trying to describe. It's called 'Little treat culture', and it refers to the habit of rewarding oneself with small, enjoyable things as a form of self-care or to cope with stress, often seen as a way to find joy in everyday life. Predominantly practised by Gen Z, this culture rose in the wake of the pandemic, perhaps in response to the accompanying stress. The hashtag #littletreat was trending on TikTok in the latter half of 2023. Some people wonder if the indulgence has been stretched too far. As one viral tweet put it: *Little treat culture is getting out of hand. You don't need an $8 coffee because you did laundry.*[6]

'So, does your family ever say why are you ordering so much. . . ?' I continue my interrogation, fascinated by my interviewee's line of thought.

'All the time,' she interrupts. 'They are like, don't waste money. A 30 per cent commission is added, so it becomes expensive. But it is so addictive because when you see how convenient it is, you kinda want to do it again and again. It doesn't require you to visit a place or interact with people for real. It's just straightforward. The Uber guy will come, hand you the food and go. He won't even speak to you. So, it's very convenient.'

'So, you'd rather not speak to anyone?'

'Ya, that's like a bonus. I guess it just saves time. Reduces small talk. Horrible way of putting it, though,' she shrugs.

Her friend Darshini, sitting across the table, is a soft-spoken girl from a small town in the south who is in Colombo to work. She stays in a paying-guest accommodation where she can cook. 'But I feel too lazy since I leave the office at 7 or 8 and reach home at 8.30 or 9 p.m.,' she says shyly. So, she ends up ordering dinner and sometimes a snack, while lunch is through PickMe or Uber Eats at the office with Anaya and other colleagues.

'On Uber Eats, they've introduced Uber Gold, where you've to pay a monthly subscription fee, and they remove the delivery fee for you. Pick Me Pass also exists. It's a good incentive. But we've done no cost-benefit calculation. It just feels like we've got a deal,' says Anaya.

Gen Z's experimental YOLO (you only live once) attitude to life is also shaping the very structure of the restaurant industry. Their enthusiastic embrace of food delivery has made some food entrepreneurs ponder the relevance of the physical restaurant. If youngsters who drive the eating-out market prefer eating restaurant food at home, why incur the overheads and operational strain of running a restaurant?

Though trained as an automobile engineer, thirty-five-year-old Karan Tanna had always been attracted to the restaurant business because growing up, he had watched his parents run a small restaurant in Veraval, Gujarat. It was a smart career shift because Tanna's turn as a restaurateur has won him several food business awards and featured him in magazine listings like 'Forbes 30 under 30' and 'GQ 40 under 40'. After running a company that managed franchisees of American food and beverage brands, in 2019, Tanna became an internet entrepreneur and founded Ghost Kitchens. 'Ghost kitchen' is a term in the contemporary restaurant business that refers to a commercial kitchen used exclusively for preparing food for delivery or takeout without a physical dining space for customers. Some cloud kitchens work for multiple brands. For example, a burger for an American franchisee could be prepped on the right counter while biryani for a Mughlai restaurant is packed on the left. Some restaurants operate cloud kitchens for delivery orders, while the restaurant kitchen can concentrate on dine-in customers. Some other food sellers do not have a physical restaurant and only work from a cloud kitchen.

Speaking to me on a video call from Mumbai, Tanna, who does not have a physical restaurant but only operates through cloud kitchens in Mumbai and Ahmedabad, says that he ventured into this because he realized that the growth and penetration of food delivery was going to be immense in future, making cloud kitchens a promising business opportunity.

'It has less capital investment. Third-party aggregators enable the discovery of our brands and the last-mile delivery. So, we only have to focus on the kitchen part. Running a kitchen in a locality with cheap rent has much less overhead cost than running a proper restaurant. You don't have to have street-facing premises; you can be on the second floor of a building on some lane in a suburb,' he says.

Is it easy for the customer to trust a brand that only operates from the cloud, whose physical outlet she has never seen? How do customers know that the pizza from a reputed brand we are ordering comes from the city outlet or the cloud kitchen? Tanna tells me that they don't care either way.

'Millennials and Gen Zs don't have any kind of a burden or influence of legacy brands as much as, you know, the earlier generations had,' Tanna says. 'So they are very open to experimentation. Their minds are tweaked to discover brands online. Not only food but also shopping, furniture, shoes, everything. They are not burdened by the fact that we have never seen a restaurant with this brand. If a new pizzeria opened in their neighbourhood, they would visit it, right? Similarly, they discover internet restaurants online and are willing to give cloud-based brands a chance. And the market is governed by young people.'

Midnight's Children

The popularity of online food delivery is inextricably linked to the simultaneous explosion of entertainment options. Modern-day nirvana is when each family member stares into their screen, earphones plugged in, and the whole world descends into that 5×5 rectangle. With the advances in subtitling, nothing feels foreign any more, whether it is

Korean mini-series, Pakistani dramas, arty Malayalam fare, Telugu masala, avant-garde Hindi content or Hollywood superheroes. We are wonderstruck, as Yashodha might have been when she asked her toddler Krishna to open his mouth and saw the entire *brahmaand* (universe) inside it. Accompanying this visual feast is any cuisine of the world that you can summon with a few flicks of your thumb. There you are in your living room in Delhi or Dhaka, watching a K-drama, lying on your couch and munching on a taco. The world is quite literally at your fingertips. It sounds like no big deal because it has become so normalized. It is, in fact, a socially transformative moment in human history because never have entertainment and gastronomic pleasure been so democratized, affordable and accessible.

Keshav Reddy, Hyderabad

Keshav Reddy,* who is forty-five, is a mid-level software engineer. He lives in Hyderabad with his homemaker wife and two young children. Since his office allows flexi-time, on most days, he leaves for work in the afternoon and returns by 10 p.m. By that time, the family is asleep. Dinner is waiting for him on the table. After the meal, the most enjoyable part of Keshav's day begins. He moves to the couch in the living room, and for the next few hours, he lies there undisturbed, immersed in his favourite OTT shows. At some point during this self-indulgent, blissful time, he opens the Swiggy app on his phone and starts scrolling, wondering what he can order as a midnight snack to enhance his pleasure of solitary TV time. Sometimes, it is momos; at other times, it is masala peanut chaat, stuffed kulchas or something from KFC. It depends on what is available from the restaurants that are open that late. The options are limited at that hour, but the dish determines his choice, not the restaurant's proximity. If he wants momos, he will order them, no matter how far away the restaurant is. He has time on his hands because he sleeps only by 3 a.m. And food delivery works all night, waiting to serve customers like him.

At 7 a.m., he is up again to drop the kids at the bus stop. When I visit his apartment for the interview, he sits up on the couch where he has been catching up on sleep after his morning fatherly duties and sheepishly straightens his clothes.

What drives him, night after night, to order food online and watch Netflix at the witching hour?

'You see,' he smiles gently, his thin frame slouching. 'All day there is office work, then I have to drop the kids off in the morning. This is my "me time"—just my space in a busy day to relax and do what I want.'

I ask Suparna, his wife, who is running a mop all over the house, if she objects to his lifestyle because he is spending too much or because of potential health risks from eating outside food every day.

'I keep telling him, but he does his own thing. Anyway, they are all thin in his family, so he won't put on weight,' she says. 'He doesn't overeat; he just wants variety,' she adds in his defence.

I ask her when she has her 'me-time' and if it includes online food delivery.

'My time is between 1–3 p.m. before the children come home and after everything else is done. That's when I sit in front of the TV. But I don't order outside food much. Maybe biryani a couple of times and occasionally pizzas for the kids.'

Is Keshav ever worried about the health risks of his nocturnal snacking?

'I don't go by everything they keep saying in the media. One day, milk is bad; another day, bread is bad. I eat what I want. I don't keep doing health check-ups on my own. They did it recently in the office, and it was all fine. I don't do any regular exercise. Sometimes, I play table tennis or shuttle (badminton),' he says, evidently bored of the contemporary health phobias.

Nishesh Kamath, Mumbai

Nishesh Kamath,* forty-five, is a director in a software services company. Both Nishesh and his wife Anita are my classmates from school. In October 2022, I spent a night at their place in Andheri while visiting Mumbai to sort out some bank paperwork. Anita and I were catching up after dinner. It was nearly midnight when the bell rang. 'Who's come so late at night?' I asked.

'Must be Swiggy,' Anita was blasé. 'Nishesh has to order something every night.'

'But he had dinner with us . . .' I said, trying not to sound shocked.

'Yes, but still, he orders something for himself to eat while watching TV or reading,' she replied.

Soon, Anita went to bed because she had an early start the next day, and I was looking forward to my own thirty minutes of mindless doom scrolling of YouTube shorts, my pre-sleep ritual, the way some people put on meditation music to lull them to sleep. Its 'infinite scroll' feature, where content continuously loads as users scroll down, encourages me to lose track of time and keep browsing. Finally, after drowning in 'information overload', I put the phone down.

When cell phones became popular at the dawn of this century, I had a blue Nokia button phone and became an ardent texter. Always fond of a good conversation, this seemed like a great way to interact with similarly inclined people. It circumvented problems of calling only at a convenient time or being unable to talk because someone else in the room was asleep. One could text away into the night, composing witty replies and overusing punctuation marks to denote emotion, as smileys had not yet come into the keyboard. The blue light became a constant companion, and the two of us got closer after smartphones arrived.

I could still see the muted light in the living room when I was about to put the phone away and go to bed. I peeped out and saw Nishesh on the couch in the living room, a half-eaten box of sandwiches next to him, watching a Netflix show on low volume. I sauntered in, curious to know more about his post-midnight indulgence.

Nishesh muses that his mind associates the combination of food at midnight and a book or a movie as a sort of forbidden pleasure that goes back to his late teen years when he would often do his own thing after the household slept. He would forage in the storeroom for snacks like chakli or chips, take them into his bedroom and settle down with a novel and a packet of munchies. It was his own little, innocent, secret bedtime ritual. Now, at forty-five, he feels the Swiggy and OTT routine gives him the same comfort he got in his teens with snacks and books. He admits that not all food lends itself well to delivery. Pizzas may not be hot, naans wilt, and chaats turn soggy. However, through practice, one learns what works from where.

Pre-lockdown, he would pick up something from his favourite haunts when he would go to his office. After 2022, many IT companies have embraced work-from-home, and he needs to visit his physical office twice a week. How would he get his post-dinner dinner then? That's when the food delivery boy comes to the rescue, ringing the bell at midnight in the Kamath household and bearing the treats Nishesh's heart desires that night.

How Dining In Became the New Dining Out

The rise and rise of 'affordable indulgence' in India

Kishore Biyani, the founder of Future Group, one of India's leading brick-and-mortar retailers that owns brands like

Pantaloons and Big Bazaar, knows a thing or two about India's consumers. In episode 11 of the popular podcast, 'WTF is' conducted by startup poster-boy Nikhil Kamath.[7] Biyani is insightful about the class indulging in value-added consumption (i.e., basics + some more). Biyani asserts that anyone who has domestic help is part of the consuming class and pegs that number at about 10–12 crore in India. That is still only 7.5–8.5 per cent of a country with the largest population in the world.

However, according to several estimates, this class has grown and continues to swell its ranks rapidly. To cite some examples, according to 'Indus Valley', an annual report on trends in the Indian economy brought out by the venture capital firm Blume Ventures, three-fourths of retail consumer spending is on groceries. But spending on things considered non-essential but desirable, i.e. 'discretionary spending', is also rapidly rising, zooming from 13 per cent in 2000 to 21 per cent in 2022'.[8] As per Goldman Sach's 'Affluent India', i.e. the group of individuals with an annual income greater than Rs 1 million, has tripled from 20 million in 2011 to 60 million in 2023 and is expected to touch 100 million in 2027. The study corroborated this with data about credit card possession, flights taken, postpaid mobile connections and payment of income tax and found that whichever way we see it, the number of affluent Indians is spiralling upwards rapidly.[9]

PRICE, a think tank that regularly presents macroeconomic trends, declares boldly in one of its reports on India's middle class, 'India is growing immensely wealthy'[10] and predicts that the middle class, which drives consumption in the country, will become one billion-plus strong by 2047, the hundredth year of independence.

One evening in Mumbai, I meet Rama Bijapurkar at her home in Breach Candy. Bijapurkar taught market research to my class at IIM-Ahmedabad and is skilled at untangling the messy threads that make up 'consumer India'. I ask her why people are spending so much on outside food. She believes that though economic slowdowns come and go, over the long term, prosperity has increased. 'Many more Indians today have more money to do everything, everywhere, all at once and the data about rising incomes is reflected anecdotally all around us,' she observes. 'My mother used to say, are you a Tata or a Birla (to spend so much)? Today, I could be a Tata, Birla, next-door neighbour, my plumber, my carpenter, they're all making money. Incomes have increased and eating options have expanded at every price point. So, with ten rupees, you have many choices, as with a thousand. It's a positive double whammy—incomes have grown and so have options across the spectrum.'

'If I look back at my life five years ago, the amount that I used to spend on eating has maybe doubled or tripled. Maybe because my income has increased or because I have less time or because many choices are tempting me to order out or go out to a restaurant,' says Karan Tanna, in a personal interview, asserting that both online ordering and restaurants are thriving. Restaurateurs do not see any drop in footfall, while entrepreneurs like Tanna, who have cloud kitchens and rely only on online delivery, are also seeing business grow.

The rise of 'affordable indulgence' is only valid for India. In other South Asian countries, the post-Covid recovery has been volatile and slow, blighted by political upheavals in Pakistan and Bangladesh and an economic crisis in Sri Lanka. Academics I spoke to in these countries estimate that the consumers willing to spend on restaurant food for pleasure and convenience would be a thin layer of urban society, comprising youngsters like Qurat and Anaya. A professor in Sri Lanka told me, 'We are talking about a thin slice of Colombo, not even Kandy. And even in Colombo, I doubt someone like a teacher can afford to use these apps. It must be only youngsters and those in corporate companies.'

Food—the desi superstar

Food has always occupied centre stage in our cultures. Anyone who has visited an elderly aunt or uncle will recall being asked worriedly, 'But what about your food?' My house has a running joke about an aunt who would halt any plan for an outing with an anxious inquiry about how we would manage our '*saapadu*' (Tamil for meals).

Food in the subcontinent is not just for physical survival but also has a spiritual component. In the fasting month of Ramzan, Muslims attempt to purify themselves and refrain from sensual pleasures, including eating and drinking. Values like piety, charity, hospitality and honour are linked to different feasts. For example, a marriage feast symbolizes honour and hospitality, while Ramzan represents piety and charity. A famous invocation before food, from the Bhagavad Gita (*ahaṁ vaiśvānaro bhūtvā* . . .) says it is divine energy that fires up the digestive process and makes this miraculous system work day after day in all the living beings of the universe.

From respect and reverence, our relationship with food has become expressive and passionate. Everyone appears to be engaged in a rollicking affair with food. With Instagram, every chaat and cupcake is described as a gustatory poem and photographed with adoration previously reserved for fancy dishes in a Michelin-star restaurant.

Anjali Bhatia, a professor of sociology at Delhi University, has conducted several inquiries into the food and eating habits of the Indian middle class. Describing the smorgasbord of choices in food available, she writes:

> The diversification and dynamism of the customer base of those eating out is matched by a proliferation in the variety of foods on offer. Continental, North Indian, South Indian, Mughlai, and Chinese no longer describe the variety. There is now a remarkable diversity of national, regional, ethnic, local, global, and industrial elements in the hamper comprising Tibetan, Italian, Afghani, Lebanese, Korean, Japanese, Bengali, Kashmiri, Gujarati, Goan, Maharashtrian, Rajasthani, North-Eastern, and Punjabi cuisines; branded/unbranded and homegrown/American fast food; pan-Indian, regional,

and local varieties of snacks and sweets; vegan or organic food; and tea, coffee and pastries. Food items such as samosas, vada-pao, chutney sandwiches, pav bhaji, golegappe, chaat, kathi rolls, chole bhature, bhelpuri, idli-dosa, dhokla, kachori, bread pakora, sambhar-vada, patties, burgers, noodles, biryani, and kebabs map the diversity of street foods.[11]

In India, specialized apps exist for sprouts and pre-cut vegetables, ready-to-eat salad kits, raw pressed juices for smoothies and fermented drinks like kombucha and kefir. Local grocery stores are packed with newer and newer brands of products like baked chips, protein-rich drinks, exotic pastes and chutneys. One magical manufacturer makes a dehydrated, powdered form of coconut, mint, tomato-onion and many more chutneys with zero preservatives, which the consumer has to mix with only a little water. I was sceptical, but such is contemporary food technology that no one can tell that it isn't freshly ground.

The spotlight on food is evident in the staggering audience for many YouTube cooking channels. Not only celebrated chefs, but a host of home chefs are also cooking up a storm. The list of top YouTubers in India, of course, has several cool Gen Zs rapping and making comic skits. But sitting pretty amidst them is also homely, middle-aged Nisha Madhulika, who cooks vegetarian food, mostly without onion and garlic,[12] along with Kabita Singh, creator of Kabita's Kitchen. Each of the ladies has over 14 million subscribers.

Across South Asia, there is also tremendous support for YouTube channels that preserve the culinary wisdom of generations and showcase traditional recipes. For example, Rustic Cooking and Tranquil Village, run by a mother and daughter in a small Sri Lankan village where they pluck local ingredients from their luxuriant backyard, has over 2 million subscribers. In all such slow-cooking channels, everything is made from scratch, cooked on a woodfire using old-world kitchen equipment like clay or brass pots.

Many of these are community-specific, bringing alive niche dishes. On the channel Gavran-Ek Khari Chaav, a toothless *aaji* (granny) and her daughter-in-law demonstrate rustic Maharashtrian cooking while speaking in a lilt characteristic of western Maharashtra. In a video where they prepare a fish kalvan (intensely spicy Kolhapuri curry) with fresh catch from the Warana River that flows in the region, viewers gush, '*Ekdum jhakaas dish*! I will definitely try too!' 'Love u Ajji. Missing those days when I used to visit my grandma.'

One might wonder who is watching this in the time of quick commerce. But even these channels have tens of thousands of fans, evidence of how technology, whether it is YouTube, Instagram or delivery apps, has made food take centre stage.

On a nippy January afternoon, I meet eminent journalist and ace writer on food trends, Vir Sanghvi, at his home in Delhi's Defence Colony to ask him how the food scene is unfolding in India. Why is ordering online growing, but the restaurants have people lining up too? And who is watching YouTube food channels if the kitchen is shrinking? Are the same people doing all things, or are they different segments?

Containing his annoyance at the noise from a neighbour's drilling machine, he shares why he concurs that food is the new fashion.

'More people are eating food prepared outside the home than ever before. More unusual dishes that were never part of home food are reaching Indian consumers more than ever. Sushi was never expected to work in India as it was assumed that Indians will not eat raw fish. But what we've done is instead of Nigiri Sushi, which has rice and raw fish in it, our chefs have put their own spin on it and created sushi rolls which have cooked fish and masala in the centre!' he laughs. 'So, whole new categories of food are being created, the way Indian-Chinese was a few decades ago, because more Indians want to eat outside food and are waiting to try new stuff. (Sanghvi had spotted the Indo-Chinese wave in food when it happened and memorably named it Sino-Ludhianvi.) Sanghvi's view is that online ordering has not impacted restaurants because the clientele and dining habits have changed. More than families going together for a meal, youngsters are the primary clientele for restaurants. 'They go out to restaurants mainly to get a drink, come home, order a biryani and switch on Netflix. That's why even restaurants that did not have a bar earlier have now opened one.'

I ask him why YouTube chefs are so popular if most people eat and drink outside. Who is trying out their recipes?

Sanghvi argues that even there, people were looking for new things or new ways to make old things. The adventurous global palate of the present-day consumer is still evident.

'Even celebrity chefs like Ranveer Brar will make dishes that people have not eaten before. Let's take shakshuka. It's a North African dish of fried eggs on tomatoes that, growing up, none of us had ever heard of. Yet every younger Indian knows what it is because Ranveer offers the recipe. Avocado toast is another example. Food habits have changed in a way that defies logic.'

'Many things are happening together,' he continues. 'I'm not saying it is necessarily better. But the range of options available has grown, and the range of ingredients available has expanded. The adventurousness of home cooks, especially younger ones, is incredible.'

Platforms are also changing our dietary habits by facilitating the procurement of ingredients. About a decade ago, even a relatively simple ingredient of Thai cuisine, like lemongrass, was not readily available. One had to find a particular upmarket grocery or urban farm to get it. Not anymore. Platforms like Amazon and Flipkart make gourmet ingredients available in a flash.

'I used to get so much food from abroad, like all kinds of exotic mushrooms. I don't need to any more. Now I click on the phone, and they deliver them by the next day,' Sanghvi remarks.

The Modern Workplace

The International Labour Organization (ILO)'s 2022 global report on work–life balance defines long hours as regularly working more than forty-eight hours per week.[13] According to the report, globally, 31.1 per cent of employees (as opposed to self-employed) worked more than that, and the proportion was the highest among the occupational groups of 'sales and service workers' and 'managers'. When regions were compared, South Asia was at the top spot with a sizeable 70.3 per cent of employees working more than forty-eight hours! In the private sector, work hours constitute not only hours required to complete assignments but also hours spent in the office or with office people to demonstrate commitment to the organization in the hope of advancing one's career.

The same ILO report confirms what we know anecdotally, i.e., that long work hours create work-family imbalances and reduce mental well-being, resulting in stress, anxiety and lower job and life satisfaction.[14] Damning evidence that corporate life and its inherent competitiveness can be stressful and physically and emotionally draining is that an entire generation has come up with a subversive strategy to deal with this. Tired of what they see as unreasonable pressure, Gen Z workers are practising 'quiet quitting'—a term used for those employees who deliberately adopt a minimalist approach to work, putting no more effort into their jobs than necessary. In response to Infosys founder N.R. Narayana

Murthy's remark that young Indians must work seventy hours per week, there was widespread furore.

'No time to socialize, no time to talk to family, no time to exercise, no time for recreation. Companies also expect people to answer emails and calls after work hours. Then wonder why young people are getting heart attacks?' Dr Deepak Krishnamurthy, a Bengaluru-based cardiologist, wrote on X.[15]

Yet in India, startup turks like Ola's Bhavish Agarwal offer thumping support to punishing schedules, saying Murthy's seventy-hour work week should become 140 hours to build in one generation what other countries have built over many.[16] In January 2025, the chairman of Larsen and Toubro inspired an avalanche of memes and heated discussions when he said people should work for no less than 90 hours.

Other honchos stated publicly that refusing to work on weekends is not acceptable and that Indians need to contribute to the country's economic growth as South Koreans did (South Korea, mistakenly held as an ideal, brought in a new labour law in 2004 following the adverse effects of its brutal work ethic).[17]

Thus, when Keshav returns home at 10 p.m., his children and wife are already asleep. How is a mid-level corporate executive returning from a day of deliverables, presentations, dealing with boss and coworkers, client calls, operational hassles of project management and so on, not to mention traffic, parking and other stresses of metropolitan life, to unwind? In the pre-Internet days, they would have eaten dinner kept on the table and curled up with a book. But now, tired executives like Nishesh and Keshav rely on the apps, winking at them to pick up the phone and destress.

The way our cities have grown

Trying to recall how food from outside became so central to their life, Qurat-ul-Ain reminisces about her childhood when the city was a different place.

'When I was growing up in the early 2000s, our family used to go out four times a week—yes! I am not joking! My father (who passed away in 2020) loved to eat out. We used to go by car and return on foot because after eating oily nihari, haleem, biryani, parathas—it was better to walk! Slowly, we stopped going out together because the five siblings became busier and busier, and we had our circle of friends with whom we would also go out. Money was limited, so we couldn't eat out with friends and again with family! Nowadays, we visit restaurants about twice a quarter, I guess, because everyone has their schedule. My mom has never been a fan of eating out. I order quite a bit online, at home, and in the office for lunch, so after that, I guess going out again is too much.

'When I was in school, going for English-style picnics was a thing,' Qurat-ul-Ain continues. 'We used to go to a park and spread a tablecloth, carry food and drinks with us. But no one goes to parks or has picnics these days because the city has become more violent. You don't feel safe doing these outdoor activities any more.'

A sprawling megalopolis of over 20 million people on Pakistan's southern tip, Karachi has been plagued in recent years with political violence, social unrest and the threat of the Taliban. In his book set in the city, *The Scatter Here Is Too Great,* Pakistani novelist Bilal Tanweer describes Karachi as 'broken, beautiful and born of tremendous violence'.

Qurat surmises that as life outside became more and more threatening and uncertain, people preferred to seek enjoyment within the familiar spaces of the home, which is also one reason for the popularity of food delivery apps.

Rapid urbanization and economic expansion have put enormous strain on intracity travel. As public transport proves woefully inadequate in South Asian metropolises, private vehicles, especially two-wheelers, have saturated the road infrastructure. Mumbai, Dhaka, Colombo and Karachi are up in neon lights as cities that have gone through an era of unrestrained urban sprawl and motorization through the last decades of the twentieth century.

Karachi, for instance, has expanded fifty times since the creation of Pakistan in 1947, resulting in unplanned urbanization that adversely affects public transport, road safety and air quality. Like in Mumbai, which is compared to densely populated commercial capitals of other countries, in Karachi too, going for an outing to a restaurant, negotiating traffic, finding parking and returning home battle-weary robs the joy of a family outing. Food delivery comes as a blessing in this scenario.

Food has become an affordable indulgence for many because incomes have risen, and the 'consuming class' is growing, especially in India. Among this consuming class are those who find pleasure in online food ordering. It consists of many demographics, such as Gen Z seeking variety on their plate and middle-aged office goers who find solitary midnight snacking destressing after handling the pressures of the modern workplace. OTT is a sweet accompaniment that has emerged simultaneously, bringing both the restaurant and cinema hall to the living room couch. The unpleasantness of driving through chaotic traffic in poorly planned cities makes cocooning ourselves at home even more attractive. Why step out when a dizzying array of choices is available at various price ranges with just a few taps on the phone? It is hard to imagine that this is a region where famine and starvation existed right until the 1970s.

GUILT

What Happened to *Ma ka Khaana*?

Western feminists may have condemned the kitchen as a site where oppressive gender inequalities play out. In contrast, scholars from indigenous, non-white cultures of Mexico, Korea and Africa counter that the kitchen is, in fact, a place where women have complete control and make all decisions, from arrangements for the daily menu to assigning tasks to sous chefs. Kitchens are also often creative spaces where women cook for enjoyment rather than only to fulfil a duty. For example, Marvelene Hughes writes in the influential book *Food and Culture* that for African American women, cooking has not been oppressive, routine or drudgery but instead has given women a possibility to express love, nurturance, creativity and sharing, which became a route to escape the painful realities of racist oppression.[1] In her new book released in 2024, *Praise Song for the Kitchen Ghosts*, Cynthia Wilkinson, a poet and professor, sees the kitchen as a place of power, stating, 'The kitchen was where the secrets were spilt, plans were made, advice was given, all while preparing mouthwatering meals.'[2]

My *patti*, tethered to the kitchen from dawn till dusk, would also cook for fun, trying out snacks like murukkus (fried rice flour snack shaped like jalebis) and making papad-style rice crispies, which were laid out on cotton dhotis on the terrace, where the hot southern sun would dry them.

The kitchen can be many things to a woman—a hot, sweaty, tiresome jail, but also a canvas to produce and display her culinary art, a place to find joy in mixing ingredients and to create beautiful dishes for the people she cares about. As the kitchen's importance shrinks and more meals arrive from outside, do mothers worry that *maa ka khaana* is replaced by *kisi aur ke maa (or baap) ka khaana*?

My teen son is the only Zomato/Swiggy enthusiast in my house. Even though he limits himself to ordering Mexican food once a week, I feel a pang when he declares he is buying his dinner from outside. Why? Is my cooking bland? Is the food we make at home somehow inadequate? There is never an occasion when I have welcomed his choice and not tried to talk him out of it. I desperately suggest comfort food or volunteer to whip up something exciting.

I shamelessly hard-sell the nutritional value, looking up another app to read aloud the number of grams of protein in beans, *paruppu usli*, arhar dal or whatever has been made in my kitchen that day. He is unfazed and carries on with the order while reminding me how a burrito from California Burrito (an Indian chain started by an American) is a fully balanced meal, is freshly prepared and has no preservatives.

I know this already. Yet I would prefer the order frequency to be reduced to only twice a month. I am not even sure what I am objecting to here. When the health argument doesn't hold water, I make some noise about spending unnecessarily when there is food at home. But essentially, I think, as a mother, I don't want to cede control of my family's meals to outside forces. It is so easy to make this a habit. Today, it is a weekend dinner; soon, it could be weekday ones.

But I am on slippery ground with food delivery apps spawning like characters in Minecraft. Small voices of protest are hastily submerged by the unstoppable tidal wave of technology entering the dining room. AI-powered apps plan menus according to a person's preferences and nutrition goals and save us from slipping into decision fatigue by thinking of what to eat. Smart refrigerators track food inventory and suggest recipes based on available ingredients. And robots are rapidly being developed to become full-fledged cooks.[3]

Health

Historically, Sri Lankan food consisted of green leafy vegetables, fibre-rich cereals like finger millet, roots, tubers, green leaves, fruits, vegetables, spices, animal fats and fish, all of which have many health benefits and medicinal properties.

Diversity and balance are also evident in the composition of the Indian *thali*, which has representations of the six tastes (sweet, sour, salty, bitter, pungent and astringent) considered necessary for a nutritious meal. Every region has a localized thali based on the same concept of all tastes on one plate. Unlike the 'unlimited thalis' of contemporary Indian restaurants, the original thali consisted of pre-set portions of dal, rice, seasonal vegetables, fermented food such as pickles, raw food like chutney, pachadi or koshimbiri and a little dairy.

Nepal's Thakali meal showcases the thali tradition beautifully. When I first landed in Kathmandu and saw many restaurant boards with the word 'Thakali', there was a moment of cognitive dissonance since, in my native Tamil, 'thakali' means tomatoes.

I wondered if some enterprising Tamil migrants were importing tomatoes from India and selling them in speciality stores. Later, I learned that it refers to the meal format of the Thakali community in the mountainous Mustang region. As the Udipi community did in India, they came to urban centres and set up Thakali restaurants, serving their kind of thali, which quickly became mainstream fare. The sheer balance of the Thakali meal is admirable. Items now only found in homes, such as *karela* and greens of mustard and radish, and have been deemed boring by Indian restaurants, made a welcome appearance. Everything was laid out in small portions. There was always mushroom and, typically, only dal was served on repeat. In every Thakali restaurant I visited, a small serving of mildly sweetened curd was included instead of dessert. It's as if the thali was saying—that's all you need; that's all anyone has ever required in regular day-to-day meals.

Moving away from these sensible dietary choices, all of South Asia is undergoing what is called a 'nutrition transition'.

A study published in 2024 in the prestigious academic journal *The Lancet* declared that the South Asian region is in a nutritional transition—where traditional locally sourced diets dominated by low-fat, high-fibre foods have been replaced by the consumption of ultra-processed foods high in saturated fats, sodium and sugar—that puts them at increased risks for non-communicable diseases such as coronary heart disease, cancer and diabetes.[4] This is a grave finding because it has been confirmed that underlying genetic and physiological factors have, in any case, made South Asians more prone to these diseases than other populations.[5] Combine this predisposition with a dietary shift to fatty, nutrient-poor food, and we have an impending public health catastrophe.

The nutritional transition has happened due to economic growth, urbanization, and globalization, which saw the entry of multinational processed food companies, the preference for convenience as dual-income households increased, and effective marketing made such food highly desirable. Trade liberalization made it easy to import high-calorie, nutrient-poor foods from Western countries (e.g. tinned cheese, canned juices, candies, soft drinks and sugary breakfast cereals), which were then sold cheaply in supermarkets.

The World Obesity Federation's 2023 atlas predicts that 51 per cent of the world, or more than 4 billion people, will be obese or overweight by 2035. The maximum increases in obesity are expected to be from low- or middle-income countries in Asia and Africa. In India, 11 per cent of all adults will be obese, as per the report, predicting a similar range of 11–15 per cent for other South Asian countries except Pakistan (21 per cent) and Bhutan (20 per cent).[6]

Restaurants, being commercial establishments, cut costs by reheating oil, making food more appealing through a host of additives and cutting corners wherever possible. Cornflour makes gravies thicker; food colour gives chicken tikka its orange hue; old *daal* can be disguised as new with a fresh tadka; accompanying salads might be cut in a dark street behind the *dhaba* in less than hygienic conditions. To put it mildly, the average restaurant kitchen in our part of the world is not exactly a haven for health and hygiene. Regular consumption of this food puts the body at risk for bacterial infection, gastric trouble, weight gain and eventually the development of chronic conditions like diabetes, high blood pressure and heart disease.

To some extent, eating outside food was mitigated in the pre-app era. Going physically to a McDonald's, Burger King, KFC or even the dhaba round the corner with the best chole bhature this side of the Yamuna required going to the establishment, finding parking space, waiting in line, placing an order, digging the cash out of one's pocket to pay for the order, waiting for the food and coming home. This required a certain amount of time and effort and was, in fact, more time-consuming and inconvenient than cooking something at home. That helped limit the consumption of greasy, cholesterol-laden food.

Food delivery apps remove so many of these deterrents. Ordering grease bombs now requires just whipping out one's smartphone and pressing a few buttons. One's credit card information, address and favourite orders are saved. There isn't even any need to speak to a cashier or the delivery boy. Besides, apps are designed to make users order more through offers, discounts, combo packs, etc. Customers are looking for a bargain—getting more for less cost, and when the food arrives, they end up overeating.

Malavika Banerjee, fifty-two, co-founder of a sports management company in Kolkata, would get a lunch dabba from home and still order in because it was a young office, and ordering in was the norm.

'Just to pig out and try new things,' she says when I ask what her motivation was.

Then she realized that her weight was creeping up, and it took a forced stay-at-home after a hysterectomy to break the habit. 'When I was at home, I began to appreciate the difference when you stop eating out and just eat *ghar ka khaana*. I felt much lighter and more energetic.'

The WHO's European Regional Obesity Report 2022 asserts that ordering in is a factor. Revealing that well above half of European adults and one in three children are either overweight or obese, it flagged meal delivery apps as possibly contributing to obesity by encouraging sedentary behaviour.[7]

When Neeraj, an IT engineer in Kathmandu, had just started working, he used to practice callisthenics and go to the gym, which made him watch what he ate. But as he became busier at work, he grew more careless about food and had no time for exercise. 'I became heavily dependent on online food delivery apps. Even on my two days off from work, I would order online. I think now that I should cook for myself in the evening,' says Neeraj. 'My parents came to my flat and noticed a lot of plastic boxes and bags from various food vendors. They suggested it's not a good habit and I should stop.'

It could be argued that the individual must exercise self-control and order healthier options. However, the cost of nutritious foods—such as fruits, vegetables and animal-sourced foods—is typically higher than that of foods dense in fats, sugars and salt.[8] Food from restaurants serving organic or healthy, low-fat, low-carb, high-protein food costs more than standard fare in any country, and for those barely starting their careers and staying away from their parents, the item's price is an important consideration when they order in.

In Karachi, Qurat-ul-Ain's mother struggles with excess weight and is diabetic. 'I know I am at risk too. But don't have any time to exercise. I joined yoga and Zumba classes, but can't sustain them. Yoga studios are not cheap here. So, eating out often, no exercise, diabetes risk—my mom says to cut down on online ordering. That's tough, so I try to do portion control,' Qurat-ul-Ain shrugs.

While food apps merely encourage sedentary behaviour, quick commerce is like giving us a tranquillizer shot that leaves us flopped on the couch in torpor, only rising to open the door when the delivery boy rings the bell. Ironically, the target audience for these apps—mostly the under-forty, upper-middle class—also wear fitness trackers on their wrists and try to complete 10,000 steps! Those trips to corner shops that now seem like a long trek would arguably have contributed to that target. According to a new Lancet Global Health study, half of India's adult population will be physically unfit by 2030. Physical inactivity has jumped from 22.3 per cent in 2000 to 49.4 per cent in 2022, of which 57 per cent were women, 42 per cent men.[9]

Excess

Growing up in Mussoorie, smoking was an occasional, furtive indulgence for Aarav Tiwari, a twenty-eight-year-old lawyer in the Supreme Court. He would join his friends at a local paan shop and puff away, secure in the knowledge that their parents had no idea about their antics. Even in law school, about five or six years ago, he would only light up by walking to the corner shop and getting a smoke.

When he is at the court, he doesn't carry a packet. He has a deal with the paan shop around the corner, where he has paid the *panwallah* for twenty cigarettes in advance. Every time he goes and smokes one or two, the panwallah sends him a message on WhatsApp to record how many cigarettes are down, and when it is zero, Aarav renews the deal.

'This helps me restrict my smokes because I have to make an effort to go down and buy a cigarette. If I had a packet, I would pull it out and light up.'

But at home, when he orders through a quick commerce app, one can't order separate sticks, so it is always a complete packet. How would he have managed the late-night cravings for a cigarette without the apps?

'Well, if the delivery system was not there and I had a craving for a smoke at midnight, I guess I would have just turned over and slept. Of course, I wouldn't leave home and start searching for cigarettes at that hour. It would be too much of an effort.'

There's a moment's pause, and he admits, 'Obviously, one smokes more, I guess. Because it has become so readily accessible.'

In a sub-Reddit group of Gurugram, a young man seeks help to escape the grip that food delivery apps seem to have on him:

I am a working male. I'm addicted to ordering food from Zomato & Swiggy. I have been trying to quit/keep it in check for 2 years now but to no avail. I order in almost daily even though I live with my parents and food is cooked at home. Sometimes twice a day. The ordering experience has become too smooth imo [in my opinion]. Fixing a meal for yourself takes effort, and the bland taste of home-cooked food, as compared to the junk that I order, also doesn't help. The repercussions are multi-pronged. This is affecting my physical, mental as well as financial health. I have tried a lot of things like uninstalling the apps, not renewing gold (membership), and eating before I'm hungry, but I end up coming back. I'm still trying. There must be others dealing with the same issue. Please share tips.[10]

Sub-Reddit groups of different Indian cities have threads by young working folks worried about health and high prices of ordering restaurant food but unable or unwilling to cook. A woman in Bengaluru living in a co-living arrangement without amenities or time to cook is sick of ordering healthy food on Zomato. She asks for recommendations for a meal service that will supply mainly salads. A man in Chandigarh is worried and seeks suggestions for newer restaurants in the city to break the ennui he feels because of frequent ordering.

With delivery at one's fingertips, it is accessible for children who have grown up with mobiles since they were toddlers. During the pandemic, Zomato sent an email targeted at children titled 'Hey, parents not letting you order?' encouraging kids to order food secretly. The mail helpfully provided a cheat sheet to the kids to convince their parents to let them order. One of the tips was that kids should patiently wait until their parents fell asleep, then sneak in the order and enjoy it in their room quietly. The marketing campaign was roundly criticized for encouraging children to be sneaky and secretive. The campaign went live in August 2020 when no vaccine was in sight. Parents were angry that in their hurry to pick up the order and run in before being spotted, kids were liable to be negligent about the usual precautionary measures of sanitizing the packaging surfaces.

Prof. R.S. Khare, a pioneering sociocultural anthropologist and a professor emeritus at the University of Virginia, now eighty-seven, has written about how moderation is a fundamental gastronomic principle of the Indic civilization. Portion control was inbuilt as it was impossible to have too much of so many dishes. Dietary balance was embedded in the ideal of *niyamita ahara* or a regulated meal. Overeating was both morally undesirable and personally harmful. Fasts were a way to control meals among Hindus, Jains and Buddhists. A Buddhist monk can eat only the amount necessary to sustain life. A Jain monk is not to be bothered with taste or any aspect of the food except that it is edible and available.

From there to a whole nation ordering enough biryanis in 2023 via Zomato to fill eight Qutub Minars, as the company humorously noted that year,[11] we have indeed come a long way.

Circadian Rhythm

'Occasionally, I think that maybe I should stop this lifestyle of sleeping just four hours every day,' says Keshav, the Hyderabad IT executive who sleeps at 3 a.m. after a night of his favourite food and OTT.

Circadian rhythm is a phrase that has been made mainstream by sundry medical folk trying to spoil the

Netflix party by waving red flags about disrupting our body clocks. The word circadian comes from the Latin phrase 'circa diem', meaning 'about a day', referring to the physical and mental changes a living organism experiences in a twenty-hour cycle. The human body's circadian rhythm or sleep-wake cycle tries to take cues from the environment, such as food intake, physical activity, social interaction and whether it is light or dark. Nearly every tissue and organ has its circadian rhythm synchronized to day and night, and a master clock in the brain controls all of these.

According to the Sleep Foundation, light is the most critical signal the body relies on to decide whether it is sleeping or waking time. So, at 2 a.m., if we are watching Netflix and munching on pizza, the body receives both light and food. Thinking that it is supposed to be awake decreases the production of the hormone melatonin, which puts us to sleep. Besides, the blue light emitting from smartphones has been shown to suppress melatonin production, disrupting the sleep-wake cycle and impairing cognitive function.[12]

The body clock regulates sleep, appetite, hormones, temperature and wound healing. Left to itself, the circadian clock would take its cues from when the sun flooded the house with light and when it set, steeping it in darkness. For instance, people who work according to the natural rhythm have a finely tuned hunger psyche. An anthropologist who observed labourers working on a rice field in south Karnataka in the 1980s noted how they could tell time by how hungry they were because the transit time of food in their bodies was in sync with the time of the day.[13]

The discovery of electricity messed with that rhythm because people no longer relied on sunlight and could be awake even after sunset. Even then, there wasn't enough reason to be awake late into the night, and everyone dozed off a little after supper.

Cell phones awakened our inner owl, but the confluence of OTT and midnight food availability completely upends the circadian clock and demands a complete reset. Moving around, eating and engaging the senses when the body isn't primed to do so is now implicated in a whole host of health conditions, from lowered immunity to diabetes, depression and even cancer. A study by the Wilmot Cancer Institute studied the effect of circadian rhythm disruption on cancer cells, each of which has its twenty-four-hour cycle.[14] They found that a gene called MYC oncogene, which exists in many types of cancers is alerted and shuts down the circadian rhythm in cancer cells. This gives them an advantage and helps the tumour progress. The lungs are mainly under tight circadian control and seem particularly vulnerable to a disrupted biological clock.

The Latte Factor

The latte factor is creeping in for young professionals who are ordering in heavily. A concept popularized by authors David Bach and John David Mann in an eponymous book,[15] the idea behind it is that the little things you regularly purchase can cut into your budget more than you might realize. For example, the $5 you spend on a latte today may seem small, but $780 over 12 months is not. When millennials and Gen Z spend more on outside food than they would have, the latte factor slips in, and before they know it, they've notched up a bill that busts their budget.

Earning about 30,000 per month, Elizabeth, who works at a think tank in Kochi, pays Rs 9000 as rent and spends 12,000 on food, half of that on online ordering. She feels the pinch despite restricting her per-meal bill to Rs 150–200 and signing up for the platform's Gold Membership, which offers discounts and zero delivery charges. She realizes that cooking at home would be far cheaper but cannot summon the enthusiasm given her current work pattern.

Not very far from Elizabeth, across the tropical waters of the Laccadive Sea, Gayatri, who is twenty-eight, moved to Colombo from Kandy to join her brother, who was already working there. The siblings have taken up a small annexe in Nawala, an upmarket residential area and split the rent. Back home in Kandy, their mother and a cook would ensure hot, home-cooked meals were always on the table at mealtimes. But in Colombo, the apartment has a small functional kitchenette, making it hard to cook regularly. They don't have a refrigerator, so every meal is ordered through PickMe Food or Uber Eats—rice and curry for lunch and *kottu* or pasta for dinner.

Though Gayatri is grateful for the availability of these apps, she says it has been tough money-wise to eat healthily. The island's economy was under the worst financial crisis of decades in 2022. I witnessed the impact of the devalued currency in the week I spent in the country towards the end of 2023. The wads of cash I kept withdrawing from the ATM vanished like water vapour rising over the Indian Ocean. From January 2024, the government increased VAT to 22 per cent, making restaurant food even costlier. Observes Gayatri:

> Online food has made my life easier because my life has changed drastically since moving from Kandy. But financially, I have found this to be very challenging. In some ways, cooking at home would be cheaper. So, sometimes, if I am short on cash, especially towards the end of the month, I try cooking instead of ordering online. Even though I share the cost of food with my brother, sometimes it becomes a little too much. It is also because I try to save at least 10,000 from my salary each month. That is a practice I had even before I moved to Colombo. Buying healthy food in Colombo is also very expensive. A salad would cost well beyond 2000 rupees [LKR], and I usually spend at most 1200 rupees per meal. Of course, we get rice and curry for lunch, which is relatively healthy. If anything, our dinner is erring a little on the unhealthy side. Even if we buy unhealthy dinners, I can still compensate for it by making a healthy side dish like salad. But I admit that I do not do that often. I also would like to be more health conscious regarding food, but right now, I cannot afford it.

In Pakistan, petrol prices increased by 145 per cent from PKR 101.42/litre to PKR 248.74/litre between 2012 and 2022,[16] causing an increase in delivery rates as well. Qurat-ul-Ain's mother, Farida, a schoolteacher nearing retirement, disapproves of the expenses. 'You girls work so hard—commuting forty minutes daily one way—it's hard-earned money. Why blow it up like this?' she scolds.

Apps are designed to be highly engaging, using features such as notifications, alerts, personalized content, reminders and gamification to capture, retain and maintain users' attention.[17] Several scientific studies have shown that smartphone addiction is associated with reduced grey matter density in the brain's frontal cortex, which is responsible for decision-making and impulse control.[18] Poor judgement leads us to make poor choices, after which we are awash with guilt and self-loathing.

But guilt is a post-facto emotion. You only feel it after the deed is done. Cain killed his brother Abel out of jealousy and bore the burden of guilt forever. Yudhishthira, the eldest Pandava, experiences profound guilt after the dice game, leading to his brothers' exile and Draupadi's humiliation. Angulimala, a notorious bandit who killed many, meets the Buddha, feels deep remorse for his actions and becomes a monk. More prosaically, in contemporary life, compulsive use of delivery services can induce the guilt of overindulgence or adversely affect one's health by being out of sync with the natural body clock. Expenses mount every time a notification from the app prompts another purchase.

A habit that is hard to shake off is formed slowly, almost surreptitiously, and more guilt is experienced in a vicious cycle. The silver lining is that guilt can also catalyse self-awareness and awaken users to exercise better judgment in buying behaviours.

GRATITUDE

On a winter night in Paris in 2008, two friends, Travis Kalanick and Garrett Camp, came out of LeWeb, an annual tech conference and couldn't get a cab. They wondered how easy it could be to request a ride from one's phone. That epiphany led to the birth of Uber, and the idea that one could seamlessly move from being a software professional or writer to a cab driver captured people's imagination. The 'Uberization' of the world's economy began, where people could do a 'gig' whenever they wanted. In the summers one could be a farmer in the village and in the winters come to the city and drive a cab.

As stated previously, we owe the idea of the 'gig' to jazz musicians carrying instruments and performing at bars and cafes. The digital era of the late 1990s spawned remote job platforms, allowing people to earn money by providing services on an on-demand basis either in place of or in addition to full-time jobs. In 2021, 16 per cent of Americans reported earning money through online gig platforms and for about a third of them, this was their main source of income in the previous twelve months. In the US, millennials and Generation Z together account for about half, or 49 per cent, of those working in an independent capacity.[1]

Even before the advent of digitalization in day-to-day life, gig work was always thriving, especially in our part of the world with its massive informal sector, constantly buzzing with activity. Freelance journalists, tuition teachers, professionals who painted their phone numbers on public walls along with their names and occupations (for instance, 78xxxxx901, Raju, plumber) and many others were all part of the gig economy. These are all skilled workers hawking their competencies for piecemeal jobs and getting paid per unit of service sold (like per article or hour of tuition or tap repaired).

Some gig workers who have signed up on tech platforms have chosen to remain stationary, while others move from place to place to deliver a product or service. Those who work from home and take up gigs are in specialized professions like, for example, graphic designers and translators. They are a substantial but invisible workforce, sitting in their homes worldwide, tapping away on their keyboards. The other set, who form the focus of this book, are the ones we see all around us, the e-commerce agents wearing the company's T-shirt and riding two-wheelers.

How many of these workers are out there?

No one knows for sure because the model is such that someone can log in and out, work for six months and take off for the next six. So, other than the company that hires them, no government agency has any database of these workers. But one estimate that serves as a baseline figure is offered in India's premier think tank, NITI Aayog's 2022 report[2] on the gig economy. According to this report, between 2020–2021, there were 77 lakh (7.7 million) gig workers in India, comprising about 1.3 per cent of the total workforce. According to the Centre for Monitoring Indian Economy (CMIE), platform workers form 2.4 per cent of the total urban workforce.[3] Pakistan has an estimated 7 lakh platform workers[4] and Bangladesh has 3 lakh delivery workers.

A World Bank report of 2023, though speaking only of online gig workers, acknowledges that there are no systematic ways to estimate how many people work in the gig economy despite its emergence as a growing segment of the workforce.[5] The word on the street is that there are far more people than official estimates suggest, who are logging in and out of apps.

Many docked their ship to the gig economy after tossing about in stormy seas, as it were. Their reasons for taking up gigs through tech platforms maybe varied, but these workers felt an immense sense of gratitude for these opportunities that came during hard times.

Victims of Covid-19's Economic Catastrophe

When the Covid-19 pandemic gripped the world in 2020, the job losses and poverty it induced made it the worst-ever economic crisis. The world had teetered back to normalcy when the Russia–Ukraine War broke out in 2023, followed by the Israel–Gaza War in late 2023. These events, but most notably the pandemic, had a ripple effect on the global economy, slashing jobs, reducing remittances from abroad, bringing families to their knees and sometimes snuffing out their only source of livelihood or the primary breadwinner. As job losses accumulated, more people joined the informal economy to survive the economic downturns. Assets lying unused were monetized. People with an extra floor rented it out through Airbnb—those with a vehicle logged on to a transport app to drive people around.

In India, close to a million drivers and cleaners of private transport (buses and taxis) were estimated to have lost their jobs[6] when work-from-home became the norm and schools moved to the online mode during the two years of the pandemic. Many newly unemployed people enlisted as cab drivers on ride-hailing platforms such as Uber and Ola. Less-educated migrants and low-pay workers could not do remote work on computers and were left to brave the risk of infection and take up jobs that required physical presence. Several joined food delivery companies such as Zomato and Swiggy and e-commerce companies such as Amazon in distress-driven employment.

'I belong to a good family,' Radha Vallabh Sharma tells me more than once. It is August 2023, and we are sitting in the basement of the building leased out to cyber cafes and real-estate brokers just outside Gandhi Nagar Railway station in Jaipur. Here, a cramped room in the basement with many blue swivel chairs serves as the office of the Gig Workers Association of Rajasthan.

Sharma is from a small town near Brindavan, Uttar Pradesh. His family had a successful business supplying construction materials for infrastructure projects, but it was severely hit during the pandemic and suffered considerable losses.

'Huge sums of money, close to 50 lakhs, were held up with contractors who could not pay us. My brothers and I had, in turn, borrowed money from the market. So, essentially, our business was finished. I realized I had to figure things out by myself. I came to Jaipur in 2021 to start a new life, hoping to give my family a better future—my wife and son. I also didn't want relatives and friends back home to know that I have become a cab driver or delivery boy,' Sharma continues. 'I belong to a good family. It's just that life took an unexpected diversion after Covid.'

Since his only asset was his motorbike, food delivery seemed an obvious choice. He had heard that one could earn a decent amount of money to help him cover the house rent of Rs 5000 and his son's school fees.

'As soon as I stepped into this industry, all my pent-up wishes of buying something extra for my family started getting fulfilled. I was making about Rs16,000 per week. After deducting for petrol, I would be left with about 12,000 a week. In the next week, I made Rs17,000 and I thought, Wah! There's no limit to this. As long as I keep working hard, I can make good money!'

Ex-Manufacturers

Some economists are of the view that with a slow and steady decline in the manufacturing industry, data has become the engine of economic growth in this century. Hence, companies that rely on IT, data and the internet for their business model (digital economy) are steering economic growth. Manufacturing became more complex with globalization, especially walloping small entrepreneurs. The asset-lite model of the tech startups came as a relief to many of them.

Chinthaka, who is thirty-three, lives with his wife, four children and parents in the suburb of Pannipitiya, Colombo. He is a qualified accountant and acquired additional entrepreneurship management and hotel management diplomas. At some point, bored of his accounting job, he started his own apparel company with eighteen employees. But it had to be shut down in 2018 because the Sri Lankan government started allowing the import of ready-made garments instead of only raw materials as it was previously. 'So the competition in the domestic market increased because my production cost was higher than the price at which the imported ready-made garments were sold.' To cope with this, Chinthaka started importing finished garments from China but ran into losses. 'I lost about LKR 70,00,000 because there was a mismatch in the quality between the samples and the stocks I received. So, I sold the stock at a lower price. I also sold my vehicle and paid back my debt completely. I had to shut down the company. Then I purchased a Prius and registered with Uber.'

Those in Distressed Economies

Shiva Rasaily, twenty-nine, is from Okhaladunga in eastern Nepal, a district made famous by the song, *Mero*

Pyāro Okhaldhungā (My dear Okhaldhunga), composed by the legendary Nepali poet Siddhicharan Shreshta. But in Kathmandu, Shiva's life is not even remotely romantic. He lives with his parents in Sukumbasi Basti, a squatter settlement. During the day, he works as a school bus driver, but his income is insufficient, so after his day job, he assumes the avatar of a delivery boy with the food delivery platform Bhojdeals.

Shiva begins the day at 8 a.m., driving the children to school. Then, throughout the day, he has nothing to do and spends it relaxing at school, surfing the net on his phone. By 4 p.m., he drops the children to their homes and logs on to Bhojdeals for nine hours straight, winding up at 1 a.m.

Shiva is a man on a mission. 'I dream of building a small house and moving out of the Sukumbasi area. I am not receiving any help from any quarter, but I am still trying my best. This is all I can do because I lack education. All I know is driving—what other options do I have?'

He feels that an app like Bhojdeals has come like manna from tech heaven, giving him a means to grow his income.

'My father and mother used to do labour work, but they grew old and had to stop. My income from the part-time job has become very useful for them in this situation of scarcity.' He has only good things to say about Bhojdeals. 'They pay the staff fairly, providing payments on time. Additionally, they provide fuel for the bikes. It's a good arrangement, and it feels rewarding to be appreciated after putting in hard work.'

When I meet Yeshu Thakali, senior vice president and head of Global Rides for Pathao, in his office in Kathmandu I ask him what he thought was Pathao's most significant contribution to Nepal.

'We have entirely transformed how people move in Kathmandu. We've created a viable opportunity for someone who doesn't have anything to do but is in financial need to start earning easily and quickly. We did a survey recently where we found that we added about 20 per cent to restaurant sales—in addition to what they were already doing. I think that is a commendable achievement for us. We are making people's commute easy, creating employment opportunities, and helping local businesses.' he says.

After years of standing outside employment agencies, paying middlemen and queuing up outside offices to submit applications, facing caste, region or religion-based discrimination in hiring, the platforms' low entry barriers are nothing short of wondrous. Anyone can sign up irrespective of class or creed. There are no interviews or job applications to fill in. You upload a driver's license on to the app on your smartphone and you're on. The phone soon starts buzzing with orders.

Ailesh, a Zomato delivery executive, is the first person I chatted with for this book. I was curious because he looked much older than the usual delivery executives milling around in the building. I discovered that he was fifty-six and used to be a collection agent for a bank, impounding vehicles of loan defaulters. In comparison, he found this job a breeze. '*Halka kaam*' (light work) is how he described it. '*Thoda* English *aana, thoda* chatting *aana* (some knowledge of English, some ability to speak and communicate)' were the talents required to be a delivery worker, he said. The chatting, I realized later, referred to the ability to talk, not to the customer, but to customer support on the app. But why would he run around so much at this age to support his small family of himself, his old mother and his wife? 'I got two daughters married, so I took some loans,' he said, solving the mystery. 'They are on my head. I'll quit this job once I am done paying them off.'

Waqas Azam has been driving his autorickshaw in Lahore for eighteen years. He says he has never had a better time professionally. Especially now, after Uber and Careem, inDrive has come in and disrupted old models through a bidding system in which a customer bids and the driver in closest proximity who accepts the bid wins the order.

'Ever since technology came into the fray, *Alhamdulillah, maza aa gaya kaam mein* (work has become delightful),' he says, seated inside his auto in a sky-blue salwar kameez. 'We used to run behind passengers asking, "Miss, where would you like to go?" and ladies used to get scared if we followed them. But since the apps came, we can park our auto in the shade, and passengers find us automatically; we don t need to go after them.'

Nugegoda, outside Colombo, was once a marshland surrounded by an elephant-infested forest of Nuga trees and canals teeming with crocodiles. Criminals tried before the king and found guilty were ordered to be 'nugeng egodaha

arang pala (taken beyond the Nuga forest to be killed)'.[7]
Now, it is a satellite town of Colombo city, full of office
buildings, cafes and traffic. This is where the head office of
PickMe is located. PickMe is a homegrown company backed
by the International Finance Corporation; it was launched
in 2015 and has become Sri Lanka's largest ride-hailing and
food-delivery platform, a worthy rival to incumbent Uber.
I was at the office to chat with Isira Perera, COO of PickMe,
to understand the journey of the business.

In the course of the conversation, Perera shares that
PickMe has 1,00,000 drivers on its platform, many of
whom work on the platform part-time after a full-time
job elsewhere because things are tough in the ongoing
economic crisis that began in 2019 and was made worse
by the pandemic and political upheaval. Retirees are also
signing up, either to supplement their income or to stay
engaged post-retirement. 'The drivers who work 8–10
hours a day make about 3000 (Sri Lankan) rupees a day
which is quite good. Some have earned really well and
they have gone on to buying two, three vehicles also,' says
Perera.

In Sri Lanka, workers are grateful to Uber and
PickMe not only for the gig opportunity but also for the
compassionate approach the platforms took during and
post the pandemic.

PickMe has endeared itself to its drivers by offering
insurance coverage for drivers as well as their families. 'We
have paid 5–10 million Sri Lankan rupees in insurance
claims. It covers not only death and permanent disability

but also childbirth and loss of a parent as these are the pain points in a driver's life which interrupt his cash flow because he cannot work for a few days,' Perera says. PickMe's highest-rated drivers get discounts at retail stores and fuel stations and free school supplies for their children.

Twenty-five-year-old Keshan finished school in Kegalle and moved to Colombo for higher studies. From second year onwards, students had to find accommodation on their own. Not wanting to burden his parents with the boarding fees, he registered on Uber Eats, '. . . because of flexibility. I can ride as and when my lecture schedule permits me.'

In Sri Lanka, if it is a cash transaction, the worker has to deposit the commission into the company's account via an ATM machine. Saleh Rislan, an Uber Eats delivery worker, had a sizeable amount of commissions accumulated, which he could not pay to the company. 'As a pandemic relief measure, Uber wrote off what I owed them and that was extremely helpful,' he says, relieved.

Hinterland Youth

In August 2023, I travelled from Poovar in the extreme south of Kerala to Kanyakumari, a two-hour drive across the state border in Tamil Nadu. I had visited Kanyakumari decades ago with my parents, and since the route was through lush tropical scenery, I wanted to retrace that journey.

I did what the locals do—took an auto to the village of Ucchakada and waited for the Kerala State Road Transport Corporation (KSRTC) bus, which would take me to the town of Kaliyakkavilai, the hub for Kanyakumari-bound buses. I was bracing myself for a long, uncertain wait at the Uchhakada bus stop, but within ten minutes, a KSRTC bus rolled in. I climbed on to it and betrayed my outsider status by asking anxiously, 'Will it go to Kaliyakkavilai?' The bored driver waved me in. The breeze from the swaying palms and Kerala's verdant scenery made it a most pleasant ride for Rs 20. As the bus crosses from one state to the other, the script on signboards changes from Malayalam to Tamil, and slowly, one sees more vehicles with registration numbers that begin with TN than KL. The varieties of bananas and stacks of coconuts don't care for administrative boundaries and remain just as abundant along the route.

Kaliyakkavilai's bus station is a busy place. A local Jesuit college is the epicentre of higher education for the rural students around the town. The bus stop is teeming with students, primarily girls, heading home after the day's classes. I approached the tin shed that serves as the office of both KSRTC and TSRTC (Tamil Nadu State Road Transport Corporation). A metal sheet divides the small space into two cubicles, so no interaction is possible between them. As I pose my queries in Tamil about which bus to take to Kanyakumari, the TSRTC folks respond more readily. 'Our green colour direct bus to Kanyakumari is coming,' they said and ensured I caught it.

It was a cloudy day and so the legendary sunset of Kanyakumari was not visible. But the tourists didn't seem to mind. There was a lot more to keep them in high spirits. On the left was the Bay of Bengal, where the gigantic Thiruvalluvar statue and Vivekananda memorial rock are situated. Ahead was the Indian Ocean and, somewhere in the distance, Sri Lanka. On the right was the Arabian Sea. Maybe there is a colour difference when the light is right, but the waters were uniformly grey that day. Behind was the temple of the Devi, whose dazzling diamond nose ring reportedly served as a lighthouse for travelling ships of yore. Someone was playing Ilayaraja's hits from the 1980s while tea and coffee vendors and sellers of artistically cut mangoes sought customers.

I had skipped lunch and subsisted on roasted peanuts. Now, my stomach was growling. So, I opened my Swiggy app and was surprised that delivery was possible even in this remote town. I ordered a small pizza and cold coffee, the bestsellers of a nearby cafe. Then, I sat down and tracked the progress of the rider on the map, fascinated at how technology makes a middle-class convenience available in the oddest places. In twenty minutes, Karthik arrived, bringing my meal to a rock on the last metre of the 3214-kilometre length of the land.

I smiled broadly and exclaimed in Tamil, 'Oh! *Vandutingala*! (You've arrived!)' I tipped him, pleased with the unique experience that he had enabled and clicked a selfie with him against the seascape. To Karthik, it was all in a day's work, and he seemed a bit puzzled by my excitement.

Karthik is a civil engineer, about twenty-five years old, and overqualified for the food delivery job he had been doing for two and a half years. He didn't intend to do this, but he along with many of his classmates could not find a suitable job, even though they were ready to move to other cities. His mother and grandmother depended on his income as the trio lived in a rented house and owned no other assets. Kanyakumari is a small tourist town and so, the business was seasonal and dependent almost entirely on tourists. A dozen delivery boys were doing about fifteen daily orders each. He was keenly looking for an alternative that aligned better with his education. I ask him what he would have done without this job.

'Then I would just keep writing emails to companies, like I do now, and hope they respond,' he smiles.

To many youth in the hinterland like Karthik, platform work has come as a placeholder while they wait for better jobs. It has also instilled professional pride and self-esteem among them.

Back home in Hyderabad, I met Koru (which means 'sun' in Meitei language) from Manipur who works as a bathroom cleaner in Urban Company. Working for about ten hours a day Koru manages to earn Rs 50–60k per month cleaning bathrooms, kitchens and chimneys. When he came to Hyderabad, he worked as an apprentice for a fortnight with his brother-in-law who does the same job with the platform. Then he enlisted independently on the app and now there is a fifteen-day waiting period to book his services. 'Customers are willing to wait for me because they have seen my work. Especially when it is around Diwali, there is a huge booking rush!' His chimney cleaning skills are most sought after. 'Because I have a technique. People are astonished at how quickly I am able to clean. They ask me what chemical I use, but I say sorry, that's something I can't tell you. That's a trade secret.'

Women Workers

Preeti Gupta, a beautician with Urban Company in Hyderabad, came home in response to a booking I had made. As she got the hot water ready for my pedicure, we made small talk and found that we had both moved to Hyderabad from Delhi around the same time. She and her husband were a gig couple, as he drove for Ola and made more money than he ever did in Delhi-NCR, which she said was packed with cabs because of which he did not get many bookings.

'*Bhagwan ki krupa se mera* rating *kabhi kharab nahi hua.* (By the grace of God, my rating has never been bad.) It was always above 4.8 because I always do a good job,' she said and added matter-of-factly, 'If someone gets a bad rating, the company gives them a few chances. Of course, after two to three more bad ratings, they fire the girl.'

Preeti was appreciative of the job with Urban Company because it offered her a steady income with flexible timings. Every month, she circled the dates she wanted to work and conveyed them to her manager, who would slot her in for those days with no questions asked. There was medical and accident insurance. She planned to keep working there as long as her health allowed.

She was making a little nest egg with the money she earned to buy a house in Hyderabad. Her husband was putting aside money to build a floor above his parent's home in Kolkata, from where they both hailed. 'If I am going to be working here, why should I buy a house there? Let him do what he wants. I want to buy here. I like Hyderabad more. It's peaceful, and the people are nice,' she said.

I agreed, and we were quiet for a while. She slathered lotion on my foot and started rubbing it in. I broke the silence by asking her if her husband got upset about her not sharing her money. 'No, because I don't even bring it home. I put it in my Kolkata account, which my mother had opened for me. I go and physically put it in the bank. I don't have any online banking or card for that account, so I am not tempted to withdraw anything!'

Platforms have been transformative for women workers, both financially and psychologically. Some years ago, it would have been unthinkable for a beauty parlour girl to dare to follow her dreams of acquiring an asset and having the financial ability to fuel them. Indian women's asset ownership is notoriously low. The National Family Health Survey-5 (NFHS-5) of 2019–21 indicates that more men, as compared to women, own property. Overall, 42.3 per cent of women and 62.5 per cent of men own a house, whereas 31.7 per cent of women and 43.9 per cent of men own land either alone or jointly with someone else.[8] Gig work helped elevate the self-esteem of women like Preeti by enabling financial independence and the holy grail of work–life balance.

Ganga is a thirty-eight-year-old single mother of a fourteen-year-old daughter in Colombo. When she was without a job after Covid, a friend suggested becoming a rider for Uber Eats because she already had a motorbike.

'This job is much better than a traditional 9–5 job because it has so much flexibility. You can report to work according to your schedule. For example, on Sundays, I choose not to work and spend time with my daughter. There is no one instructing you what to do. I can run my errands on the job as well. My workday starts at around 7.30–8.00 a.m. First, I drop my daughter off at her school in Gampaha town, and then I log into Uber and wait for orders to come through. After school, my daughter takes the bus back home. Then I work maximum until 5.30–6.00 p.m. Some days, I get off work earlier than that. I do not work at night because there are only two females at home, so for reasons of safety.'

The only downside she sees is that she is always on the road, which her family is unhappy about. However, her daily income of about Rs 2000/day is enough to meet the needs of her small household, even after deducting fuel and vehicle expenses. She also benefitted from an Uber Sri Lanka scheme called Diriya Kantha (women of courage), which provided female drivers who met weekly targets additional financial compensation. Nevertheless, she admits there are risks associated with being a woman driver and hopes the platform would pay attention to helping them feel safer.

Sigal in Kathmandu is an area known for a smaller version of the famous Swayambhunath Stupa. There is a small square lined with shops selling touristy T-shirts, pictures and Buddhist flags. Sarita Joshi Bajracharya has a small manufacturing unit here making keyrings, bags, bike covers, car covers, handloom Dhaka coats and tote bags. As a young girl, Sarita had always been fond of dresses and would cut up her mother's old sarees and create clothes. The hobby became her livelihood when she learnt sewing formally and set up a tailoring unit with a dozen workers. A few years ago, a woman's organization helped her to register her business in Daraz Nepal. 'I am indeed obliged to Daraz. Before my business was registered on Daraz, I was mainly selling to friends and neighbours. But now my reach has expanded so much! I employ many more people in my unit. My aim is to grow and give employment to more Nepali youngsters so that they don't have to go abroad to find work,' says Sarita.

Tania Akhter, who is twenty-six, is a national-level player at Bangladesh Skating Federation. On a Zoom call—joined by Rituparna, my research associate in Kolkata who does the translation—Tania narrates a story of agency and liberation from suppression made possible by her employment in a small app-based startup in Dhaka. Tanina came to Dhaka in 2017 from her home in Khulna district to escape marriage as she was keen on pursuing her sports career. The one skill she had was riding a bike and, through a friend, she learnt of Lily Rides, a bike taxi startup exclusively run for women passengers with women riders.

The job gave her the flexibility to engage in sports activities, and a few years later, she found a job as a skating instructor at a school. Till 2.45 p.m., she works at the school and then moves to work for Lily Rides, co-ordinating the orders for the day, earning around 20,000 Bangladeshi taka per month. Earlier, when she was doing more rides herself, customers would wait even two hours but insist that only Tania come to pick them up. An all-women group makes her feel safe and as if she is in a family environment; the owner, Syed Saif, is a mentor and friend. All the girls are loyal to Lily because Saif has been with them through tough times—like in Covid when Saif tried his best to pay them salaries even though business was driven to the ground. Tania wants to remain associated with Lily in whatever small capacity and help grow the business.

Tania is stocky, wears short hair and rides a motorbike in a conservative society. How does the world react to her?

'Out of 100 women, just two maybe are riding motorbikes. So people stare at me for sure, but they don't dare mess with me!' she smiles.

Girls like Tania are, however, an exception. Working for digital platforms while staying at home finds far more favour with women as it requires no mobility and no stepping out into the public space, which women prefer to avoid for fear of risk to their safety.

Digital work offered by micro-tasking platforms enables hundreds of low-income, predominantly rural women to earn a supplemental income from their homes by being 'voice participants'. In June 2022, I visited Kolkata to see some women making money by speaking on their phones.

Sharmila, forty-four, is a resourceful, dynamic woman in Attabagan, a low-income neighbourhood in Garia. In the past, she has connected her neighbours to various livelihood opportunities. Sometime in January 2021, she found a new way to make a living that required them to merely read out 750 lines in Bengali on an app called Karya and get paid a Rs 1000, a substantial sum for the below-poverty-line families that inhabit the area. Karya is a smartphone-based digital microtask platform incubated in Microsoft Research, Bengaluru.

Voice search is growing exponentially in India, as one can observe when Uber or Ola drivers speak out the name of the destination they have to go to. It's quicker, comes more naturally than typing and avoids spelling errors. To build such voice-enabled interfaces, machine learning has to be fed thousands of hours of voice data in Indian languages, using as many intonations and variations in pronunciations as they can find. That's where voice data suppliers like Karya, I-merit or the Australian Appen come in. They offer 'voice-based microtasks' to low-income people who can speak a regional language and sell the resulting voice database to companies making products based on voice and speech recognition technology. E-commerce giants are particularly interested in vernacular voice interfaces since they aim to lure digitally diffident online shoppers in small towns for whom the predominance of English on websites is a barrier.

On a humid afternoon, a group of women who have tasted success through digital work have assembled in the bare pink room of a resource centre in Garia in anticipation of more. Women, in particular, have taken to digital work because of its inherent flexibility of time and space. Amazon's Mechanical Turk, which crowdsources digital microtasks, such as image annotation, claims that around 35 per cent of its workers in India are female. Some are motivated by the thrill of earning an income for the first time, while for others, digital work provides an alternative to physically taxing occupations. First-time participants are reluctant to sign up because a job that involves the phone triggers fears of hackers accessing their personal and financial information. Public service broadcasts about such 'phishing attacks' have amplified leading to deep suspicion about earning through the phone. For people who are used to being paid only for doing physical labour, digital work sounds too good to be true. Coordinators like Sharmila Di are vital links who help convince them to come on board.

Growing up in the Sundarbans, Kabita Guha was good at volleyball and keen on joining the police or armed forces. As wage labourers, her parents couldn't imagine such a future for their daughter, and that dream died when Kabita got married at twenty-two. Now, at thirty, she is thankful to find a means to earn without leaving home. Voice data generation offers Mamta Ghosh, forty-one, extra income to make unplanned purchases for her teenage daughter. For some, like Seema Das, thirty-five, two rounds of work on the Karya app earned the same as her previous tailoring work did but without the hip pain caused by hours of working the sewing machine.

Someday, a person in a remote village of Arunachal Pradesh may say, 'Switch off the TV' in Idu Mishmi, a Sino-Tibetan language spoken in the state by a tiny minority, and the voice assistant will follow the command. Making that happen are droves of low-income Indian women speaking into smartphones, from the slums of Mumbai to rural Nadia in West Bengal, and a clutch of tech companies.

In 2023, 10.7 per cent of Nepal's labour force was unemployed, more than twice that of the South Asian average that was 4.5 per cent that year.[9] The default employment option for a young Nepali person of working age and lower economic strata is to leave home and find a job in India, the Gulf or South Korea. Delivering food packets or conveying passengers on a bike in Kathmandu Valley allows him to earn a decent wage, do an honest day's work and stay close to his family instead of joining the remittance economy.

Sri Lanka has been reeling under an economic crisis that began in 2019, brought on by tax cuts, a poorly managed shift to organic farming, and a series of devastating events such as the 2019 Easter bombings and the Covid-19 pandemic. The island ran short of fuel as it ran out of foreign currency to import it. The fuel shortage caused petrol and diesel prices to rise dramatically. Inflation soared and people could not buy even essential commodities. The economic hardships resulted in the 2022 Sri Lankan protests and the political upheaval which ousted the incumbent President[10].

Small businesses especially in tourism and hospitality were the worst hit and had to downsize.

In Pakistan, as political turmoil raged since the ousting of Prime Minister Imran Khan in April 2022, food and fuel costs spiralled upwards, the currency depreciated sharply and the cost of imports increased.

An uncertain geopolitical climate has had a ripple effect even on technical and managerial cadres. As clients in the West cut spending, India's top software firms had fewer staff in September 2023 than they did in January of the same year. This was the first time in twenty-five years that such a shrinkage of workforce was witnessed in the country's IT industry.[11]

Thus, slow post-Covid recovery and the resultant economic distress apart from political and global instability, have led to thousands getting displaced from their old jobs and joining platforms to take up delivery or driving as occupations. The gig economy has provided livelihoods to throngs of workers when they needed it most. For them, the apps have been nothing short of a magical invention that transformed their lives, for which they are immensely grateful.[12]

ANGER

Income and *Izzat*

Income

The amaltas trees in B.K. Dutt Colony, New Delhi, are spilling over with boughs of golden flowers in the harsh June sun. This colony is like an impostor between Lodhi Colony and Jor Bagh, posh areas home to high-ranking bureaucrats and retired corporate honchos. This is a modest enclave where the recently formed government of independent India had given Partition refugees subsidized houses. It has the standard elements of old-style Delhi colonies—a park, a Mother Dairy booth and low-rise residential buildings. A street-side temple happily encroaches on the road.

I have come to meet Kamaljeet Gill, national secretary of the Indian Federation of App-based Transport Workers (IFAT) and president of the Sarvodaya Drivers Association of Delhi (SDAD).

Kamaljeet's house is a 1BHK (one bedroom-hall-kitchen) home on the third and last floor of a building, which, if it were in Mumbai, would be called a chawl. He is an imposing, swarthy man with a thin moustache and a slicked-back ponytail. We sit in a living space illuminated by a dull tube light. Under the gaze of departed family elders whose photos stare down at us, Kamaljeet tells me how he acquired the reputation of a troublemaker who has been banned from working for all leading ride-hailing companies.

He begins by giving me some background. 'I became a cab driver twenty-three years ago. These foreign companies like Uber started coming in 2013 and found that this country is full of greedy people. I consider Ola a foreign company because its money is from abroad, even if the founder is Indian. So, knowing our greed, they gave all the drivers an Apple iPhone for every car that enrolled and about Rs 5000 as a joining bonus. Some fleet owners enrolled ten cars and got ten Apple iPhones plus cash. Business started rolling in. They used to pay us Rs 2 a minute for waiting, Rs 100 as base fare and Rs15/km. The commission was also low. Clients and drivers were happy with this nice, new service. People from the company used to call us the previous night and ask sweetly, "Will you be working tomorrow?" Uber gave us the phones, so they said we should log in to the app for ten hours, and whether we get orders or not, we'll pay Rs1800 a day. Uber just bought us all, and Ola followed the same pattern.'

In December 2014, two years after the Nirbhaya incident,[1] a twenty-seven-year-old woman was raped by an Uber driver leading to the cab aggregator's ban in the national capital.[2] During the ban, Uber had kept giving money to all the drivers enlisted previously.

'How much?' I ask, expecting it to be a subsistence amount for drivers to tide over the loss in income.

'What can I say,' replies Kamaljeet, a little bashfully. 'I had two cars, so I used to get Rs 25,000 in my bank account weekly. Drivers were making a cool one lakh in 2014, just sitting at home. And we would also make more money driving for Ola, which was paying handsomely.'

When Uber returned to Delhi roads in January 2015, it lowered the rates from Rs 10/km to Rs 6/km. Payment per trip went from Rs 400 per trip to Rs 375 three weeks later, then finally to Rs 350 per trip by the start of 2015. Then, they stopped paying per trip, counting only for the number of kilometres covered. In September 2015, about fifty drivers vandalized Uber's Gurgaon office. Kamlajeet who was at the vanguard of the disruption says, 'An FIR was filed and I was locked up with some others for a day in Sector 29 Gurgaon police station.'

Media reports between 2014 and 2017 about drivers protests confirm that payments to drivers fell dramatically in those years as the ride-hailing companies found their feet in the market and felt assured that they would have a steady supply of drivers. One report in the *Guardian* has a driver in Delhi complaining that Uber used to pay Rs 2000 as a per-day incentive if they completed a dozen trips, but this was cut back to just once a week for doing forty to fifty rides and they hiked their commission from 20 per cent to 25 per cent by end December 2016.[3]

February 2017 was Kamaljeet's moment. Joined by another union, he led 300 drivers in a protest in Jantar Mantar demanding that the Rs 6/km rate be increased because metered taxis charged Rs 16/km and autorickshaws charged Rs 8/km. 'How can we survive on Rs 6/km after paying the mandatory 20 per cent cut to the company and 5 per cent as tax?' he said to the press, which covered the protest because it inconvenienced city dwellers. Kamaljeet went on a day's hunger strike at the venue.

'I became a famous man after that protest! The Delhi High Court has passed a restraining order against me saying I can't go anywhere close to the offices of these cab companies.[4] You're sitting next to a celebrity!' he laughs. Indeed, in April 2017, the Delhi High Court issued a perpetual injunction against union leaders from stopping other drivers to work with Uber, staging *dharnas* (protests) and causing violence outside Ola and Uber offices.

'When Kalanickji (Travis Kalanick, the then CEO of Uber) came in December 2016, we *gheraoed* (surrounded another person or place with a group of protesters) him in the Uber office in Gurgaon. If you ever meet Travis Kalanickji, he'll remember me.' In classic Delhi bombast, Kamaljeet imagines that the protests he led contributed to Kalanick quitting soon afterwards.

'Last year, we protested when petrol prices hit the skies. CNG prices were Rs 80/litre and petrol costed Rs 100/litre—*chalo koi baat nahi* (that's all right). At least our conditions are better than Pakistan's,' he says. 'Now we drivers have only one demand from platforms—that they reduce their commissions by just 5 per cent from 25 per cent to 20 per cent and the government raise the tariff to 18/km from the current Rs10/km because fuel prices have gone through the roof. *Bas.*'

His wife, Sukhbir Kaur, enters with a tray of masala chai, biscuits and snacks. She's excited that I've come from Hyderabad because her future sister-in-law is Telugu.

'Sukhbir makes the best chai ever,' Kamaljeet adds. The couple have two sons. 'My younger son is in Class 11. He is trapped all day on the internet. Net *ka matlab* trap (internet means trap). You enter it and get entangled in its world of apps. We've again become *ghulams* (slaves). First, we were slaves of the British; this time, we are enslaved by these internet companies.'

Kamaljeet runs a small second-hand car sales business and petitions for restrooms, first-aid and parking space for ride-hailing cab drivers. 'Even if a person dies, we have to jump through hoops to get compensation for his family. Once a driver had been smashed by a BMW and died, we surrounded the car and made the customer pay Rs 32 lakhs to the family. The company gave nothing. God knows who scares the victim's family; each time they tell us just go away, we don't want any compensation.

'I am fighting against this on behalf of the poor drivers who had mortgaged their wives' jewellery to buy cars because the job attracted them. They thought they would earn money, educate the kids and buy a car. Now, they can barely pay the monthly instalments, and the jewellery is long gone.'

'But I've met many who are earning much more than they used to,' I say to counter him.

'Let's do the calculation,' he says, taking my pen and notepad. Suppose a man drives for 20 kilometres. He will need fuel worth Rs 100. The company pays Rs 15/km, i.e. Rs 300, to the guy. If you deduct the commission of 25 per cent and the fuel cost, he will be left with Rs 125. And usually, they pay lesser than Rs 15. I am just being generous.'

'So, if the earnings are low, why are more and more people joining in?'

'Because they don't realize that you have to spend hours on the road, make ten such trips and then only you can earn about Rs 1000 to 1200 daily. And they do some offline trips to save on the 25 per cent commission, which is bad because the customer's security is compromised.'

Less than a year after I had tea with Kamaljeet Gill and his wife, I chanced upon a crowd-funding appeal titled 'Please donate for brave heart Kamaljeet Gill'. The accompanying picture showed Kamaljeet lying in a hospital, eyes closed and tubes attached to him.

The post read, '*For over ten years, Kamaljeet struggled day and night to organize Ola and Uber drivers in Delhi. He was there when drivers met with accidents, got robbed or died, or at the police stations when they were in trouble, or leading them in dharnas or meeting the minister with drivers' demands. He became an all-India leader of drivers when elected as the vice president of the Indian Federation of App-based Transport Workers (IFAT). Today, Kamaljeet, the brave heart, is fighting to save his own life. Suffering a brain haemorrhage, he is on ventilator support at AIIMS Hospital in New Delhi. He never found time to attend to his family, which is now showing. The family is in dire need of money for medical treatment and to survive. He was always*

there for the drivers. Today, he and his family need us.
Please, let's all rise to the occasion and contribute generously
to support Kamaljeet in his hour of crisis.'

Only Rs 1.5 lakh had been collected. Eventually, he
came home, but he was completely paralysed on his left
side, and the family had no insurance coverage.

The drop in income is the main cause of angst among gig
workers in India. This has happened because companies
have withdrawn the carrots they had used to lure workers
when they first attempted to establish themselves in
India. The number of people joining these companies has
exponentially increased. Consequently, the market has
become fragmented, and the share of business for each
worker has fallen. Far too many cars and delivery workers
wait for their phones to buzz with an order. Meanwhile,
customer behaviours for some services have also changed
post-pandemic. For instance, some women who were not
going to parlours earlier because of the fear of contracting
Covid have now returned to their usual salons. Restaurants
were a no-go zone during the pandemic, and food delivery
executives were in demand to fulfil orders. Once the
pandemic ended, restaurants started filling up again.

One of the attractions of gig work is the temporal
freedom to work when you want. There is no requirement to
complete a specific number of hours. A driver in Delhi tells
me, 'I love being in my car and cruising along. Sometimes,

I stop for chai. If it's too hot, I take a nap, and again, when I feel like driving, I log in.' Women workers appreciate the flexibility that allows them to arrange their schedules and attend to domestic responsibilities.

But here's the hitch. While workers can choose the specific hours to earn the requisite income, they are obliged to put in more than ten, sometimes as much as sixteen hours. A journalist from the English daily *Deccan Herald* signed up as a food delivery worker for a day to get a taste of what such a job feels like. 'A "decent day" is when they earn Rs 600, and a "good day" is when they make Rs 1000 to Rs 1500, and this requires being on the road for twelve hours at least. "Bad days" can be really bad,'[5] he writes in his article.

For most South Asian workers, platform-based employment is not a side hustle but the primary source of income in which they are engaged for the entire day, sometimes working for longer than five years. In 2023, I partnered with an NGO that works in the area of labour rights called Janpahal, to survey gig workers nationwide on various aspects of their jobs.[6] Of more than 5000 polled workers, a mere 3 per cent work under four hours, 12 per cent work four to eight hours and a staggering 85 per cent work above eight hours a day as drivers/riders. Within that, 21 per cent work more than twelve hours to earn the desired income. Workers above forty enter the platform economy, work longer hours and stick to the job longer, possibly because it is harder to find alternative employment with age. Something that started as a 'gig' is now permanent.

Permanent gig work is an oxymoron, a contradiction in terms that should not be possible but is a stark reality.

Mohammed Asif is a balding man in his late thirties who works at Foodpanda in Lahore. He makes PKR 40,000 a month, but only if he works fifteen to sixteen hours daily.

'Working for sixteen hours is not sustainable, but we have no choice because of the situation in the country. Even educated people are becoming delivery boys. We can't give any time to the family. Once we reach home, we are so exhausted with all that driving that we can barely stay awake. Next morning, get up, wash your face and run. *Zindagi motorcycle tak hi mehdoot hoke reh gayi hai* (Life is limited to the motorcycle),' he says poetically.

'We spend a lot of kilometres just "emptily" driving,' says Krishna in Jaipur. He was referring to 'deadheading', which in ride-hailing jargon is the distance cab drivers travel with no passengers between rides.

Krishna has worked for all the apps but has quit everything to join the protests against the platforms. 'When we drop off a customer in a less habited area, for example, in the outskirts, about twenty kilometres away from the city, to get to the next ride we have to travel at least five to six kilometres to reach a more habited area. Once you reach there, you hang around and still don't get a ride; you wander for another couple of kilometres. But what will we get paid? Only the twenty kilometres that was part of the ride. Sometimes, the location is wrong; it's not exactly where the customer is, and we roam around finding the right spot. All those kilometres add up, and we aren't paid for that.'

It must be said that only workers in India were unhappy with their income. In other countries of the region, by and large, workers were grateful to have a means of earning in a slow economy, as the many examples in the chapter 'Gratitude' demonstrate. But in India, the high commissions, the rising fuel costs, the glut of workers and the debt burden for those who jumped into the job recklessly and took vehicles on loans have disappointed many, who feel the gig didn't live up to their expectations. The prospect of earning a windfall became illusory as more workers joined in and the company tightened its reins.

'Madam, let's go offline,' says Shyam sheepishly. He was an Uber driver who had come to take me to Hyderabad airport. Offline meant making a private deal with each other, bypassing the app. If I agreed, he would cancel the trip on the app but continue with the ride at the same price. I doubt there is anyone in the subcontinent who uses app-based transport regularly and has not received a similar proposal from the driver. In Nepal, Pathao bike riders will drive up to bystanders on the road and ask 'Pathao ho?' which means hop on, I'll drop you for the same price as on the app. This countermove is an anti-establishment form of resistance against the high commissions charged by the intermediary. In Bangladesh, such an arrangement to bypass the platform is called khaep and is not limited to ride hailing but practised by workers on all types of platforms.

When I argue with Shyam that there is no need to take it offline, he pleads that of the Rs 700 that will be billed to me, he will get only about 450. The commission he pays Uber was higher for airport trips, and he may have to return empty.

'Bookings are less during the month end. That's when we do all this. Otherwise, if there were enough bookings in the city to make the same money, who would want to come all the way to the airport?'

The son of groundnut farmers in rural Telangana, Shyam has been a cab driver since Covid. Earlier, he was working as a delivery person for Swiggy, but after a coworker was killed in an accident, hit by a tipper truck on a busy junction in Hi-Tech City, Shyam was too traumatized to use his bike. He bought a car on loan and turned to cab driving.

'After lockdown, too many drivers are there. KCR gave free cars to Dalits under the Dalit Bandhu scheme,'[7] he says, referring to K. Chandrashekhar Rao, the then-chief minister of the state. 'Thousands of cars have joined Ola, Uber and Rapido. But there aren't enough passengers. Many people in IT companies have shifted to working from home. Night shifts have been reduced. Companies are putting out their cars. Autos and bikes have been added. Before lockdown, there were only a cabs.'

In this tough market, occasionally going offline saves the driver the commission he would otherwise pay the company, the ethics of it be damned.

Izzat

It is May in Tirupati. The mercury has crossed 40 degrees Celsius. My family and I are back in the hotel after *darshan*, which anyone who has been to this popular pilgrim site knows is a physically exhausting project. Phones are whipped out, and after some discussion over the menu, an order is placed on a food-delivery app. A mild-mannered, bespectacled man arrives in the lobby a while later. Nagendra is about to leave after handing over the food to me, but I'm curious to know what food delivery means in a pilgrim town. Who orders and when? Is there enough business and so on?

Nagendra answers shyly, throwing furtive glances at the other guests going in and out. He is an electronics engineer from a government college. Still, there were no suitable jobs in Tirupati, and he was obliged to stay in his hometown because his father was unwell. His sister is married and stays elsewhere, so he is left to help his mother be a caregiver for his father and oversee the construction of their new house. He has been stuck in this job for nearly three years because of domestic constraints but hopes to quit soon. It's not about the money, Nagendra explains. Because even if he had taken up an engineering job, he would have earned the same 30–40k per month that he manages to make here. It's about lack of respect, he says. No one respects a delivery boy.

The perceived lack of respect makes Sai Kumar avoid wearing the company T-shirt. Sai Kumar is a twenty-year-old student at an engineering college in Hyderabad. In the morning, he attends classes, and in the late afternoon up to midnight, he does food delivery. He lives with his widowed mother, a domestic helper and his brother in his grandmother's house. The house that the family had booked under a government housing scheme was in Mehdipatnam, a Muslim-dominated locality politically controlled by the Muslim party All India Majlis-e-Ittehadul Muslimeen (AIMIM). However, the Bharat Rashtra Samithi (BRS) floated the Dalit Bandhu scheme[8] when they were in power; hence, some tussle resulted in the project getting stuck. Money was tight because both his mother and brother had fallen ill and notched up daunting hospital bills. He was studying data science but wanted to become a full-stack developer. Food delivery was an interim gig that no one except the immediate family knew about. Not even the neighbours in the low-income settlement he lived in.

'Because if they know, they'll think instead of studying, this boy is doing this kind of job. That's why I don't wear the uniform. *Shy feeling hota* (I feel shy),' he says speaking like a typical Hyderabadi.

The uniform is a contentious element of the job, at once bestowing an identity but also announcing the wearer's occupation to everyone on the road. A few are proud of the association with the platform while some are outright embarrassed.

'Drivers of other vehicles mistreat delivery boys. I don't want people in a traffic signal to address me as "Hey, Swiggy! Hey Amazon!"' a delivery worker in

Patna remarks. Another questions why he should do free publicity by wearing the T-shirt for a company that doesn't even recognize him as an employee.

Balakrishna, forty-five, drives a pick-up van in Ahmedabad for Porter, the packers and movers app.

'Porter wanted us to put a poster on our vehicles as branding for them. Workers are told that those who put the poster will get an order ten seconds prior than those who don't. Every month, we have to upload a photo of this poster to the app to show that it is still there. If the poster is torn, you must buy a new one for Rs 1000 or 1200. I tore away the poster. They call everyone . . . telling that if you want more orders, do this branding for us—especially new ones who get attracted to such schemes. Older people know it's nonsense. When we do private work and customers see this poster with all the rates written, they think this is much cheaper. They move to Porter. If we are doing work at Rs 1000, Porter will give it at Rs 600, and the job will go to them. By doing branding, you fall into a special category.

'Initially, this poster used to be free, but now they also charge for that. Once, we had organized a protest outside the company office about all the exploitation, the high commissions and the matter about the poster. The couple of people who breached the security and went into the office got caught in the camera. The bosses identified these workers and sent them to jail. Everyone contributed, and we collected Rs 50,000 and got them out.'

Rambling, private residential spaces, enclosed by a wall and heavily guarded gates or 'gated communities', have become the most visible urban form in Indian metro cities. Entry inside these societies is not allowed unless a resident approves the entry on an app or the intercom. Not being able to contact the customer after reaching the destination also happens sometimes in 'cash on delivery' orders when the delivery person cannot move until money is collected.

Even after the entry clearance is obtained, reaching the customer who could be living twenty to thirty floors above is a hurdle race. Almost all societies have separate lifts for visitors, which are typically overcrowded and have long wait times. Societies are often sprawling spaces; hence, once a delivery person enters the gate, sufficient time is spent walking or driving around trying to find the customer's block or tower. Sometimes, the bike is not allowed inside the society, and the delivery person is obliged to park the vehicle outside, which leaves him feeling anxious about the vehicle's safety when he goes up to the customer's residence and delivers the package.

While it is stipulated that delivery personnel should not carry more than 30 kg of weight, this is often exceeded. Urban Company beauticians and masseurs, who are almost always women, must carry along a bulky box containing bulky equipment required for the job. Manual work, such as lifting heavy weights, becomes scarcer as one goes up in the job hierarchy. Carrying weight on the job is seen as a coolie job, lowly and animal-like and hence associated with less respect. The Hindi word *majboori*, i.e., helplessness in a choiceless situation, was used frequently by workers I spoke to—carrying heavy weight was troublesome but had to be done to earn a livelihood.

This erosion of dignity that happens almost imperceptibly but regularly and the bearing down on workers through patently unfair practices is depicted beautifully in the movie *Zwigato,* directed by acclaimed actor–director Nandita Das. As a small-budget film, it was only released in the festival circuit and, until the time of writing, was not available on any OTT platform. Through a common friend, I secured a private screening. I was astonished at how the film authentically captures numerous aspects of a food delivery worker's challenging life. Kapil Sharma, better known for his comedic ventures, convincingly plays the role of Manas, a worker for an online food delivery platform called *Zwigato* (a clever portmanteau of actual company names). At the film's start, Manas hopes to do ten orders a day and earn a lot of money. He even reluctantly participates in a scheme where he has to post a selfie with the customer to earn an extra ten rupees per delivery. But within days, things spiral out of his control. One day, when he lads up at a house to deliver a pizza, the customer who had over ordered by mistake, blames and insults Manas, eventually giving him a poor rating. His ID gets blocked based on the complaint which begins his financial slide. But equally palpable is the hit on his self-respect as he performs his work in a society that thinks nothing of heaping indignities upon those who have been pushed to the margins.

The Blocking of IDs

On Diwali 2022, Radha Vallabh Sharma quit being a food delivery worker. It had been a year since Sharma had visited his parents and siblings back in Uttar Pradesh, but he elected to work and earn some money instead of going home. The festive season was a boom for online food ordering, with consumer goods companies luring customers with discounts.

'In Jaipur, many roads are blocked during Diwali because different events are happening, and the police put up blockades. Invariably, orders come from people in these areas because they don't want to step out and tackle the roadblocks. I had to deliver an order to a customer in one such area. No matter what I tried, I kept going in circles getting stuck at yet another road where the entry was closed. Google Maps wasn't helping; it directed me through some roundabout way that involved driving many more kilometres. I spoke to the customer, who was kind and understood my situation. So, I went to the closest point possible, and he walked up there and collected the packet from me. No sooner had I given him the packet that the phone buzzed with another order. I reached the restaurant, picked up the order, and found that my bike's rear tyre had a puncture! Maybe it was God's hand. I called up customer care and explained my predicament. The girl at the other end insisted that I somehow reach the location. I said listen, the roads are blocked, I have a flat tyre, please assign someone else. But they didn't have anyone else nearby because most riders, except desperate ones like me, were on holiday. I called the customer and took him into confidence. He was cool about it and told me to cancel the order. I did that, but imagine my shock when the company blocked my ID. I was in touch with the support team and the customers had no complaint. I had a genuine reason because of which I could not reach the assigned spot. Why should they block my ID?'

Blocking of ID refers to the company effectively disallowing the workers from using their app to get customers. As punishments go, it can be the harshest because, for these workers, every day earnings matters in meeting their monthly requirements.

His younger colleague Gaurav narrates how his refusal to go to a place cost him heavily. Late one evening, he had put his status as 'go to home' in the app. This is done by the rider in the last hour of his shift so that the app will only send him orders that lie enroute to his home. But he got an order to deliver to a university campus off his path and in what he calls a 'jungle area'. He called the support team and asked them to cancel the order, reminding them he was within his rights to cancel one order daily. 'But they insisted I should go. We got into an altercation, and after that, I woke up the next day to see that my ID was blocked. It has been blocked for months now. I put it on Twitter, but nothing happened.'

In contrast, traditional taxi/auto drivers can wave you away if they don't want to visit your location. A joke about Bangalore's notoriously whimsical auto drivers depicts Einstein with the caption 'Refused Nobel'; Marlon Brando

'Refused the Oscar'; then there's a picture of an auto driver with the caption 'Refused to go to Brigade Road' (a Bangalore locality). Behind the humour is a comment on how completely autonomous the local taxi/auto driver is in deciding his spatial coordinates.

Stumped by the App

For all the technological sophistry behind the scenes, the app underperforms in the most crucial moments or proves useless when a worker wants to understand why his payment was less than expected.

A few months after my Kanyakumari visit, I was in a similar setting in Sri Lanka. While researching in Colombo for this book, I was free on the last day, and Galle seemed inviting. Galle is a port on the island nation's southern tip. (Maybe I was a seafarer or maritime trader in a past life, but I have a thing for the land's end.) I took a bus from Colombo to Galle that whizzed past the exact scenery one sees in southern Kerala and arrived there promptly in two hours, as promised by Google Maps. It is a city where, in a sickeningly familiar theme, first the Dutch, then the Portuguese and finally the British fought each other and the locals to mark their territory. After each battle, the winner built a bit of the Galle Fort—an extension, a lighthouse, a dungeon. The fort has been turned into a hip district with cobblestoned streets, cafes and art galleries resembling a Monte Carlo or Luxembourg neighbourhood.

A king coconut in Lanka contains double the amount of water than that in the tender coconuts you get in mainland India. Though I had drunk from one of them, I got hungry after roaming around the fort, the serene Japanese Peace Pagoda situated on a hill on the other end of the bay and walking on the sandy beaches of Unawantuna. There was no time to eat in the many beach cafes because I had to catch the bus back to Colombo at 7 p.m. I reached the central bus stand and wondered if Uber Eats would deliver fast. An iced coffee sounded practical to take along on the bus without creating a mess. I chose one from Jaya Stores, which would appear in twenty-five to thirty minutes but could be earlier, the app said. Google Maps showed the store to be only fifteen minutes away. It would cut it fine, but I fill my life with these silly adrenaline rushes, so I ordered and paid LKR 1353.

It was 6.40 p.m., and dusk was giving way to a darker-hued sky. The bus was starting to fill up. Vehicles honked. Our conductor was yelling 'Colombo, Colombo' at regular intervals. The man outside the adjacent bus was way more aggressive, shouting 'Kalutara Kalutara' as if people would change their minds and get on to his bus only because he was louder. The scene could have been from any city in the subcontinent.

Meanwhile, Jaya stores had not yet packed the coffee. I stood outside the bus, looking at the phone nervously every few seconds.

6.50! Finally! The coffee had been packed, and Lalith, the rider assigned, was ready to leave. It was *Mission*

Impossible, the Lanka version. Would he make it? Maybe the bus would start a minute or two later?

Lalith had left and was coming towards my location. I was watching the map unblinkingly. There he was, come on, cross that signal! *Chalo, chalo, jaldi chalo* (hurry up) . . . I thought, sending him speed vibes, the way people on social media send 'positive vibes' if someone is ill.

6.59! He was almost there! I then got a message: 'Where r u?' Lalith wasn't calling for some reason, which I thought was good because we'd have wasted time negotiating the language barrier, as most workers I met spoke Sinhala.

'Bus stand. Standing on the main road. Blue T-shirt.' I typed back fast.

7 p.m. Our driver climbed into the seat and revved the engine.

'Bus is leaving. Fast.' I walked a few steps left and right, looking out in the failing light for a motorbike and a man in an Uber Eats T-shirt.

'I am near the bus stand.' Lalith wrote back.

'Where??? I am here! On the main road. Colombo bus.'

To my horror, the animation on the app showed that he was moving further away!

7.04. The last of the passengers was inside. The conductor indicated that I needed to get in too.

Reluctantly, I did and continued looking out the window in case the delivery boy would ride parallel to the bus, holding the cold coffee up like a trophy. I would put my hand through the window, lean over and pick it up. I guess I have watched too many Bollywood movies. The bus turned the corner, and nothing so dramatic happened. The rider merely cancelled the order.

I wondered why the rider was circling in the same 500-metre radius where I was standing but couldn't find the exact location. I realized through conversations with gig workers that it happened frequently because of glitches in the app, even when their internet signal was strong.

In Kathmandu, Bibek Kunwar, a cab driver with Pathao, complains how when the customer's location is not exact, the cabbie has to roam around to locate the customer, which costs money that neither the customer nor the company pays for.

In my study with the NGO Janpahal, we included a question: 'Have you ever had a problem because the app is not working properly?' The responses were educative. A quarter shared that the map would not load properly, an equal number pointed to errors in showing the drop/pick-up location, 28 per cent said they had experienced the app hanging, and the rest of the respondents said there had been delays in indicating that a ride was completed or that payment has been made. Less than 2 per cent said that they had never faced an issue.

NASA launched the Mars Climate Orbiter mission on 11 December 1998 to study the Martian climate and atmosphere. However, during the orbiter's approach to Mars in September 1999, a navigation error occurred due to a mix-up in units of measurement. The spacecraft's navigation software used English units (pounds-force-seconds) for thruster performance data, while the ground-based software used metric units (newton-seconds). This discrepancy led to inaccuracies in trajectory calculations, causing the spacecraft to enter the Martian atmosphere at too low an altitude. As a result, it disintegrated due to aerodynamic stresses and the mission failed.[9]

The point is that even the most advanced and powerful technologies with grand ambitions can have limitations and shortcomings. Apps are merely trying to deliver packages to customers. From the vantage point of a worker, technology is the almighty force that selects, allocates, optimizes, prices, penalizes and calculates every metric possible, holding workers in a tight, invisible rein. And yet, it can malfunction while in use, leaving workers even more mystified about the nature of this beast.

In the web series, *Super Pumped: The Battle for Uber*, which is based on true events, an Uber employee asks aloud after a presentation, 'Is this legal?' The room erupts in derisive laughter. It wasn't cool to care about regulations and laws in Uber's initial years under Travis Kalanick. *The Uber Files* refers to a trove of over 1,24,000 confidential documents ranging from 2013–17, which were leaked to the *Guardian*. They tell the inside story of the unethical and illegal practices the tech giant resorted to in its desperate bid to force the cab service into cities around the world.[10] It may not be a stretch to imagine that Uber's unapologetic, hyperaggressive approach set the template for how platforms should win markets.

Though other platforms have not come close to creating the kind of fracas that Uber did then, the idea was established that new tech businesses are disruptors of the game, rather than enablers. And when the old order is getting destroyed, some collateral damage is inevitable. The ones crushed under are the last links in the shiny, new-age tech assembly line—the delivery workers and drivers. They bear the brunt of the business strategy to grow the market by appeasing only one stakeholder—customers.

Unlike AI, human beings are messy, troublesome creatures with demands and ideas of *izzat* (respect). The ones on platforms are now increasingly raising their fists, angry at being sold snake oil stories about how much they would earn and how easy and flexible the job is. They are bristling at unilateral decisions that result in the termination of their earning opportunities and how the app and the tech they are asked to deify is, in fact, sometimes quite like them, whimsical and irrational.

At least until drones come in, the anger of the workers will have to be heeded.

FREEDOM

Freedom from the Kitchen

Binu Sharma, Kathmandu

Bhaktapur (also called Bhatgaon) lies east of the Kathmandu valley. It is a city packed with art, architecture and cultural heritage dating back to the early eighth century. The Durbar Square is a visual treat of pagodas, shikhara-style temples and Buddhist monasteries. E.A. Powell wrote in his book *The Last Home of Mystery* (1929), 'Were there nothing else in Nepal save the Durbar Square of Bhatgaon, it would still be amply worth making the journey.'[1]

'Bhat' means cooked rice in Nepali, and Bhatgaon is 'Rice Village'—a name given to Bhaktapur because it has always been a fertile, rice-cultivating area. When I reach Durbar Square and step out of the cab, I see pink-cheeked women in bandanas, winnowing paddy manually. They throw the mounds of paddy up in the air using a winnowing fork so that the lighter chaff blows away in the wind and the heavier grain falls to the ground.

Minutes after watching this age-old scene, I had a conversation in a café about tech-enabled food delivery with Binu Sharma, who is forty-one. Binu lives with her husband, Sumit Sharma Sameer, and helps run their media company. 'Apps like Foodmandu and Pathao have made life much easier, especially when I get home late and tired, not knowing what to cook. I order from these apps, and they deliver food within an hour. It is so helpful when we have guests and all of us are entering the house together! These apps save the day. If my little boy wants to eat momos, they are delivered in thirty minutes; it would have taken me hours if I had to cook them.'

Online food delivery gives urban working women a breather from the non-stop treadmill of meal preparation that generations of women have endured. My paternal grandmother, for instance, presided over a large household of eleven children and a husband who earned a modest living as an advocate in a temple town in Tamil Nadu. Family lore abounds about how she ran the kitchen like a well-oiled machine in the 1940s and 1950s, despite little help and no electric appliances. Meal after meal would be produced to accommodate varying time schedules, nutritional needs and fussy palates. This was the era of unannounced guests arriving suddenly from other towns and staying on for days to watch a temple festival. In the spirit of 'atithi devo bhava' (a guest is God), all of them would be fed to their heart's content in my grandmother's kitchen. There were no restaurants to buy food from if she was tired, no way to supplement the food by getting one dish from somewhere else and nothing except temple *prasadam* would come in as an ingestible from outside. I think she might have appreciated an occasional order from Zomato or Swiggy if it had existed in her time.

Shobha Rani, Patna

For sixteen years, Shobha Ranjan, who is forty-eight, ran a beauty parlour and a cybercafé in Patna, which she claims was Patna's first. Then, a couple of years ago, she got tired of running the beauty parlour because customers expected her to attend to them personally, though she had helpers. The cybercafé is still running, and in addition, she works for an NGO that represents street vendors, which requires her to go out of the house for a few hours a week. Her children are working professionals in other cities, and her husband, a businessman, leaves for work early and returns after 9 p.m. Though she packs a *dabba* for her husband, she deliberately makes just enough for him because she doesn't like to spend much time cooking in the kitchen.

That means, at lunchtime, she is alone, and there's nothing to eat at home. Out comes the phone, and lunch is ordered in almost every weekday afternoon. Each meal costs about Rs 500–700, and chicken dishes are a favourite.

Does she worry about the money spent? Does her husband comment on the expenditure?

'*Nahin*. Sometimes, he doesn't even know,' she giggles. 'I feel I have worked a lot and have been careful about money. Now, I feel it is my time to enjoy life. I don't fret about the expenses. I am done with that kind of thing. I also don't want to cut costs to save up for the children. Let them figure out their own lives! If they know parents have stashed away money for them, it will weaken their efforts at making a success out of their lives.'

And what about health concerns?

'I eat healthy stuff at breakfast. I do some exercise. And I am not convinced that those who starve or deny themselves good food are any healthier,' she says, giving a few examples to support her argument, particularly of her mother-in-law, who, at 72, heartily partakes of the lunch that Shobha orders whenever she's visiting from the village.

Ordering in hasn't stopped her from going to restaurants with her girl gang a few times a month. 'That's a different experience that continues.' But the other women are not food delivery junkies like she is. She points out a crucial difference.

'They are not working. They don't earn an income. When you ask your husband for money, there will be questions—*kyon chahiye? Kya karna hai?* (why do you need it?)—I have always been a working woman. No one has ever asked me a single question about what I do with my money.'

The town of Passau in Germany, close to the Austrian border, sits at the confluence of three rivers: the Danube, the Iz and the Inn. The place where the rivers meet is one of enchanting beauty, combining gently flowing waters, rolling hills and church spires in the distance. As I was admiring the landscape, my eyes fell on the sculpture of a young woman, installed at the edge of the water. Stepping closer, I read the plaque. The sculpture depicted Emerenz

Meier, a Bavarian who lived in the nineteenth century and came to be known beyond her region for her narratives and poems. A verse of hers on the plaque read:

If Goethe had to prepare supper and salt the dumplings
If Schiller had had to wash the dishes
If Heine had had to mend what he had torn, to clean the
rooms, kill the bugs
Oh, the menfolk, none of them would have become great
poets

Women across the world have yearned for free time from daily cooking and cleaning and embraced anything that would allow them a little leisure.

This explains the success of ready-to-eat convenience foods and time-saving appliances, such as the wet grinder to make idli-dosa batter that sent south Indian homemakers aflutter with excitement in the 1980s. Delivery apps are enabling them to taste that same sense of freedom.

The kitchen, once a sacred place, has diminished in importance and is yielding more and more to the might of technology to bring any cuisine into the house. In an 82-page note to investors, ominously titled 'Is the Kitchen Dead?' investment bank UBS echoed many other studies and forecast that online food ordering sales are expected to boom globally.[2] After surveying 13,000 consumers across countries, the report forecasts delivery sales to grow annually by more than 20 per cent, taking it from $35 billion in 2018 to $365 billion by 2030. The kitchen, it asserted, would become slowly redundant as more meals are ordered home.

A cartoon by renowned illustrator Hemant Morparia hits the nail. It shows two high-rise residential buildings—one called Zomato Enclave and the other called Swiggy Enclave.[3] A property broker, while showing the building to prospective clients, markets it by saying 'In these we have two bedrooms, a hall and NO KITCHEN!'

Syed Tahmid is one of the founders of OnNow, Bangladesh's only Silicon Valley-backed food startup. His company employs home chefs who supply meal kits and are trained to prepare the dish when an order comes in from a customer.

On a Zoom call from Toronto, where he lives when he is not in Dhaka, he tells me that he dreams that the kitchen slowly curl up in the corner and die. 'Cooking every meal daily in your kitchen is the most unproductive activity. In the West, around 50 per cent of meals are ordered from outside. In Singapore, working couples returning home pick up something on the way. Their kitchens are much smaller than ours. The trend has yet to catch up in South Asia, but it will. My father ran a food business and wanted my mother to participate and contribute to it. But she could never take time from preparing meal after meal for the family. Why should you? Somebody is doing it for you now, and it's possibly tastier.' I argue about healthier home food, and he reasons that healthier options are multiplying. 'As younger people start living away from home, they will choose not to cook if they can help it. There are so many other things they have to do, like scrolling through Instagram reels for two to three hours,' Tahmid says unironically.

Dolce Far Niente

The Italian idiom *dolce far niente*, literally meaning 'sweetness of doing nothing', was trending globally after it was enunciated in a scene of Hollywood movie *Eat Pray Love* (2010). Delivery apps have enabled several cohorts to do nothing except press a few buttons on their phones to bring essential household items home. Most of them are youngsters from small towns trying to hustle and build a life for themselves in big cities without a familial support system.

Youngsters have been going to big cities to seek their fortunes for a long time. The most iconic cinematic depiction of such a person is Satyajit Ray's *Aparajito*, where Apu arrives in Kolkata from his village to chase his dreams. Apu lives in a boarding house, one of the '*messbaris*' that flourished in the first half of the twentieth century in Kolkata to provide accommodation and meals to migrants who came to the city for jobs or education. In Mumbai's chawls, people from the same provenance invariably share rooms. A boy from a village in Ratnagiri district would move into a chawl where a relative or a member of the same town had already established a base to continue his way of life and cultural practices. Food was provided by *khanawals*, or community kitchens run by women. Since families were close-knit in earlier generations, a newbie starting out in an unfamiliar city could easily stay with a relative. When my father moved from Trichy to Madras to study law and prepare for the civil services in the early 1960s, he stayed with his eldest brother's family, who were just about managing financially but supported him wholeheartedly.

Today, young people who live alone in rented places and hostels power the online food delivery business in cities. In July 2021, Zomato reported a decrease in the demand for food delivery across India, attributing it to the demographic who went back to their hometowns when companies asked them to work from home.[4] Hyderabad and Bangalore's tech industries have led to more nuclear families and single-person homes as professionals from other cities flock to these metros. Eating wholesome home-cooked meals involves a fair amount of work—meal planning, grocery shopping, cooking and clean-up. In the pre-app era, working moms and even single young people did this labour, mostly because they did not have a choice. Now, apps allow them to experience the freedom of dolce far niente once they get home.

Elizabeth Koshy, Kochi

Elizabeth Koshy, who is twenty-four, is one such migrant who moved from Trivandrum to Kochi to join a think tank. She shares her rented apartment with another girl who works in the same organization. Both leave the house on time to punch in (yes, punch in!) by 10 a.m. and stay on till 8 p.m.—a ten-hour workday.

'By the time we return, we cannot cook. We simply flop on to our unmade beds and order in,' says Elizabeth.

For that reason, on weekdays, 50 per cent of the sales of a food delivery app are at dinner time, compared to only 35 per cent at lunch because lunch is often eaten in office cafeterias.

Neeraj Chhetri, Kathmandu

Neeraj Chhetri, twenty-eight, is a networking engineer in an IT company in Kathmandu. He studied in Bangalore and became used to food apps during his years in India. 'Staying alone and busy throughout the day, when I return home tired and needing meal options, I find these apps convenient. I was happy to find Pathao foods here.'

Young migrants to the city have rarely cooked because they are too busy studying or working. Technology has replaced the old support systems that offered comfort to those away from home.

Nilan and Miriam, Colombo

A little before Christmas in December 2023, I made an appointment to meet Nilan one evening in Tea Avenue, Jawatta Road, an upmarket area in central Colombo, because my contact told me Nilan was an avid online food customer. Tea Avenue is a rambling, two-tiered lounge. At 7 p.m., it is crowded with team meetings in progress around laptops, yet it has the languorous air of colonial clubs. All varieties of in-house blends of Ceylon teas are aesthetically arranged on a shelf. I order masala tea and was asked to choose between fresh, powdered and condensed milk, options I heard for the first time. I was occupying myself thus until Nilan arrived with his wife Miriam, apologizing and explaining that they had landed at a different branch of Tea Avenue close by.

Nilan is a stocky man aged 30, while Miriam, who is half-American, is a petite woman of the same age. They were both warm and pleasant, and we were chatting like old friends within minutes. Nilan is a communications manager in an apparel manufacturing factory in Horana, which lies ninety minutes south of Colombo. Miriam is a content creator who works from home.

'What's for dinner?' is a question that men have been asking their wives forever. But when Nilan comes home at around 7 p.m., totally bushed after the long day, he asks Miriam, 'What do you want for dinner?'

They met through their church, married in 2015 and live by themselves. They have almost always been ordering in. Before the food delivery apps came in, they ordered from Burger King thrice a week. They only cooked at home for about four months when the pandemic coincided with the petrol crisis in Sri Lanka in 2020. That's eight years of procuring almost every meal from outside. For dinner, it is Chinese fried rice or biryani or shawarma, and for lunch, it is the traditional rice and curry package, which in Sri Lanka comes in the set format of steamed rice and some curries, all wrapped in a banana leaf. The couple sources everything mostly from local eateries in a deliberate attempt to support small businesses in the island's ongoing economic crisis.

'If I were to ask you the most important reason why you don't cook, what would it be?' I ask them.

'Because I am lazy,' laughs Miriam. 'I feel a little guilty because it's unusual for a wife to never cook, but I also work through the day. I need to be in front of the computer for eight hours.'

'But you could cook too,' I tell Nilan.

'That's true. I did cook when we were forced to during the pandemic. But I come back at 7 every day, I am awake for two hours and then I am out like a light,' he says. 'It's a tough job. Every day, I have to walk from one end of the plant to another. The plant is a huge—15 acres—so on a regular workday, I clock 10,000 steps. And there are only two people—me and another person. The apparel industry is on a downturn. We haven't hired anyone in the last two years. So, I have to keep performing . . .' he laughs.

Quick-Fixers

Nargis, Lahore

In Lahore, Nargis Bibi is delighted to use Foodpanda's instant grocery service. At the end of an uneventful interview, she suddenly realizes precisely why she is so happy with the service. Going out to the shop, even to buy a packet of milk, requires her to don the burqa in the conservative milieu she lives in. Home delivery of groceries liberates her and those Muslim women in the subcontinent who would rather not wear the burqa.

Hafza, Karachi

Online ordering of groceries has freed women in ways the founders would have never thought of, such as from the peculiar constraints women face in joint families.[5] Customarily, the women of the house are formal with the head of the family and male members other than their husbands. The kitchen is the responsibility of the women, with the eldest matriarch often deciding the menu and the daughters-in-law executing it.

Hafza, who is twenty-five and newlywed, lives in a joint family in Karachi. She works from home and has no time to buy groceries, so she depends heavily on Pandamart, Foodpanda's grocery delivery arm. The joint family setup makes a difference because before she was married, she would tell her brother or father to buy something, but as a new daughter-in-law, she prefers to be more formal in her marital home. 'You can't just tell your brother-in-law or father-in-law to go to the shop to buy stuff,' she says. Pandamart saves the day every time. She can be discreet and efficient in managing home and work.

Aarav Tiwari, New Delhi

'Paan or Smoking needs? We have them all on Blinkit app,' says Blinkit's website.[6]

Aarav Tiwari has responded to the call. The twenty-eight-year-old Supreme Court lawyer in Delhi has a hectic twelve-hour workday that involves appearing in courts, going to the office of the senior lawyer he is attached to and visiting clients. He is entirely dependent on Blinkit and Swiggy Instamart because even after the cook arrives and finds the fridge empty, he can order online and the paneer or vegetables will arrive before she finishes kneading the atta. And if he needs a smoke at midnight, the apps will deliver that too.

When he's home after a long day and wants a late-night cigarette, he orders on either of the fast delivery apps, and a packet arrives at lightning speed. 'Because I know the apps are there, I don't have to stop to buy a pack. It's not something I give a thought to.'

Mobility Freedom

The Arbitrariness of Local Transport

Before the arrival of ride-hailing platforms in India, customers relied on autos and yellow/black taxis (the fabled *kaali-peeli)* whose owners/drivers were unionized and used to dictate terms to transport regulators often. They would use strikes as a negotiation tactic to pressurize the government for more favourable fare revision.

One can still see this in Goa, where belligerent taxi unions have ensured that Uber and Ola don't function. The only possibility of mobility for a visitor who does not want to rent a car is to hire a private cab whose rates make one want to stay in the hotel room. Every resort has a taxi driver gang—the only way to describe the men who menacingly hang around outside the hotel's gates. If a hotel guest calls for a cab from outside, tries to hail one which has come to drop someone off or even shares a cab with another passenger, woe betide her and the driver. I once naively made a deal with a family headed towards North Goa from our South Goa hotel (this division is almost as sharp as the two Koreas). We agreed to split the fare, which at around Rs 2500 or so and is 80 per cent of the airfare I had paid to come from Hyderabad to this picturesque tourist trap. When I got into the front seat, a few men arrived and started taking a video of the driver, warning him that if he dared to take two sets of disparate passengers in the same car, they would report him to the union. The hapless driver begged me to step out, which I had to for his sake.

It gets even more weird in Ladakh, which, like Goa, does not have Ola or Uber. If a group of tourists has rented a car and driven up from Delhi, local cab drivers descend upon them and demand to see the car papers and the driver's license. If the driver's last name on the license is, say, 'Sharma' and the car papers say that the car's owner is also a 'Sharma', they will let the group go because that is proof that you are likely driving your car or maybe your brother or father's. Otherwise, they will bully the driver and not let the car pass because they have rented a car from another city and deprived the locals of business.

Thus, places where ride-hailing is not an option are a throwback to a time when customers could be held to ransom by local transport unions who fixed prices arbitrarily and left passengers with no choice.

In June 2023, Sri Lanka's aviation ministry allowed PickMe and Uber to operate at the international airport near Colombo after tourists complained about taxi drivers overcharging and harassing them. Old school drivers who drive metered tuk-tuks have been fighting for the right to control public transport in tourism hotspots and violently attacked ride-hailing drivers.[7] Isira Perera, Pick Me's COO whom I met in Colombo tells me, 'These guys were ripping off the customers. Their way of doing business is to wake up in the morning, do a couple of rides, try to earn 3000 just from them and then not do anything for the rest of the day. Maybe do drugs and that is how they would spend the day.' PickMe sees all traditional tuk-tuk and cab drivers as potential partners and is working with the government to onboard them on to the platform.

Broken Streets

In his award-winning novel *A Fine Balance*, Rohinton Mistry describes a street in Mumbai thus:

'On the first day they sat in awe on the stone steps outside the shop, watching the street and seeing a universe of frightening chaos. Gradually, they perceived the river of traffic in the street and, within it, the currents of handcarts, bicycles, bullock carts, buses, and the occasional lorry.'[8]

'Traffic churned through the street with wondrous and mysterious efficiency—a ballistic dance of buses, trucks, bicycles, cars, ox-carts, scooters and people,' writes Geoffery David Roberts in *Shantaram*,[9] again about a road in Mumbai.

These passages could, in fact, describe many streets in South Asian cities even today. Stray dogs, street vendors, haphazardly parked cars, cows and the air thick with the smell of exhaust fumes, sweat and dust complete the chaos.

Understandably, no one wants to walk if they can avoid it. Ride hailing's key feature of point-to-point pick and drop frees users from walking on broken, dirty, poorly lit streets to a bus stop, metro station or even down the road to hail a tuk-tuk/auto rickshaw.

The democratization of app-based travel

The inclusion of bikes and autos on ride-hailing platforms, where there were only pricey cabs earlier, has democratized app-based travel. Men and women (only in Nepal though, where women use bike taxis freely) from lower-income groups ride pillion and whiz through the traffic. It serves them in ways that local transport simply cannot, like during a last-minute rush or to access a place much further than a bus stop. Pathao Nepal which operates in Kathmandu and Chitwan has 5 million app downloads while the floating population of Kathmandu Valley is an estimated 5 million[10] which means virtually everyone, including tourists, has on their phone.

Ashok Banjara nearly missed his enrolment in the master's course he had applied for at Tribhuvan University, Kathmandu. He was enjoying himself at the farewell party of the college he was graduating from when he received a call from the university. 'I was informed that it was the last day for admission, and the deadline was noon. I thought that the admission was open for the whole day. There was very little time, and I needed to rush. I was in Baneswor and had to reach Kirtipur, about ten kilometres away. I booked a Pathao bike, and fortunately, I arrived on time. I realized if I had been late by even fifteen minutes, I would not have got admission that year!'

Cars are inefficient in hilly regions or semi-rural parts of Nepalese cities where roads are narrow or unpaved. That's why Pathao motorbikes are the default mode of transport. 'Buses stop 500 metres away from a destination. But if I am on a Pathao bike, the driver will drop me at the entrance gate, and I don't have to walk. Besides, local buses stop and start anywhere and waste time. But if I have a Pathao, I can tell the driver to speed up if I am late. It's like owning my vehicle!' says Banjara.

Women

Ride-hailing has been a godsend for women in regions like ours, where gender-based violence in public places is still alarmingly high. The simple feature in the app of sharing the ride information with someone has liberated women in South Asia to venture out after dusk, which was not encouraged by families in the pre-ride-hailing days. In Pakistan, it is an unspoken rule that when a female passenger gets into a Careem or InDriver cab, she shares her ride information with someone in the family and whoever expects her at the other end.

The inclusion of autos has made women hire them, knowing they need not face the stress of bargaining. A six-country study on women passengers and ride-hailing by the IFC (World Bank Group) in 2018–19 cites cost transparency as a critical reason for women choosing app-based transport.[11] Bargaining with the driver is a rite of passage every South Asian learns to do when hiring an auto. It is a tiring process whose worst-case scenario is a nasty, street-side argument, and the best case is that the driver will refuse the ride and drive off. A loud streetside harangue with the male driver or being stranded on the road waving down one vehicle after another are unpleasant experiences, especially for female passengers. Ride-hailing removes that possibility entirely by deciding the fare upfront.

The multi-country study by IFC found that ride-hailing provided women passengers access to places not served by public transportation or where they felt the existing options were less safe.[11] Apps inform passengers about drivers' identities and ratings, reducing uncertainty for passengers. Some have introduced new features, such as panic buttons, that were unavailable in traditional taxis.

Physically Challenged

Perhaps the most significant contribution of ride-hailing has been making People with Disabilities (PWD) travel confidently. Being a physically disabled person in a low-income country is one of the most disadvantaged intersections to be on. With poor walking infrastructure and public transport and an overall insensitivity of the public to anyone vulnerable, the physically challenged often could not dare to venture out. As the stories below demonstrate, ride-hailing has helped them reclaim their space in the city.

Nir Shreshta, visually impaired, Kathmandu.

Twenty-four-year-old Nir Shreshta is a visually impaired man working as a programme officer at the Blind Youth Association of Nepal in Kathmandu. Much of his work involves conducting outreach activities to raise funds for the association and organizing training programmes to enhance the independence of visually impaired people.

As a student, Nir relied on local transportation from college to his rented accommodation. At that time, there were no apps, but equally, in his student life, he had no pressing commitments and didn't need to be anywhere urgently. However, in 2019, when he finished college and entered the workforce, he became actively involved with the Blind Association and started attending programmes and events. During this time, ride-hailing apps like Tootle and Pathao were already available, and he started using them whenever he needed to go to unfamiliar places.

'All the ride-hailing apps are accessible to visually impaired people and are easy to operate. While using the application, I haven't faced any complications. It has helped me save time and reach places punctually. I can't ride by myself. Taking public vehicles is challenging. One has to keep asking for help from passersby about which bus stop it is, which bus comes there, etc., since all this information is inaccessible. Footpaths and roads are poorly managed, and accidents like crashing, falling and injuries often occur while changing buses and stations. It is dangerous, and my shoes and clothes get spoilt, affecting my appearance at events. Private taxis are costly. As an alternative, ride-hailing apps are very convenient in cost, ease and reliability. They have become an integral part of my life, and without these apps, I can't imagine how I would manage my day-to-day life. Though I spend a significant ten to fifteen thousand [Nepali] rupees on it, I think it is money well spent.'

Ramesh, spinal injury

Ramesh,* who is thirty-three, lives in Kottawa, in suburban Colombo and is a lecturer at the university. A spinal and neck injury limits his mobility. The left side of his torso is fragile, so he can't walk or climb staircases without solid support. He is forced to manage things with one hand and a weak left leg.

'I entirely rely on Uber and PickMe to commute now, especially to and from home to the University of Colombo. I rarely take the bus any more. And I cannot take the train because of my limited mobility.' Travel forms a significant portion of his monthly expenses because ride-hailing cabs aren't cheap for daily commutes. 'Especially because there is surge pricing during peak hours. It is significantly more than it ought to be,' he smiled. But Ramesh isn't complaining.

In the pre-ride-hailing era, Ramesh found the experience of travelling by public bus terrible and anxiety-inducing. He would never know if the bus would allow him enough time to get in and out, whether he would find a seat, or if he saw a seat, would the bus wait until he hoisted himself on it. He used to get yelled at by drivers and conductors for taking too long to get in and out.

'If the bus pressed on the brake too hard, as is the case often with Sri Lankan buses, there was a significant risk of me falling out of the bus because of my weak torso. But even then, I continued to take the bus because I had to report to work daily. Thanks to the apps, all that is history.'

For young working people living far away from their families or strapped for time, online food/grocery delivery is a blessing they did not ask for and never knew they needed.

Preparing meals and feeding the family is a major part of the domestic work, and women spend significantly more time on it than men do. A UN report called 'World's Women' is released every five years, and the South Asian region continually fares as one of the worst in terms of the division of labour between the male and female members of the household.[12] Urban working mothers juggle rigid work timings, transportation schedules and myriad household tasks but get no respite from the cultural expectation that mothers should produce hot, tasty food for the family. They are enthusiastically embracing the genie who appears with a few taps on the phone and liberates them from routine cooking and grocery buying.

In an ideal world, mobility is a personal freedom that allows us to move about as much as we want and go to any place at any time. However, in reality, many forces restrict our mobility, not the least of which is the urban infrastructure of the cities we live in. In almost all South Asian cities, traffic is unruly, public transport is woefully inadequate, pavements are broken and streets poorly lit and encroached upon. While these conditions affect everyone, women, children, senior citizens and people with disabilities are especially disadvantaged. In many ways, ride-hailing has freed them from their mobility constraints and enabled them to reach places in the city that they were unable to earlier.

OPPRESSION

The Almighty Algorithm

Franz Kafka wrote in Prague in the 1920s. His work was based on the existential philosophy, and thinkers like Kierkegaard and Nietzsche greatly influenced him. In Kafka's worldview, the individual constantly struggles against an indifferent and often hostile world. This struggle can never be fully won but must be fought continuously nonetheless, even in the face of bleakness. His tragicomic stories act as a mythology for the modern industrial age, as they show the relationships between systems of arbitrary power and the individuals caught up in them.

A hundred years after he wrote his stories, the relationship of gig workers with the algorithm that powers the app on their phones is symbolic of Kafka's philosophy. Every action is judged by people they can't see, according to rules they don't know. In an ironic twist, Kafka is also the name of the software that processes real-time streaming data and helps platforms do big data analysis. Algorithms are step-by-step procedures for solving a mathematical problem, pioneered by Persian polymath Muhammad ibn Musal al-Khwarizmi, who lived a thousand years before smartphones and the internet. The word 'algorithm' is, in fact, a Latinized version of the latter part of his name.

In the context of platforms, algorithms are the rules, signals and data that govern the platform's operations and take an optimal decision at every juncture. Other than the platform's technocrats, no one knows about the logic encoded into it. The algorithm's primary function is to allocate the worker who can best service a request, such as match the driver/rider optimally with the customer, find the closest delivery person to pick up and drop off a grocery or restaurant order and so on. But it is much more than that. The algorithm is invisible but omniscient, omnipresent and omnipotent force—an *antaryami* (all-knowing).

Naveen Konella* has spent five years in food and grocery delivery company operations. As he had just quit one of them and joined a different industry, he was willing to speak candidly about how the tech works behind the scenes.

'There is a first mile and a last mile in logistics. The first mile is when the delivery boy gets an order to pick up a package from a restaurant. He does not get paid to reach the restaurant. His payment calculation starts once he picks up the order and proceeds to the customer's location. Algorithms are designed in such a way that they will try to ensure the first mile is shorter than the last mile. So, it will choose from among the pool of delivery agents who, at that time, are close to the restaurant. But in peak hours, if there is no delivery person close by, they extend the radius and look for someone a little further away who is free.'

When a girl in Mumbai's Andheri West orders a lasagna from an Italian place in Lokhandwala, the algorithm starts looking at the delivery boys around the area. So, if Ram Dayal has driven into Lokhandwala, he, along with Kanhaiya Lal, Prem Kumar and Arbaaz Ali, who were already there, come into the consideration pool. Who gets the order depends on a host of parameters such as exact location, proximity to the restaurant, typical speed of delivery, how promptly he delivers and how customers rate him, to name a few obvious criteria. Within seconds, an optimal decision is made using a calculation embedded in the algorithm's logic, and one of the men hears his phone ping.

'Every few weeks, managers study the data, tweak the algorithm and introduce a new rule. Rules are always designed to enhance customer experience. Customer is the God, whether it's quick commerce, food delivery or ride-hailing. Sometimes, the new rules impact the payment structures of the delivery fleet, and they get angry and go on strike. The changes are not intended to lower their earnings. However, the company cannot bear losses, and the customer is a priority. So somebody's got to pay,' says Konella.

That 'somebody' is the worker. Workers are mystified about the functioning of this digital antaryami. Rajesh Singh,* who has worked for Swiggy and Zomato, was baffled by the inscrutable logic of the app and finally decoded it as biased against older workers.

'In the initial stages, the company drives you crazy. *Pagal kar deti hai.* You get lots and lots of orders. Even if fifty other riders are sitting around, the newbie's phone will buzz. You're on a high. You work twelve hours, thirteen hours, fourteen hours, keep taking orders, driving around from restaurant to customer, back and forth. Of course, it affected my health. Madam, you'd be surprised if you saw my old photographs before I started this job. I had a gym body, my waist size was 32, and now it is 28. I have lost so much weight just overworking, running here and there, and the cash kept rolling in.' But then, after a few weeks, Rajesh found he was working just as long, maybe more, but his weekly earnings had dropped from Rs 16,000 to 12,000. He thought maybe, for some reason, business was slow, and there weren't as many orders as before. Then, slowly, the earnings dropped to Rs10,000 per week.

Sometimes, you are the pigeon, and sometimes, you are the statue. After flying high as the pigeon, Rajesh found that he had become the statue; newer riders were flying over him, and he was covered in droppings. He would sit outside the restaurant and see another worker coming from two kilometres away and taking the order. From thirty-five orders a day, he started getting twenty orders, severely reducing his earnings. It dawned on him that the honeymoon was over. '*Brahmit kyon kar rahi hai humein*?' he asked angrily. '*Brahmit*' means to confuse someone, to make it hard for them to know what is happening. 'Why isn't the company giving us the work it used to when we joined? Why is it confusing us?'

Eighteen-year-old Rinku in Delhi, who delivers food, observes, 'Just when the target is going to be completed, and one becomes eligible for incentives, we start getting orders late. We've to wait for hours to get a single order.'

A few months later, when I was in Kathmandu, I got some clues on how to solve these mysteries. On a pleasant afternoon in October, I met Sixit Bhatta at Dhokaima Café in Kathmandu's Patan area, which has a lovely courtyard and garden setting. Sixit is the creator of Nepal's first ride-hailing app, Tootle. It was also the first bike ride-hailing app, which started way before Pathao in Bangladesh and Rapido in India. I say 'was' because Tootle wrapped up after running for about six years, from 2016 to 2022.

Sixit knows a thing or two about how the algorithms of platforms work because, as an electronics engineer with experience in the telecom sector, he created the Tootle app with his team and made all the decisions about the logic on which it should run. There were some things that Tootle could have done, but Sixit decided not to step over the ethical line, which he thinks is part of the reason they couldn't compete with the game's present-day champions. For instance, it is possible for a ride-hailing app to visually show many more vehicles in a location than there are in reality so that when the customer opens it, she feels that there are many cabs and stays on the app. The fact that this is possible to do was proven in 2017, in a *New York Times* exposé which unveiled how Uber was manipulating data to make these 'ghost vehicles' appear on the screens of certain regulatory officers or competitors whom it did not want to give a ride to.[1]

'But we didn't do things like that because I didn't start Tootle to make it into some humungous, million-dollar valuation. I was just fooling around with the tech out of curiosity to see where it goes. But everyone in the business does it.'

He likens the creation of an algorithm to two people creating the same dish with the same ingredients but with different desired outcomes. 'The mix and match of the parameters could be likened to a recipe. If my mom makes chicken curry with chicken, tomatoes, onions and spices, her desired outcome would be to create a likeable dish while ensuring her family's health. But if a restaurant cooks the same dish, the aim is taste, customer approval and profitability, and so the chef will play around with those ingredients differently. Similarly, there are different metrics you could use to build your algorithm—newness in the system, ride completion ratio, ratings and so on.'

Sixit demystifies Rajesh's bafflement at being ignored by the app once they approach their targets or become older in the system.

'You set a challenge for riders that if you do ten rides, you get 500 bucks,' Sixit continues. 'Then you make them run around for a while, and after nine rides, you don't give them the tenth ride, which will give him the extra 500. Because if he gets it, you will lose money.'

'When a platform enrols new riders, it wants to change their behaviour,' Sixit continues. 'You want to get them into the system by giving them 200–300 trips and get the dopamine going. Once they are used to it, they get into the same pool of the oldies. No one cares about the people in the system because the company knows they are not going anywhere. Even if they quit, there will be others.'

This aspect of the platform economy is a jarring antithesis of something workers are culturally attuned to—age matters. In this part of the world, in any profession, the person who is older in the system symbolizes wisdom and experience, not someone who has outlived his utility and must be disposed of. In traditional skill-based occupations such as masonry or weaving, skills, knowledge and experience of those already working in the area would be transferred to the newbie over time. Even in a roadside mechanic shop, an *ustad* (expert) will train a *chottu* (novice/apprentice). He will acquire his stature only after the chottu has paid his dues by dirtying his hands with motor oil for many years. Therefore, it is counter-intuitive and incomprehensible for workers that a new guy is more valued than one who came into the job earlier.

Sixit, who was part of G20's Think20 in 2023 when India held the presidency of the G20, is a passionate advocate of responsible AI. He prophecies that the algorithmic divide is far more dangerous a chasm than the digital divide. The digital divide was visible because one knew who had access to computers or the internet and who did not. However, in the platform economy, he points out that we have an algorithmic divide, which is far more insidious because algorithms are opaque and invisible.

Algorithmic management is the term used to describe the way digital labour platforms organize and coordinate extremely large groups of workers and customers in an automated way. As the algorithm constantly watches, it knows when drivers take passengers on offline rides. A driver in Trichy, Tamil Nadu, explained that the company would know if he came to a customer's building in response to a cab request and then logged off from the app. It's a dead giveaway that he's made a private deal with the passenger. Besides, if they track the location of his mobile through his phone number, they know he's headed for the airport, which was the destination the customer entered when booking the ride. It doesn't take a detective to fit the pieces together. And here, the entity watching is a super sophisticated computational algorithm that relentlessly monitors, controls and instructs drivers. In another paradox characterizing gig work, workers are seemingly autonomous but controlled by an unseen force, George Orwell's Big Brother, pumped with steroids.

The award-winning British movie *Sorry We Missed You* (2019) details the oppressive nature of jobs in the gig economy. Set in the industrial town of Newcastle in the UK, the film features Ricky Turner, a working-class man who lives with his wife Abby and their two children. Abby is a healthcare worker visiting seniors and end-of-life patients in their homes. Ricky hears that a delivery company has an opening and signs up. The interviewer tells him he will be an 'owner franchisee', a master of his destiny. 'You won't be working for us; you'll be working with us,' he says, handing over a device that will monitor Ricky's every move. Unknown to him, it is a Trojan horse containing the seeds of the family's ruin. Ricky proudly tells his family that he will be 'in business'. He sells the family car that Abby was using for her visits so that he can buy a van because they reckon it is an investment for a better future for their family. But soon, things go south. Ricky works excessively long hours, but the earnings often fall short when factoring in fuel, van maintenance and other expenses. His intense work schedule strains his relationships with his wife and children. The pressures of meeting delivery targets and insecurity about the future take a toll on Ricky's physical and emotional health, leading to a poignant climax.

The film shows the new working poor, a neo-proletariat—the people who work all day and are still not able to afford a decent living. While earlier, capitalism hid exploitation behind a labour contract, digital capitalism hides it behind the veneer of self-employment. The film may be set in the UK but it could easily be the story of a gig worker in Asia.

Suppressing Protests

Sangam Tripathy, a veteran transport workers' activist, shares what happened when they got some women gig workers together one cold December day in 2022 to protest at Jantar Mantar, a sixteenth-century observatory in New Delhi that is now a popular spot for *dharnas*.

'Because female drivers have many more constraints than male drivers. Many of them are widows or sole breadwinners in the family. The protest got a lot of press coverage, and other unions and women's rights NGOs came to the *dharna* to show solidarity. While we were happy with this, the brunt was borne by five women drivers who found their IDs blocked by the evening. This is how the companies penalize the workers. They stop your ID, so you can't return to work the next day. It's the punishment they give to those who protest.'

Christmas was close, so the corporate offices, inaccessible to workers in the best of times, became even more so as many staff were on vacation. There was a person in Uber that Shaikh Salauddin, general secretary of the All-India Gig and Platform Workers Association, had built contacts with, so he called her and requested that the matter be sorted. By 1 January, the IDs were restored. 'Except for these informal contact points, there is no legal official person one can approach,' says Tripathy. 'The company's stand is, why should I talk to any workers' union? These are not even our "workers" to begin with.'

The gig workers I met in Jaipur share in angst that workers start getting calls from the company not to attend these protests whenever they begin a mobilizing effort. Strange things reportedly start to happen. Like, an ID blocked for months gets activated on the day of the protest.

'In our WhatsApp groups also, somehow the team leader sneaks in, and those who know he's present, feel scared to express themselves openly. Even if some disgruntled workers are roped in to organize a protest against an unfair action by the company, it quickly peters out as every day of work is income earned for these workers. Except for those whose IDs are blocked by the company, time spent striking, is time lost in earning. As Tripathy likes to say '*Roz kuan khodna hai, roz paani peena hai*' which translates to 'unless you dig a well every day, you will not get water to drink'. Strikes quickly dissolve also because the company credits some money into the accounts of striking workers to buy a temporary truce. A manager in a food delivery company sneered when I informed him of an impending strike in his city the next day, 'Tomorrow the company will put some money into their account and they'll all come back to work.'

No *Mai-Baap*

Platforms do not recognize workers as employees. They are termed 'independent contractors' or 'self-employed partners'. As the COO of an app company said 'our partners are people who use our technology to earn money for themselves, just like you use a telecom service on your mobile phones. The commission they pay is the fee for our technology.' There is an inherent hypocrisy of an arrangement where workers are disciplined by the firm despite not being employees of the firm and for referring to the workers as 'independent contractors' when they enjoy far less freedom than the truly self-employed. Such a classification allows the company to keep an arm's distance from taking responsibility for workers' safety and welfare, despite them spending many years making the company's business grow.

'If I want to become a delivery worker or cab driver, I only download the contract in the app, which runs to more than 50 pages, and check the box which says "I agree". And mind you; it's all in complicated English full of legalese that even folks like us won't understand easily,' says Tripathy. Tripathy and a few lawyer activists have read many of the contracts and find that the terms and conditions keep changing slightly. Sometimes, the stranglehold gets tighter; at other times, more liability is quietly shifted to the worker. 'I have not found a single place where there is any onus on the platform. Everything is on the worker,' he says.

Hanuman Sahay is a stocky, wizened man from Nagar district in the Marwar region of Rajasthan wearing a faded red oversized shirt and a white *gamcha* around his neck. Many years ago, he came to Jaipur to earn a living as an auto-rickshaw driver. Once Ola and Uber came in, Hanuman found that 'the luxury *savari*', or the high-value customers who travel from the airport or tourists who would book the auto for the entire day, moved to the more comfortable cabs. This left only the low ticket, short-ride passengers for auto drivers.

'Everything has a phase. Something comes in, captures the public's imagination and has a high. Then it goes down, and something else takes its place,' he says philosophically.

He read the winds of change and, about three years ago, moved to Porter, a tech-enabled logistics company in the business of intracity and intercity delivery. He drives a three-wheeler Tempo, an auto with a carrier for transporting household furniture, carts of fruits and vegetables or light industrial goods, etc. He was making Rs 40,000 to support his family of six if he worked twelve hours a day '*imaandaari aur lagan se*' (sincerely and diligently). Despite that, about 40 per cent went into fuel costs, vehicle maintenance and wasteful driving that was unremunerative, Hanuman says.

But all that was par for the course for a man nearing sixty who has held many kinds of jobs in his life. What got his goat was the sheer indifference and callousness of the company when he faced a situation earlier that month.

'It was on the 3rd of June. I was at a customer's house. Sometimes, customers want you to help load or unload things, though strictly speaking, it's not our job. But they say we'll cancel the order if you don't help. This was one such customer. So while I was offloading the machine parts that were in my vehicle, I cut off half my finger,' he says, upholding the bandaged index finger of his right hand for me to see. 'It's on my right hand, so I feel especially handicapped.'

I had vaguely noticed that he had an injury but had not paid attention. Now, I was shocked to learn that under the bandage, there was only a small stump of the finger left because of an occupational accident.

'It was some kind of wheel with sharp edges. As I was removing it, half the finger got cut and fell to the floor. There was a lot of blood. I put the fallen part in my shirt pocket and drove to the hospital. The customer offered to take me there, but I thought I'd rather go alone. I called up my son, and he rushed to the hospital. I was taken to the trauma ward. But the doctors there could not rejoin it and put stitches and medicine on what was left.

'We called the company for financial help and narrated the incident that happened that morning, but they said there is no provision for such help since we are not company employees. Thankfully, I had taken a Chiranjeevi health insurance policy offered by the state government. You only have to pay Rs 900 annually and receive upto 25 lakhs health insurance in emergencies. I managed to use that and pay the hospital bills. In the past few days, I have visited the Porter office in Jaipur several times to ask them for some compensation, but they flatly refused.'

We click a photograph where Hanuman holds up the maimed finger to make a statement. The stump wrapped in a grimy bandage is almost a symbol that embodies the fragility of workers in the gig economy.

To understand why Hanuman Sahai feels left out in the cold by the entity providing him his livelihood, we must understand how the idea of a 'mai-baap', an authority who provides and protects, is deeply entrenched in our collective consciousness. The ancient dharma of kingship decreed that the king was the 'mai-baap'—the universal mother–father figure who protected the people. After independence from British rule, the government became the primary employer and looked after the welfare of the 'government servant' through various social security schemes. But slowly, after liberalization, even public-sector undertakings, once notorious for their swollen ranks of employees, began hiring more people on a casual or contractual basis. According to the Public Enterprises Survey reports, in March 2022, 42 per cent of employees in Indian public-sector companies were engaged on a contract or casual basis, compared to 19 per cent in March 2013.[2] These were jobs that came with social benefits but with lesser and lesser intake in the government. Much of the population, especially at the lower end, has had to get used to the idea that the mai-baap has left the scene. There is no protective umbrella and you have to find your own way to not get drenched when the rain pours.

Sougata Ray, is a former dean of the Indian Institute of Management, Kolkata and a professor of strategy and entrepreneurship at the Indian School of Business (ISB), Hyderabad. He has over the past few years been spearheading a mega programme in ISB towards developing a research-based understanding of family firms and business groups in India and South Asia.

When I ask him if family firms in India gave priority to welfare of workers, he gives me a nuanced answer.

'Dhirubhai Ambani was known to treat employees like family. If an employee's family was in distress because of an untoward accident or health crisis, Reliance officials would support them through it, visit their house or hospital, give financial aid and handhold the employee through the bad times. In return, employees swore loyalty to him and, therefore, to the company. Soon after the pandemic began and lockdown was announced, the governing board of the Tata Group took three decisions—to do everything possible to ensure that workers were protected from Covid, to not spend cash unless imperative and to not retrench any worker or vendor.' Sougata narrates another example of a family business that held its silver jubilee celebrations recently and the owner in his seventies recognized every one of his 15,000 employees–partners as part of the success story.

'But another family-owned, diversified business made a list of employees and vendors to be retrenched as soon as factories and offices closed due to Covid. So whether family-owned or not is not the differentiator. It is the embedded values, mostly established by early founders, that makes the difference.'

But those values, Sougata agrees, have been changing rapidly since India became liberalized and globalized, the two words that came into our lexicon in the early 1990s. Like him, I am a mid-1990s product of a business school. It was a heady time to be a freshly minted MBA. Economic liberalization had just set in and a new set of multinationals had arrived on Indian shores—Kellogg's, Coca-Cola, Seagrams to name a few. It was as if a new, flamboyant production was going to be launched in the economic theatre of the country and we were in the green room getting ready to step on stage and take our place in the spotlight. For our parents' generation, most of whom had worked in the government, nationalized banks or public-sector undertakings, the private sector, particularly multinationals, was an inscrutable species. They were disbelieving of the starting salaries that their children

were offered, awestruck by youngsters below twenty-five,
flashing credit cards and travelling abroad on work, things
they themselves did in twice that time, if at all. They swung
between approval for the pecuniary windfall that their
MBA children brought to the family and a vague unease
about too much happening too soon.

Soon we heard the word 'pink slip' and learnt that this
refers to a notice of dismissal from employment. In 1997,
Peregrine Capital, a coveted company during campus
placements, did in its Mumbai office that very American
thing we had only seen happening to Tom Cruise in *Jerry
Maguire*. Overnight, the company cleared the desks of
some newly recruited young MBAs, put all their things in
a box and handed a pink slip to each of them when they
arrived for work the next day. It was a glimpse of the other
side of globalization and the shaky relationship between
global corporations and their employees.

Around the start of the new millennium, it was
glamorous to work for the BPO/KPO sector (business/
knowledge process outsourcing). Swarms of young Indians
got into bizarre jobs, such as transcribing handwritten
prescriptions written by American doctors into legible
English. Or leading schizophrenic lives where Jai became
Jack at night and spoke with an unnatural nasal twang,
just so that the Americans who dialled them for customer
service could feel comfortable. There's a reason why Chetan
Bhagat's debut novel set in a call centre became a hit—it
caught the pulse of something unprecedented happening
in the world of work.

As technology advanced, efficiency and productivity became the new paradigm. These came at the cost of a certain dehumanization and diminished the quality of day-to-day interactions. A deeply felt example is the corporatization of healthcare which eliminated the entity called the 'family doctor' an avuncular, bespectacled gent who would visit the patient at home and at least in movies, reassuringly say *maine dava de diya hai, ab ghabrane ki koi baat nahi* (I've given the medicine, you don't need to worry)'. In his place is a roster of doctors in your friendly neighbourhood super-specialty hospital. Each time there is a different person in the OPD. The specialist doesn't know you as a person—your food habits, the nature of your job, whether you are a smoker or teetotaler or not. He only has a file with details of previous visits which the uniformed front office lady will pull out from the system. You are not a patient, you are an ID. It doesn't matter because you have under ten minutes with the doctor anyway. In the quest for efficiency, time is a commodity that often takes precedence over the human being. Delivery riders, racing against the clock to meet demanding delivery schedules, exemplify this struggle. Their need for speed is not just a matter of convenience but a reflection of a broader societal trend, where the immediacy of services can overshadow the well-being of those providing them.

The feeling of being lost and abandoned by the employer that Hanuman Sahai felt when his finger was cut, is emblematic of a society-wide change affecting all human exchanges—worker and employer as well as customer and seller.

Inside the Amazon Warehouse

On the sidelines of a workshop in central Delhi, where representatives of gig workers from across the country have gathered to exchange notes and plan their next move, I am introduced to Nisha*, who works in an Amazon warehouse in NCR. I estimate that Nisha, dressed in a neat salwar kameez and hair tied in a ponytail, is in her early twenties.

The warehouse is one of the twenty-five Amazon Fulfillment Centres in India. 'Fulfillment' refers to storing, packaging and shipping orders and managing customer returns and exchanges. This one employs nearly 2000 workers, mostly girls from the government's skill and placement programme for rural youth called the Deen Dayal Upadhyay Grameen Kaushal Yojana (DDU-GKY). As a partner of India's National Apprenticeship Promotion Scheme (NAPS), Amazon trains apprentices in Amazon Fulfillment Centres in warehousing and inventory management skills so that they are ready to be hired as warehouse associates and process associates.

The warehouse that Nisha works in is in Manesar, about thirty kilometres from the corporate glitz of Gurugram. Inside rural youth from Punjab, Haryana and Uttar Pradesh are engaged in a non-stop whirlwind of activity, in different processes labelled 'decanting', 'loading–unloading', 'picking', 're-binning', 'packing', 'storage' and 'sorting'—some deal with new items that customers order, and some with returned items. I have an hour-long conversation with Nisha who describes her daily work life and that of her co-workers in the warehouse.

'Pickers' have to pick items ordered by people like us, including toiletries, kitchenware and home décor for our pretty urban middle-class homes. Pushing a yellow cart, a picker scans the barcodes of the list of things to be picked and the scanner tells her the exact location of the item among the seemingly endless inventory of goods stored in rack after rack that encompasses several floors. Nisha says pickers walk at least fifteen kilometres on a typical day.

Fifteen kilometres every day? I check to see if I have heard correctly.

'Yes, sometimes twenty,' she says. 'There are floors labelled P1, P2, P3 . . . one item will be on P1, another on P4, then the next one on P1 . . . like that you end up walking for miles.'

I later read that in all warehouses worldwide, pickers walk around with a handheld device through which Amazon's software calculates the most efficient walking route to collect all the items to fill a trolley. Despite the efficient routes, a considerable amount of walking must be done.

'It's suffocating. The AC is ineffective when you are inside picking goods from the racks. We told them to install fans, or else we would not work. Only then did they oblige and put some fans.'

Nisha is a 'packer'. The schedule is punishing, beginning at 8.30 a.m. and carrying on for ten hours with two washroom breaks of thirty minutes each. Within these breaks, workers must include lunch, tea and washroom visits.

Within five minutes of logging in, she has to necessarily pack an item and one minute before breaking for lunch, again she is obliged to pack at least one item.

'That's necessary to avoid showing "idle time" and for a "strong finish" and "fast start". You can't have idle time, else your supervisor will summon you and ask—"*madam, itni der se kahan the aap*? (Where have you been all this while?)"'

The washroom breaks are strictly monitored by a supervisor who watches everyone on CCTV cameras. If someone takes more than ten minutes, they will be questioned. The fulfilment centre is, however, a massive space, and just walking up to the bathroom shaves off a couple of minutes. The washroom is not just for biological needs but is the only place where the worker can bend her legs. Back in the workstation, no one is allowed to sit during work time. To ensure that no one sneakily does, there are no chairs. An ex-worker from Amazon, Meeta*, who quit because the conditions were too harsh, sends me photos of girls squatting on the floor in the washroom, their bent heads held in their palms. Their faces are blurred, but the despair is evident in their posture. Without context, it could be mistaken for a photo of people just arriving in a refugee camp. Another photo shows two men on plastic chairs in the canteen, with their heads on the table, taking a quick snooze.

If the customer rating system of drivers/riders seems unfair and subject to arbitrariness, the warehouse worker is subject to a rating system on overdrive. There is an hourly target, and at the end of the hour, a rating is given based on the achievement of that target. Nisha tells me that for packers, the target is 240 items per hour and for re-binners, it is 500 items per hour, which must be put in different bins A1, E2, etc.

Scan, put in the bin, scan, put in the bin. Rinse and repeat 500 times an hour. About eight items a minute. Meeta, whose job was to scan returned items, had targets of thirty-five oversized items, forty-five medium items and fifty-five small items per hour. Unmet targets attract feedback from HR three times. The third time, there is no conversation; only a letter is handed out. After that, the employee is terminated, and the person is blocked, so she can't work in any Amazon warehouse. Nisha showed me a letter which has ominous phrases like 'job performance not meeting standards', 'your superiors as part of this conversation are interested in understanding barriers' and 'following is a summary of your performance . . . areas of improvement'.

She showed me a video of a packer at work, which she had secretly filmed. The packer stands at her desk and her hands move ceaselessly. She takes an item, scans the bar code, puts it in a container, tapes it, tears a label, sticks a label, scans again, tears some plastic, wraps it and puts it away. For variety, sometimes the container is a box, sometimes a plastic cover and sometimes both. Another woman, with her back to the camera, is doing the same. Both are dressed in a functional salwar kameez, hair tied neatly in a top knot to not distract from the job. Her colleague in the frame does the same. For a few seconds, the colleague comes to the other girl's desk and asks something, but her friend doesn't look at her, engrossed as she is in her work.

The workers report to 'problem solvers' (PS) for each process, above whom is a process associate (PA) and then a manager. All of them are under pressure. The worst calamity is the violation of the customer promised time or CPT. The CPT is for urgent items that must be despatched on that day. The worker has to find those items from a lot and ensure they are packed by the deadline. There are three checks on the CPT—11.30 a.m., 2.30 p.m. and again at 5.00 p.m. If even a single item marked under CPT is not packed, all supervisors will descend on that part of the shop floor with their laptops. Nisha showed me a video of a crisis when the CPT was unmet. I can see people with laptops staring wide-eyed at screens supposedly showing critical information, then yelling and moving their hands about, not unlike the last scenes of Hollywood disaster movies where the future of humanity is at stake.

Surreally, a song from the Bollywood movie *Sultan* plays in the background. 'Music is constantly played,' says Nisha. 'Else, it will be impossible to work.'

There is no shortage of people willing to face this pressure. I saw pictures of anxious hopefuls waiting in the lobby. At least a hundred are recruited every month in the facility. Some agents create a pipeline of warehouse aspirants. Selection is done through an online test followed by a translation test from English to Hindi, which is evidently to see if the person can follow instructions in English. But the girls tell me that there are other unsaid criteria. Those hired are always slim, as they are perceived as agile and physically fit to move around the expansive space, climb many floors and walk like an athlete. There aren't any fat people, even in the photos I see.

The contract is for 240 days because, according to a Supreme Court ruling, '. . . a workman who has worked for 240 days in a year in an establishment would be entitled to be made permanent'. Nisha says that a few days before the 240-day milestone, the worker finds herself mysteriously sacked on flimsy grounds. However, a fresh contract is made with the same person a few weeks later, as if that person had never worked there before. It's like being caught in the *jeevan-mrityu* (life and death) cycle and being reborn repeatedly because you haven't earned enough credit for *mukti* (liberation). Rehiring the same person benefits the company by saving them the effort of training.

Leave is a sore point with the company. Warehouse workers who took an extra day off found their ID cards dysfunctional at the gate when they returned. Although two days of leave are allowed after five days of working, on the eve of the second holiday, the HR person calls and asks if the worker wants to cancel the second leave and come to the warehouse instead to earn some overtime, an option that the financially needy worker would often choose.

Sometime in the first half of 2024, Nisha moved from being a packer to a stower (one who puts things back on the racks). In May 2024, all stowers were asked to come to the standup area at 4.30 pm. There, they were subject to a weird, cult-like practice. Their manager lectured them on how it was a matter of shame that their targets for the day had not been met. Then they were asked to stretch their right hands in front and take an oath that they would strive to meet their targets hereafter and not take breaks until it was accomplished.

This matter came to the attention of the National Human Rights Commission and an inspection of the warehouse was conducted.[3] Officials spoke to workers about their work environment and collected feedback.

After the visit, according to Nisha, targets were brought down, people were given chairs to sit on and the overall treatment improved. Even their take-home salaries improved from Rs 10,088 to Rs 11,059. But in 3–4 months, except for the small salary hike, everything else went back to the way it was before the government intervened.

The girls are from nearby rural areas and rent accommodation in Manesar in twos and threes. But soon, they find boyfriends, and possibly because they find an escape from the oppressive rural milieu, they never go back, even for a visit. Nisha's voice drops even further as she tells me about her friend who moved in with her beau, who also worked in the same warehouse. She became pregnant, and then the boy, who was barely twenty-one, got overwhelmed, quit the job and ran back to his village. Another married a boy from a different caste, unknown to her family, who would have been enraged. 'There are many cases because most of the girls are from poor, rural backgrounds,' says Nisha. In the choice between a rock and a hard place, some of them endure the tyranny of a faceless corporation to escape the patriarchal caste-ridden society back in their village.

Heike Geissler's *Seasonal Associate* was published in German in 2014 and eventually translated into English. The book describes the working life of a lowly associate in an Amazon warehouse in Leipzig, Germany, drawn from the author's own experience of working at such a job. It is remarkably similar to the daily drama that unfolds in the warehouse in Haryana. The supervisors pressing workers to work faster, the too-short lunch break in which workers gobble down their food, the workers labouring like bees, scanning and packing in a cavernous facility, constantly monitored to improve their productivity figures.

The perpetrator of this brazenly exploitative set-up that epitomizes neo-colonialism is the world's third-richest corporate. Every day, *Forbes* tracks the wealth of Amazon's founder, Jeff Bezos. We often see lists of billionaires and companies valued at multiple billions in magazines like *Forbes*. For most of us, our eyes glaze over because we can't quite fathom what that *really* means vis-a-vis our economic status.

In a viral TikTok video, Humphrey Yang helped the world comprehend the scale of these figures.[4] He visually represented what it means to possess Amazon founder Jeff Bezos' wealth by using rice grains. He gave a value of $1,00,000 to one grain of rice, making ten grains equal $1 million. Then he spent twelve hours piling up the grains required to show $1 billion and created a small hillock. But that was still nowhere close to Bezos' wealth. To visually represent Bezos estimated wealth of $122 billion, as of 2023, Yang had to pile up 26.3 kg of rice! So, one grain represents a millionaire, about three grains represent the price of, say, a Lamborghini, and an uncountable mountain of rice grains represents the wealth of Bezos. Another estimate is that if any of us earned $7000 an hour every day since the birth of Jesus Christ, we would still be unable to match Jeff Bezos' wealth.

And his company can't give a chair for a poor Indian girl to sit on?

The Dark Store

Behind the groceries that zip into our house before we can blink lies a supply chain that involves hectic, coordinated action by many invisible workers in a warehouse that we possibly pass by every day but never know exists. In the quick commerce industry, it is called the 'dark store'.

The dark store is a cavernous tech-enabled warehouse, but unlike Amazon's Fulfillment Centre, whose location is publicly listed on the company's site and even on Google

Maps, the dark store of quick commerce platforms like Blinkit or Zepto or Instamart exists in the shadows. On average, a dark store has an area of about 3000 square feet (the size of a spacious three- or four-bedroom apartment). It could be anywhere, maybe in the shopping mart around the corner or deep inside the basement of an innocuous-looking building. There is no outside signage associated with the brand; some have thick plastic curtains at the entrance. Its only giveaway is delivery boys wearing the company's T-shirts milling outside. Quick commerce companies have dark stores every five kilometres or so to meet the promise of lightning speed delivery to residents in the neighbourhood.

Inside the dark store are rows of grocery items, electronic items, cigarettes and absolutely anything that can be delivered on a two-wheeler by one rider. The store is designed to optimize picking time.

As soon as we customers book an order for groceries on the app, two people receive it—the rider closest to the store, who is assigned that task and the picker inside the store, whose handheld, black device beeps loudly to alert him to a new order whose details flash on a screen. The picker then starts running down the aisles, collecting things on the list, scanning and packing them in bags of different weight capacities. It is not easy because there are many brand variants of a particular product, with barely discernible changes in the packaging colour and design. For example, at a glance, Red Label Nature Care and Red Label tea look similar. Then, the ensemble of groceries is packed and placed in a pigeonhole near the entrance. Meanwhile, the rider who has arrived at the store gets a prompt on his phone telling him which rack number in the pigeonhole has his stuff. He scans the barcode of the rack, collects the paper bag containing his order, does a quick check and rushes off to deliver. That's how we see 'delivery in 8 minutes' on the app and smile at how extraordinary our lives have become because of tech.

But, until the robots come, it is human labour that is making the tech work. The metrics on which the humans are evaluated are unforgiving. Pickers cannot have idle time and must complete the picking and packing in under two minutes. The order must be implemented accurately to avoid returns and complaints. Speed is the deal-breaker in this industry. The rider comes to the store within two minutes. At the same time, inside the store, the picker gets the items ready. Then, the rider races against time to reach the customer and deliver within the promised ten minutes.

Riders in quick commerce companies work 12–14 hours and according to a Morgan Stanely report released in end 2024, earn around Rs 21,000 a month.[5] Pickers work nine-hour shifts and are paid a fixed salary of Rs 17,500 a month.[6] These figures might vary from one company to another, but only slightly.

Albinder Dhindsa, the founder of Blinkit, posts actively on X (formerly Twitter), as does Deepinder Goyal, founder of Zomato, which bought Blinkit in June 2022. Both are IIT Delhi alums in their early forties. They keep their posts light and upbeat, intended to draw a reaction from trendy urban youth, who are the core target of the business. For example, when Blinkit started selling high-end mobile phones, a lady challenged the company, saying if anyone ever bought an expensive product like an iPhone from Blinkit, she was willing to eat 'karelas' (bitter gourd). Dhindsa replied to her with a screenshot of some people who have bought iPhones on Blinkit and quipped, '*Karela kahan bhejna hai*? (where do I send the karelas?)' There was much applause from his followers. On special days when business hits the roof, like Valentine's Day, he updates the number of soft toys, condoms or roses ordered on the app, like sharing the score of an exciting match.

The witty banter on the page is punctuated by pleas from a worker in Indore whose ID is blocked or someone in Agra whose team leader is not responding. While Blinkit makes Hinglish puns like 'Did you know a raw orange is called a sant-raw?', Manoj*, a worker distraught about his blocked ID, with four followers who seem to have made the account only to complain, writes:

> I am not reject any order if a order is cancelled that because customer want to cancel it or customer not respond or customer is in train when the order is cancelled i am return it to the respectative restaurant i am not in fault why my id got disable see my past history record.[7]

That's how I spot Riyaaz Khan*. He has uploaded two photos of a dark store with negative comments under it, which no one had reacted to. I track him down through social media, and we speak on the phone. Riyaaz is a store manager in a quick commerce dark store in south Mumbai. He earns a fixed salary of Rs 35,000 a month.

'The money is okay. But the company will not pay so much without extracting a lot. So it's a high-pressure job. As a store manager, one has to manage an inventory of over 15,000 items—fruits, vegetables, groceries, frozen food, electronics, toiletries and many others. Three trucks come daily—fruits and vegetables, meat and other items. Items have to be offloaded and kept in the correct rack. Then there are 150+ riders and over thirty pickers who must be managed. Sometimes, if there were too many orders, I would go on my bike to make deliveries.'

He has been given a target to hire 150 riders at the rate of ten a day to build a pipeline of delivery boys to secure the store against attrition.

'How can I find so many delivery boys?' he asks rhetorically.

'That's a ridiculous number of delivery boys! Why would they need so many in addition to those already there?' I ask.

'Because the company doesn't want the packet to remain in the drop zone. It wants the picker to hand over the packet to the rider the instant he is at the window. That can happen only when there are so many riders that one of them appears at the window in a super-fast time once the order is placed. So they say you keep 250 instead of 150, but the customer must not face any delay. But if we hire more and more riders, then each of them gets fewer orders, and then they get upset, and I have to appease them. Pickers have to finish their tasks in 1.5 minutes. All these numbers are visible on the system. The manager gets questioned if a store's average exceeds two minutes. But sometimes, things are strewn around, finding an item is impossible and the numbers drop. What to do? Running a store is not easy, Madam. You're saying 35k salary is good, but it comes with so much pressure!

'The delivery boys are another story. Some get drunk on the job, and some fight with customers. Then, if we block their ID to teach them a lesson, they quarrel with us, bring along their ten rider friends and create a scene. Sometimes, they involve the local politician . . .'

Platform Sellers

There was a time when 'platform sellers' referred to hawkers sitting on the platform (footpath or kerbside as it is called in some countries) on the streets of a bazaar. Now, it refers to businesses and individuals who sell their wares on e-commerce platforms such as Amazon, Flipkart and Daraz. These sellers are called 'third party' as they are distinct from the platform, which also sells its own products, but third-party products contribute 50–60 per cent of the company's sales. The lure of the platform is that it provides the marketplace infrastructure, logistics services such as warehouse and shipping, advertising and insane customer reach. The sellers need not worry about capex, need not scout for real estate, build a website or app or set up a payment gateway. They need nothing to get onto the platform except their product.

A foray into the world of e-commerce sellers will show that the old adage was correct: Anything that sounds too good to be true probably is. Sellers are frenemies with the platforms. In return for access to the gigantic online marketplace, they deal with unethical competitive practices and unfair policies stacked against them. The platforms run a prison-like, strict and unforgiving system where those who carefully follow its rules can survive or fall off the boat, as many have.

How Do I Exploit Thee? Let Me Count the Ways

Copycat

Sellers are constantly wary of the immense asymmetry of power that the platform has because of its hold over the main currency of the business: data. Ownership of all transaction data gives the company real-time information on consumers' shopping behaviour, who likes what, which product is hot or not and all other key details of the shopper's journey. With this information and its endlessly deep pockets, it can quickly experiment and recreate a product that it knows is popular and highly rated. These products are then sold under the platform's own brand name at lower prices than the popular one. Buyers don't realize that it is able to sell at a lower price because it doesn't pay any commission unlike the third-party seller who pays about 20–25 per cent per transaction.

In 2021, Reuters published an expose[8] that revealed that Amazon was running a systematic campaign of creating cheap rip-offs of other people's bestsellers but also manipulating search results to boost its own brands (Vedaka, Solimo, etc.) in India, one of the company's most important growth markets.

Paul Chacko,* in Kottayam, Kerala is a small seller of spices, honey, pickles and other organic food products on Amazon. Most of his sales come from Amazon but not without several pain points.

'Selling on Amazon is a kind of trap,' he tells me on phone. 'Because *they* decide how much sales they want to give you, not the customers.'

In the beginning, everything was going well for him. He was selling 100 kg of green cardamoms every month when the price of cardamom was 2000 per kg. In anticipation of a good quarter, he stocked up 300 kg. Then, suddenly, his sales dropped. The stocks got fungus and had to be thrown away.

'You see, Amazon also sells green cardamoms under the brand name Vedaka. They know what the demand is for my product and who the customers are. When they see my brand doing very well, they then suppress it and show their brand to customers looking for green cardamom. When my sales dropped, they approached me to hire their account manager to boost sales.'

I ask him why he doesn't walk away from Amazon and sell through his own website.

'Because, like I told you, it's a trap. You cannot not be there . . .' he replies.[9]

Unfair returns policy

Giridhar Soundararajan is a passion-preneur in Bengaluru who converted his fascination for high-performance motorsports to his profession by founding Barrel Electric, building the country's first electric dual sport motorcycle. Before that, he founded Barrel Exhaust in 2014, which makes automotive parts and has a loyal clientele in the biker community. Like other SMEs, Giridhar got on to Amazon and Flipkart in 2017, drawn by their immense reach, since anyone who wants to buy first searches for the product on these platforms.

In four years, he was out of there.

'When I list a product, a customer anywhere can order it for cash on delivery. Our products are a little premium, and we are an SME, not a huge brand. For us, the stock is critical. Our inventory is not extensive, so we play around with our working capital. When someone places a cash-on-delivery order, the buyer does not commit to the purchase. Sometimes, the address is wrong or the customer will say, sorry, I am not in town. Sometimes, just by looking at an address, we know this guy can't be a serious buyer of our product. When we used to raise it with Amazon, we would get an auto-generated response that the address is verified, so please ship the product.'

'80 per cent of cash on delivery orders were invariably cancelled. Okay, granted that the customer is king, and it is their platform, they can make whatever rules they want. But it is my product! After the customer declined it, it would take thirty days to return it to us! So if ten such products were shipped, imagine eight of them getting returned and missing from our inventory for a month! The value of each exhaust system was about 20k, so that's about 1.6 lakh worth of goods just tied up. Sellers like us had to suffer only because Amazon has random customers abusing its customer-centric policy, and it doesn't want to do anything about it.'

This is only part of the returns saga that Giridhar faced. Some customers would pay and accept the product only to return it in a week.

Exhaust for motorbikes, once fitted, cannot be resold because once someone fits it into the vehicle and takes the bike for a spin, the carbon deposits on it will ensure it never looks new again. Ideally, they should be classified as non-returnable, like for example, undergarments are. However, sellers do not have a say in whether their products were returnable and whether they could opt out of cash-on-delivery. Once a category is chosen, the seller has to follow the template in which these parameters are pre-fixed. There is zero room for negotiation.

When the customers returned the product in a week, and Amazon finally sent it to Barrel Exhaust's office, there was a high probability of damage. Giridhar shares photos of the original fan stem, silencer, shock absorber and the ones he got after the customer returned them to show the difference.

'Either the customer is keeping a 20k item with him and returning a 2k one. Or someone in the warehouse is stealing the originals and sending us damaged stuff,' he says. In his experience, Flipkart was even worse as they had even more non-serious buyers who were fooling around with sellers, and a lot more pilferage happened during the logistics.

When Giridhar and his team would complain that the returned item was damaged, there would be no human being to speak to as usual. A 'safety claim' had to be raised in the seller's section of the website. In the few years that Barrel Exhaust was selling through Amazon, Giridhar recalls raising thirty to forty such safety claims—uploading photos and filling in all the information every time. Here's the clincher: after doing all this, Amazon would decide how much the damage was worth and how much compensation the seller deserves.

'If my product is worth 20k. And they decide that damage is worth 4k. They'd only repay me 16k. So because of them not having good-quality customers, my product is returned; they hold my inventory for thirty days, it comes back damaged and when I make a claim, the value of the loss is decided by them!' says Giridhar, in disbelief despite the incidents happening a few years ago.

Eventually, Giridhar and his team decided the 'reach' was illusory, and they would rather sell to genuine customers through their website.

Despite these obstacles, did he make a net profit through the platforms?

'On Flipkart, I made nothing. We were getting awful customers. On Amazon, I made about a 10–15 per cent margin. If I sell the same thing offline through my old website, I make 35–40 per cent.'

Giridhar found it hard to understand the calculations of what they finally received for their sales on Amazon, after the commission deductions, fee for warehouse and logistics and other mysterious levies that he terms 'the best kept secret after the formula for Coca-Cola'. Big retailers hire consultants just to be able to understand Amazon's transactions,' he finishes.

It's a jungle out there!

Within the platform seller community, it is common knowledge that both negative and positive reviews can be obtained for a fee. Neither is desirable. If a vicious competitor leaves a lot of negative feedback about the product, the scene is set for an account suspension. But viciousness can also manifest itself in several profuse positive reviews for a rival's product. Since Amazon has been cracking down on sellers who buy five-star reviews; its algorithms are trained to detect unusual spikes in positive review activity. So if a competitor leaves many positive reviews, it will draw unwelcome attention from Amazon and again lead to a suspension of the rival's account.

The barriers to entry are low and there are hundreds of courses and tutorials out there urging entrepreneurs to join the bandwagon. Hence, sellers are like cats clawing each other for the same piece of bread.

The competition makes them resort to reprehensible tactics, which seem like they are inspired from *saas-bahu* serials. These include orchestrating product returns to give the impression that the product was lousy and buyers are returning it en masse. Another below-the-belt hit is to allege that a seller has listed counterfeit or fake products. Because Amazon takes the approach of 'guilty until proven innocent' for sellers, the accounts of even genuine sellers are suspended until they are able to prove the allegation wrong. This is akin to blocking the ID of delivery workers and cab/bike drivers on the basis of the customer's version of an incident.

Sellers therefore have to watch like hawks to see that no one is fooling around with their account. Amazon is not clamping down on these practices despite the superlative tech that is otherwise always called to action.

The Buy Box

On the contrary, Amazon fans the flames of unsavoury competition through the kind of structures it has built and the fight for visibility that it encourages, pitting one seller against another.

Take every Amazon seller's obsession with The Buy Box.

Ah, the Buy Box. For an Amazon seller, having her business' name on the Buy Box is like us, as customers, having our name in neon lights on a billboard on the main thoroughfare of the city, in the sense that it becomes unmissable.

Since it is so important to a multitude of sellers on the biggest retail platform on the planet, it is worth understanding what exactly is being fiercely fought over.

So, imagine you are buying a Philips food processor. Many stockists sell this item. Once you click the product page, on the right is a white rectangle that shows the price, quantity, shipping address, 'Add to cart' and 'Buy Now'. Within that triangle, in small font is 'Sold By'. There will be only one seller's name there. That seller is the chosen one. If the customer decides to go ahead and buy the Philips food processor this seller gets the sale.

Just below that it says, 'Other sellers on Amazon'. Upon clicking, a few more sellers will appear each with marginal differences in price and shipping time. But almost no one goes there. Everyone just clicks 'Add to cart' and moves on to make the payment. Sometimes there is no option to choose another seller except whoever is displayed in the Buy Box.

The chosen one in the Buy Box is a 'high-performance seller' according to Amazon's metrics, with the most competitive price. Because numerous merchants can sell the same item, this position can be very competitive. If there are multiple high-ranked sellers for a specific product, the sellers will rotate in the Buy Box.

That tiny bit of digital real estate is what every seller is obsessed with. It's what the Cannes Film Festival or the Met Gala means to a celebrity.

Just like you can't just waltz into these prized events, sellers can't just sign up and imagine they will appear on the Buy Box. Sellers that outsource shipping and logistics to Amazon, commonly called Fulfilment by Amazon (FBA) are given preferential treatment. You need to be a quality seller with a history of satisfied customers. You should sell high volumes, have low defects, no late shipments, have sufficient inventory and be on the platform for a long time to be recognized by Amazon as a 'professional seller'.

Websites that tutor people how to be a Buy Box winner remind them that the algorithm Amazon uses to rate sellers is constantly changing. It's up to the seller to keep up to date on what the platform considers most important.

Amazon's Sellers Central, a country-wise portal where sellers discuss their troubles, is a cesspool of frustration across the world. All of them are agonized tirades and bewildered outpourings about the workings of Amazon. Shipments delayed, inventory issues, losing the Buy Box, listing deactivated, incomprehensible charges—the list is long and the complainants run into hundreds of thousands, laying bare the tensions in the relationship between Amazon and its third-party sellers. Given below is an edited version of a goodbye note from a small seller in the US, which could well be a note from a small Indian businessman:

*Calling it quit after 5 years of being a
small business on Amazon.*

After selling for five years on Amazon, we are finally calling it quits. My wife and I started this journey on Amazon almost six years ago, and each year, we keep hoping things will get better, but things get only worse and worse.

If you are a seller on Amazon making $10,000 or more each year, it is a great thing, but for most of us small sellers or businesses, you get to a point where you realize that Amazon is that big and giant pig you are taking part of fattening up, hoping one day you get a slice of bacon. But that day may never come.

With everything this platform says and does, it feels like they only want a small percentage of success to come your way but the mass majority to them. You come to a point as a seller where you realize that when, after all the time and money you invested, you only get a small percentage back.

For example, when you are selling on Amazon, depending on your niche, you will have to spend a lot of money on ads every week to make a few sales, and after all the cost of ads and fees, you are only left with a small margin. After all, this is not just it; they hold that small margin on something they come up with call reserves, paying you 15 to 20 percent every two weeks from your own funds when they get their cuts every 3–5 days. And when they finally send you that small deposit, you can't

even afford to get new inventories in. That's when you
keep investing more and more of your personal funds
and hoping that things will get better one day, but you
never do.

Amazon might be an excellent platform for big
companies and big sellers, but to a lot of small businesses,
Amazon is their biggest nightmare.[10]

Restaurants

'We are not against Zomato or Swiggy. We feel that
they are an essential part of the ecosystem. What we are
against is tyranny, the abuse of their dominant position,'
says Riyaz Amlani, the restaurateur behind eateries like
Social, Smokehouse Deli and Mocha. He is also an ex-
president of the National Restaurant Association of India
(NRAI), who held the position during the challenging
pandemic years.

During the pandemic, restaurants could only make
sales through online orders. Hence it was boom time for
online food delivery. They wanted to increase demand
by giving discounts. The more concessions a restaurant
gave, the more orders it received. It became habit-forming
behaviour among customers who gravitated towards
restaurants that gave price cuts. At the same time, while
they were putting downward pressure on the pricing, they
were also increasing the commissions they were charging
on delivery. The small restaurateur, utterly beholden to the
aggregator, was getting burnt at both ends.

The small restaurant's situation hasn't changed much, even after the pandemic has ended, as far as delivery is concerned. The algorithm is designed to bump up restaurants offering discounts, higher on the search. Customer membership schemes like Swiggy One and Zomato Gold require restaurants to offer deep discounts. It creates a race to the bottom for restaurants because such discounts are unsustainable. The platforms benefit from higher transaction volumes and the commission they earn from both customers and the eatery for each purchase. Amlani calls it the creation of 'a FOMO kind of a situation' when every small restaurant feels obliged to reduce its prices because that's what someone else is doing. Restaurants are controlled and monitored by the platform just like delivery agents are.

'So, there is this thing called KPTs or kitchen prep times, and they monitor that very closely, which is part of the algorithm. If there's a delay, they charge for waiting time, push you down on the list, and impose a penalty . . . It gets unilateral, and then we have to have a dialogue with them.'

Amlani says that the restaurant business is tricky to survive, with a 95 per cent mortality rate. A desperate restaurant owner with a choked cash flow thinks that if he comes onto Zomato or Swiggy and gives a discount, the customer will try the product, and then they will be so swayed that they will start ordering directly. But that never happens because the customer has tasted blood and become a discount junkie. As platforms have spent billions of dollars and trained customers over a decade to order on the app, no one calls the restaurant directly. Even if they do, the restaurant directs them to the app as they have let go of the boys delivering for them earlier. Despite the apparent growth in food delivery, many restaurants struggle to survive due to the steep costs of operating on these platforms. While new restaurants are onboarded each month, many others shut down due to financial pressure.

Amlani explains that there are three Ds that are important for a restaurant listed on a food tech platform— delivery, discovery and discounting. 'An aggregator typically charges 25–30 per cent to the restaurant partner for delivery. Then, the restaurant has to give a 15–20 per cent discount to be present in the customer's consideration set. In addition, they spend another 10 per cent for discovery as advertising on the platforms. So, restaurants spend about 45–55 per cent more on online orders. Thus, the number of transactions has increased because the catchment area has widened. But profitability has fallen.'

Large restaurants have bargaining power with the aggregators to reduce commissions, while the smaller ones comply meekly and suffer in silence. Amlani urges me to 'talk to the small guys' to understand their relationship with food delivery platforms.

Taking his advice, I meet Sarita Sarkar, proprietor of a Bengali speciality eatery eponymously called 'Sarkar'. The restaurant is a forty-seater on a busy main road in Hyderabad's Hi-Tech City area. The interview was interrupted many times because she was firefighting on many fronts. The previous night, pest control had been done, and the kitchen was not yet back to normal; a guest had stormed off because of a delay in service; men from a soft drinks company had come to install their refrigerator and were waiting for directions. Sarita is a petite woman in her early thirties who handled all this with incredible calmness and an unwavering smile. Later, as she narrated her story, I realized that this was because these were trivial matters compared to the kind she had dealt with and emerged victorious. Between being diagnosed twice with cancer, going through a divorce, being financially abandoned by her adoptive parents and facing irrecoverable business losses in the second wave of Covid-19, Sarita had opened and closed ten restaurants in various locations in Hyderabad. Through the ebb and flow of her food and beverage entrepreneur career, she had also received numerous awards proudly displayed on her restaurant's walls.

But it's never an easy road in the F&B business. It had been two years since she started the restaurant, and she had not yet broken even. Her cumulative losses totalled to Rs 23 lakh. She was ambivalent about whether listing on food delivery apps had helped her business.

'Because parking is not easy and given the small size of the restaurant, we cannot accommodate everyone. In that sense, Swiggy-Zomato has been useful. But their commissions have been increasing. It's now 33 per cent. Then you have to put ads to show up on the app. In the monthly report that they send me, there is a big difference between the amount of food we sold and how much they have paid me! What happened to the rest? It just goes off in various payments to them!

'Look at this,' Sarita says, pointing to a plastic packet of food kept on the counter. 'This has been ready for thirty minutes, but the delivery guy hasn't come. When it reaches the customer, it will be cold and not nice. Then the customer will either complain or return the food, and the company will call us and force us to pay the refund.'

One of the earliest factories in the United States was that of the textile industry. Children were often employed to push foot treadles and produce spindles of yarn. Here is a letter written by one such little girl to her father:

Dear Father,

I received your letter on Thursday the 14th with much pleasure. I am well, which is one comfort. My life and health are spared while others are cut off. Last Thursday one girl fell down and broke her neck, which caused instant death. She was going in or coming out of the mill and slipped down, it being very icy. The same day a man was killed by the railroad cars. Another had nearly all of his ribs broken. Another was nearly killed by falling down and having a bale of cotton fall on him. Last Tuesday we were paid. In all I had six dollars and sixty cents. I paid $4.68 for boarding. With the rest I got me a pair of

rubbers and a pair of 50 cent shoes. Next payment I am to
have a dollar a week beside my boarding . . .
  I think that the factory is the best place for me and
if any girl wants employment, I advise them to come to
Lowell.

—Excerpt from a Letter from Mary Paul,
Lowell mill girl, 21 December 1845.[11]

Oppression can hide in plain sight without even the oppressed realizing it.

The influential management guru of the late nineteenth century, Fredrick Taylor, who counted Henry Ford amongst his admirers, drew up the 'principles of scientific management' to improve industrial efficiency—break complex jobs down into simple ones, measure everything, rewarding high performance and sacking the inefficient who can't keep up with the metrics. This mechanical and reductionist approach to work, called 'Taylorism', has been critiqued for prioritizing efficiency and control at the expense of worker autonomy and dignity. In the digital age, Taylorist principles have been adapted and applied to digital platforms where every process is broken down, and workers are constantly monitored and evaluated to maximize output. This phenomenon has been termed 'Digital Taylorism'[12] or, as some scholars put it, 'Taylorism on steroids',[13] leading to the dehumanization of labour.

The lack of transparency about how and why work is allocated by the algorithm powering the app builds an information imbalance and, therefore, a power imbalance between the platform on the one hand and workers, sellers and restaurants on the other. They are termed 'partners', but it is a strange partnership where the platform makes the rules, dictates the commission, sets the price and decides which customers should be served.

When everything is codified into rules and fed into machines, there is no skill or historical knowledge that the enterprise needs. Hence, every worker is an interchangeable part and can be exchanged for another worker with little disruption. The harsh truth is that frontline workers on platforms are easily replaceable in labour-surplus countries. As a veteran labour activist quips: '*Ramlal nahin toh Shyamlal aajayega.* (If Ramlal is not there, Shyamlal will be there.)'

In the foreseeable future, all low-skill jobs are likely to be performed by robots who will, of course, not reduce output by taking lunch breaks. In many retail warehouses in Western countries, robots are already deployed to do some of the tasks that people are doing in labour surplus countries.

This is also true of the numerous small sellers who get on the treadmill of selling on the site and collapse trying to breathe. Steve Chou is a successful e-commerce store owner, bestselling author featured in *Forbes* and *New York Times*, YouTuber and podcaster with a master's from Stanford, who has taught legions of students how to sell online. 'Amazon is like a drug, a drug that promises you quick sales in a short period of time while making you addicted and dependent on their marketplace . . . things can turn on a dime and you have to make sure you have a fall-back plan just in case . . . because Amazon doesn't really care about you,' cautions Chou on his website.[14]

The fact that a few tech monopolies (Uber, Amazon, etc.) have made their presence irreplaceable to modern societies was bad enough. But monopolies whose inside workings remain opaque and incomprehensible to everyone on the outside—workers, sellers, customers and regulators—are even more frightening, raising ethical and social questions about a tech-dominant lifestyle.

ANXIETY

Speed Devils

The first thing I notice about Ranjith Kumar is the bruise on his face near the right eye and the injury on his arm. A nineteen-year-old bespectacled boy with a mushroom cut, he is a new entrant to Swiggy's workforce in Chennai. 'I joined last week,' he says. 'But a couple of days ago, my bike got hit by a truck at night. I fell off and got injured.'

Though he did not receive compensation from his employer, he's happy it wasn't his fault. If he had sped, Swiggy would have reprimanded him.

'How do they know whose fault it is?'

'They see how fast I reach from one order destination to the next and calculate the speed. If it's too high, they will call me to ask, "Why, bro? *Yenna aachu*? (What happened?)" They know everything. Right now, I am not driving and speaking to you; they'll know that too.'

He works in the daytime because, during the day, he only gets orders within a five-kilometre radius of his house in Pallavaram, close to Chennai airport. But if he were to work at night, he would be expected to fulfil orders in far-flung areas. 'It's scary to ride the bike at night,' he says. 'You can get hit very easily by guys who drive rashly.'

Ranjith is his family's main breadwinner, consisting of his ill father and his mother, who works as a domestic maid. Previously, he had been employed in a hardware shop for a salary of Rs10,000, but he was lured by Rs 5000 more that he could earn by being a delivery boy at Swiggy.

'But I am going to quit,' he tells me. 'I don't like roaming around in the sun all day and night driving is risky.'

Ranjith's fears are well-founded. Road accidents involving speeding delivery boys are routinely reported and often result in collateral damage. In July 2021, Arun E.J., a thirty-seven-year-old Kochi resident, was returning home after visiting his relative's house when a food delivery boy overtook his car from the left while negotiating a curve. Though the latter's motorcycle hit the front left headlamp of the car, the delivery boy escaped unhurt. However, Arun lost control of the vehicle, which crashed into another bike coming from the opposite direction, whose rider and pillion rider suffered severe injuries.[1]

Although food delivery companies state that they do not penalize their partners for delays, competition with rival companies forces them to take risks while driving. If there is a delay, the order can get cancelled, and the customer may order from a different app. If that doesn't happen, delays accumulate, impacting each subsequent order and compelling delivery workers to drive faster.

Attacked!

Hundreds of gig workers—Lyft and Uber drivers, and DoorDash, Instacart, Grubhub and Amazon Flex couriers—have been carjacked in the US over the years. In many cases, the would-be assailants used the company apps to lure unsuspecting drivers.[2]

In Jaipur, workers recounted an incident where a delivery boy was stopped by two people on a motorcycle who pretended to be looking for an address. As the boy came close, the driver of the motorcycle took out the boy's helmet, hit his head with it, snatched his mobile and cash and sped away. It appears that criminal behaviour has nothing to do with education. In a medical college in the same city, students placed orders through 'cash on delivery', but when the food came, they grabbed it from the delivery boy, ganged up and refused to pay.

The tensions faced on the job stemmed not only from direct interactions with customers but also from the environment. Given the industry's infancy, there is no exhaustive manual of precedents from which workers and the company can learn. Things keep happening anew and take everyone by surprise.

The attack on Priyanka Devi, one of the few women Uber drivers in Delhi, is testimony to the occupational hazards on the job. On a chilly night in January 2023, Priyanka Devi was attacked by robbers in Delhi's Kashmere Gate. When she was on her way to pick up a passenger, a brick was thrown at the car's windshield, and two men came up to her car demanding her phone, money and car keys. She alleged that the two men tried to take away the keys, and when she resisted, one of them hit her on the neck with a beer bottle. Priyanka, who needed nine stitches on her neck, eventually quit the profession. Incidents like the one Priyanka underwent, which threatened personal security, are why few women enter the transport sector.

On 11 January 2023, Mohammed Rizwan, a twenty-three-year-old Swiggy delivery boy who lived with his unemployed, ailing father and three siblings in Hyderabad, went to work as usual.[3] Three years ago, he had dropped out of college to support the family by delivering for Swiggy. As he knocked on a customer's door on the third floor of an upmarket gated society in the tony locality of Banjara Hills to deliver a food packet, he heard a dog bark. An instant later, the door opened and a German Shepherd rushed towards him. Terrorized, he started running as the dog chased him. In a moment of fear, he jumped down and grievously injured his head. Though the customer arranged for him to be taken to hospital immediately, Rizwan could not be saved.

Others point to the menace of street dogs. 'I know people whom street dogs have attacked, and in fear, they lose their balance and trip. In one case, the guy fell from his bike, and the dog nipped his ear. We wrote a letter to the municipality, but they shrugged it away, saying street dogs are everywhere and it is hard to control them,' said a labour activist.

Khyber Pakhtunkhwa province is the Wild West of Pakistan, where Pathans carry guns as routinely as

Englishmen carry umbrellas. Rahimullah is a food delivery rider working for Foodpanda in Peshawar, the province's capital. He lives in Bara, a tehsil southwest of Peshawar, where militants have been active. He relates stoically how, on his way back home one night, he was attacked by a gun-wielding gang who robbed him of his mobile and money. Fakhar, an inDrive driver in Lahore, was not lucky enough. In February 2023, a passenger shot him dead following an altercation. In Karachi, Abdul Kareem says that there were cases of snatching that happened every day. 'When orders come from Lyari General Hospital at midnight while returning, riders commonly have had their phones snatched. There are some lonely areas where things can take a bad turn at any time. If I am very uncertain, I call Foodpanda and tell them I can't deliver, and they mostly understand. Or I request the customer to walk up to where I am and collect the packet. *Dar toh laga rehta hai.* We are just working and hoping Allah will take care of us.'

Heat

Climate change is exacerbating the frequency and intensity of heat waves. Scorching summer months in all parts of the subcontinent, with the mercury touching 45 degrees Celsius or more in some places, are no longer surprising. People in physically demanding, outdoor jobs experience heat far more than others. For gig workers, working long hours on the road and trying to add more and more gigs to increase income make them prioritize work over well-being. Workers remain anxious about suffering heat strokes, which entail medical expenses and loss of earning days.

Those Crazy Customers

Brahm Prakash is close to fifty. He lives in a village in Greater Noida and has been a Zomato delivery partner for five years, a fact he is proud of.

'Do you meet any crazy customers?' I ask him.

'They are all crazy,' he says, laughing. '*Ek se ek ajeeb hain*. The ones in the villages are the strangest.' He tells me about an elaborate modus operandi that is a favourite among customers in the villages. To give a little context, Greater Noida is a suburb about forty kilometres from Delhi's south-eastern border, administratively in Uttar Pradesh (UP). As part of the National Capital Region, it is a schizophrenic town—partly urban and partly rural. The villages are embedded within the urbanized areas such that they lie cheek-by-jowl with malls and swanky villas. This forced juxtaposition has resulted in village youth adopting distinctly city mores, like ordering food online. But they gave it their own twist as if they were thumbing their nose at such new urban fads.

Brahm Prakash explains that when an order is cancelled, restaurants do not take back food once it has been packed and sent out for delivery. Many villagers have got wind of this. So, they order from these outlets and cancel the order after the delivery reaches their doorstep. They know that the restaurant will not accept the food back, so they plead with him to give the food to them and offer him Rs 100–200 for this misdemeanour. 'But I never oblige,' he tells me. 'Why should I give it to them when I can take the food to my own home? The value of the food is much more than what they will pay me! The customers in the apartment complexes don't do this, just the *gaonwalle*,' he says, laughing indulgently at his brethren.

Abdul Kareem is a delivery worker for Foodpanda in Karachi. Like workers in India did, he described how customers switch off their phones at the crucial moment when he is close by and needs to call to check directions or get clearance to enter a building. 'Sometimes they are at home but put their office location by mistake. They tell us to then drive to their home. Who will pay for that? Once, a customer ordered me to taste the pizza I was delivering to check if it was too spicy. I told him, "My job is to deliver; I am not responsible for the taste!"'

Inside the Cab

A few years ago, while interviewing people for a global project on gender-segregated transport, I spoke to a South African academic about whether women-only cabs enhanced their security. She pointed out that while more women are victims of harassment in public spaces than men are, women could sometimes be perpetrators. Despite being a renowned feminist herself, she was honest about the reverse harassment that Uber drivers in Johannesburg faced from women who stepped into the vehicle after drunken nights in pubs and bullied the driver. She had done a training programme for Uber drivers and learnt how scared male drivers were to venture out at night.

Cut to March 2023. I was in Delhi travelling from Lodhi Road to Greater Noida with Sanjay Kumar in an Ola cab at night. It was a long ride, and Sanjay was a talkative man, so we covered a great deal of ground about his life as a full-time Uber/Ola driver in Delhi-NCR. Son of Bengali immigrants to Delhi, he was now more of a north Indian and was a rare Bengali who could barely speak the language. Having been on the job for twenty-five days a month for five years, he had seen it all. So, when I asked him if he had met any oddball customers, anecdotes came tumbling out, reminiscent of what I had learnt about Uber drivers in South African cities. Here is what Sanjay Kumar had to say about the gender-based differences in passenger behaviour in his experience.

> I come across very strange customers. Especially girls. Some of them smoke in the car, though it's not allowed. I can't say a thing to them. If you ask them not to, they'll say, 'Bhaiya, I smoke daily in the cab; no one says anything. What's your problem?' Every other day, I meet someone like this. Then there are the drunk ones who come in the night. For every ten female passengers riding beyond 10 or 11 p.m., two or three will be

drunk. First, they start a conversation; soon, they lose all decorum and even put a hand on my shoulder from behind. Some girls, even if they are sober, use such bad language while sitting behind and talking on the phone to someone. They are blind to the fact that someone else is listening in front. It's hard to keep driving quietly when all this is happening.

I ask him why he doesn't avoid picking up female passengers at night since he knows they are likely to misbehave.

'I can't refuse because I can't judge whether the person is drunk through the booking! Sometimes, there are decent passengers at that hour as well. The ones who leave offices late speak politely and say thank you when the ride ends.'

'Don't you find drunk men?' I ask.

'Yes, of course. But they sit quietly, slumped in the back seat and get off when it's time to get off. I haven't faced any trouble from them.'

He goes on to cite several instances where women passengers turned aggressive.

'Some madams want to go off the route shown on the map to pick up someone on the way, so they ask you to follow a different route. If I refuse, a conflict arises. "What's the big deal? It is just a small deviation," they say. But it's not. If I don't follow the map, I will be questioned.'

Since he seems laid-back and even-tempered, I asked him how he handles such a situation. Does he also argue?

'We can't do much because in today's climate, we have to think hard before we say anything to them, or they'll complain, and that'll be the end of our livelihoods. Why take *panga*? Once the ride is over, I will never see them again. But not everyone is like that. My driver friends from UP are more hot-blooded!' he laughs and narrates an instance of his friend, a driver from UP, who drove a small car under the category Uber Go. The girl who had booked the cab brought along oversized luggage and was stuffing the car with it. The driver objected, and it became a full-blown altercation.

Was Sanjay a misogynist? With a mother, wife and daughter at home, he was unlikely to hate womenkind in general. His view that female passengers were more troublesome seemed to stem from several unfortunate encounters he had had with them. Some had cheated him of money after choosing the 'cash payment' option on the app. They had gotten off at the destination, saying that they would go home and return with cash. Then they disappeared into a building or some side street, their phones switched off and never returned. 'I am not going to run after a girl, obviously. And they know the driver is not going to wait forever. They don't get down at their building, where maybe one can ask the security guard where that madam went. It would be some friend's place. Or some gully near their home. Somewhere where one can't trace them.'

One instance where a woman passenger mugged a driver was particularly startling.

Another driver, a friend of mine, once took a girl from Hauz Khas to Chittaranjan Park at night. Midway on the route, she told him to give her all the money he had on him, or else she'd claim that he had sexually harassed her. The driver was shocked but recovered and stood his ground, saying he had only two thousand rupees but needed it and would not give it to her. She persisted, and finally, the angry driver drove to the nearest police station. The police advised him to give her the money and close the issue, saying, 'If she makes me write a case against you, I will have to lock you up for the night, and the case will go to court. You'll have to prove your innocence. We have had such cases before. We can't do anything.'

Eventually, according to Sanjay, the driver gave the girl the money and became so depressed after this incident that he almost quit the profession. He later continued, counselled by friends and family, but ensured that by 4 p.m., he logged out of the app and headed home.

Mustafa Sheikh,* an Uber driver in Hyderabad, is eloquent about the situations faced by drivers in Hyderabad with drunk women passengers. At first, I expressed disbelief at what he was saying, maybe because of my biased view of Hyderabad being a sober, more conservative city compared to Delhi.

'I'll take you with me, madam, on Friday nights and weekend nights to Madhapur, Hi-Tech City', he says in his Hyderabadi lingo. '*Bachhiyaan itni pee rakhi hoti hain, unki khud ki hosh unke paas nahi rehti.* (Girls are so drunk that they have no idea what is happening.) In such situations, who will get blamed if they lose something or if the boy accompanying them misbehaves in the back seat? It is the driver. Because the first thing the police will do is see the CCTV footage in which they will catch the car number and hence the driver.'

I ask him if there was any misbehaviour apart from drunkenness. He echoes what Sanjay had told me in Delhi, 'Sometimes, they don't even give money. Then they don't want to get dropped at the location they entered, but as per the company's rule, we have to drop them only at the location, particularly for female passengers. And if you refuse to go somewhere else, they threaten you by saying they'll put a criminal case against you, I'll do this, do that, what do you think of yourself.'

Incidents of harassment and criminal acts of violence by passengers against Ola/Uber drivers have taken place across the country, irrespective of either party's gender.

In August 2022, a twenty-six-year-old cab driver in Hyderabad, Y. Venkatesh, was brutally attacked with cricket wickets and repeatedly punched in the face by a group of seven people, including an intoxicated passenger. The drunk passenger asked Venkatesh to turn into the lanes, saying his friend would give him Rs 1000. Once there, a gang appeared, beat the driver up and confined him to a room. Somehow, Venkatesh managed to call the car owner, who was also thrashed and thrown into the room. In what could be a scene from a Telugu potboiler, the two of them managed to escape from the illegal confinement and reached a police station. Venkatesh, who had come to

Hyderabad from a small town in Andhra Pradesh barely a month ago, was planning to study for entrance exams to join the police. He attended coaching classes during the day and drove a cab at night to earn money for his tuition fees. Plans foiled, he lay in a coma after sustaining severe head injuries in what became a ride to hell and back.[4] His family struggled to pay his medical bills, and a driver association was helping them to whatever extent possible. But sadly, the same association confirmed that he died in September 2024.

I heard of another incident where a woman driver ferried a male passenger from Hyderabad airport to the city. The passenger started asking the lady driver personal questions about why she was driving a car when she was so pretty and could be doing something else. The driver reprimanded him, but the passenger continued. For a while, she was silent but finally lost her cool and told him to sit quietly until she reached the drop location and mind his own business. The passenger was snubbed, so he wrote a lengthy complaint against her, accusing her of rudeness and misbehaviour. The lady driver also complained to the police, who, like in the Delhi case, urged her to settle offline.

Drivers, of course, are no angels. Numerous cases of male drivers harassing and even raping female passengers have made headlines. Apart from sexual crimes, drivers have also extorted money. In September 2022, a Bangalore Ola passenger shared his ordeal on Twitter in which the driver did not enter the OTP but drove the car to the highway where the commuter was stranded in a cab-less area and demanded the full fare.

And not all drunks are villains. A tuk-tuk driver in Colombo says, 'Sometimes a customer will bring a beer and ask whether they can drink. I say, go ahead. I had a hire from Kaduwella to Pannipitiya. He was already drunk but asked if he could drink some more and smoke. He chatted with me through the trip and gave me an extra 500 when he got down.'

Laxman Lama is a cab driver with Pathao, hailing from Imadol, a village in Lalitpur, south-east of Kathmandu. 'There are times when more than four passengers get into the car. This is against the rule. Pathao has told us they have only an insurance policy for four passengers. If the driver allows more than four passengers, the office is not responsible for insurance if any accident happens. When we tell the customer this is against the rules, they become confrontational and say, "When did this rule come in? We have also travelled with six people. Why doesn't Pathao communicate these things properly to customers?"'

Priyantha, forty-one, in Colombo, has met some terrible customers. 'I had a Pick Me hire from Kollupitiya to Mt Lavinia yesterday. The customers were a mother–son duo. On the way closer to Dehiwela, I accidentally ran over a nail, and my tyre got a puncture. The lady started scolding and abusing me that I was not maintaining my tuk-tuk! Then she got down, got on to another tuk-tuk and left. When I ended the trip, the ride cost had accumulated to 500+ Sri Lankan rupees. But she did not pay a single cent. And I also have to pay a commission to Pick Me for that 500.'

'They are upper-class people who get in from bungalows in Cinnamon Gardens. But they do not have any manners or decency,' Priyantha continues. 'Some customers insist that I turn the vehicle and come near them if they are on the other side of the road. Sometimes, the traffic is very high, and it would take me longer to make a U-turn than for them to cross the road and get into the vehicle. But they won't budge from where they are. You cannot even make U turns in some places because it is prohibited, and traffic cops are watching. But some customers care so little about these things!'

Chinthaka, in the same city, would agree that the socio-economic status of customers has no bearing on their behaviour. 'About three years ago, I had a customer who got into the front seat of my car. When I asked him to fasten the seat belt, he refused to because he did not want his clothes to be crumpled. Then I asked him to get into the back seat. Then he yelled at me in filthy language, and I had to ask him to get out of my car. He happened to be a member of the Parliament,' he says wryly.

Women's Relationship with Ride-Hailing: It's Complicated!

Women's perception of safety or risk in a public place is partly fed by media hype about the extent of the prevailing danger in that place and partly by cultural norms that dictate that women should be under a watchful eye. Feminist mobility scholars argue that the tracking feature of ride-hailing apps feeds that narrative of the helpless woman whose every move must be monitored. In Nepal, where attitudes to women's dress and movement are relatively liberal, women passengers sharing their rides with family members is an individual choice, not a default practice, like in Pakistan.

Besides, for some women, the presence of an unknown driver, especially at night, negates the advantage that GPS tracking provides. Bhavya,* who is twenty-five, an IT professional living in Secunderabad, parties every weekend. A bunch of her girlfriends go together to the venue but prefer taking one of their family cars accompanied by a driver. Their families feel safer knowing that they are in a known vehicle.

> In the daytime, it's fine to go by cab; there are people around, but if it's later in the night and I have to travel a longer distance, I would rather travel with someone I know, like a personal driver. If I take a cab at night, I would ask one or two male friends to accompany me. Because if I am alone and the cab driver goes into unfamiliar lanes, it makes me panic. I would have to switch on the live location and tell someone, I'm here; please keep tracking me. Or I would call someone and tell them all the details of my car or maybe even make a fake call to ensure the driver knows I have alerted people.

Bhavya takes the metro to work every day. But she uses an app to summon an auto for the first- and last-mile connectivity, i.e., going from home to the metro station and back. Despite travelling on the same beaten track every day, if the driver takes a different turn on a usual route, saying that it's a shortcut to avoid the traffic, Bhavya's antennae are immediately alerted, and fear starts to creep in. She would prefer it if he took the longer, familiar route than travel on an unknown road, even for a short distance.

'You read about things happening to women so often!' says Bhavya. 'Someone was murdered, some girl was raped. A sense of panic immediately kicks in, knowing the victim was a woman. So, I'm always on alert.'

Ramya,* a software engineer in Bangalore, admits to being scared one night while using an Uber. 'It was late. We were returning from a party, and my two friends and I were sloshed. We didn't get a cab for long, so after half an hour, one driver accepted, and we sat in the back seat. Suddenly, a friend of the driver hopped on to the passenger seat. It was horrifying because we were three girls out of our heads. We called a friend and he suggested we open an SOS app and keep it ready. So, we downloaded it and kept it on standby, ready to press the button to alert the police if something happened. That's why I prefer personal cars on these occasions.'

Farah, who is seventeen and has just given her A levels (the equivalent of Class XII) in Peshawar, does not travel out of her city except on family holidays. But once, she went alone to Islamabad for a MUN (Mock UN) session.

Using Careem and inDrive apps, she felt safe in a new city because they picked her up and dropped her right at the doorstep. But on one of the rides in Islamabad, the driver started making small talk, making her uncomfortable. 'He asked me which class I was in and if I was in school or college. I think this is unnecessary. InDriver drivers have called me, texted me and sent me pictures. Once, a driver tried to call me from two different numbers. I feel harassed, of course, so I block them. I wish companies would stop such behaviour,' says the cherubic teen.

But that will not stop her from using transportation apps prolifically because she feels that by doing so, she will benefit Pakistan's shaky economy as drivers get a chance to earn something. 'And I hope they take on more women drivers. I heard they are already there in cities like Karachi and Islamabad. If there are more women drivers, more women will use such cabs, and we can also help get more women into jobs,' she concludes.

Women and Bike Taxis

Bike taxis are popular because they are easier to navigate through dense traffic and are more affordable. But they are popular only with male passengers. As drivers are almost always male, women passengers are reluctant to sit pillion for various reasons.

Bhavya always uses a cab to reach the metro station, from where she takes a metro to her workplace, although Uber, Ola and Rapido also have autos on their platform.

'Okay, it's a girl thing,' she explained. 'You don't want your face getting dusty with all the pollution and hair getting messed up in the wind when you ride an auto.'

Apart from aesthetics, women avoid bike taxis because of social censure about physical proximity to a male stranger. In Indonesia, ride-hailing leader GoJek's bikes are rarely hailed by women, prompting an entrepreneur to start a women-only service called Ojek as a parallel option.

Drivers are sometimes more worried about stricture than female passengers are. Zia, a lawyer in her early twenties in Karachi, wants to travel by bike taxi, but drivers refuse to take her on as a passenger and cancel the rides she books.

Riding pillion on a bike with a stranger can sometimes be precisely how moms imagine it, as Aruni,* who is twenty-seven and works in a private audit company in Colombo, discovered one day.

I go by train from home in Negumbo, on the outskirts of Colombo, to the office, and to reach the train station, I take an Uber or PickMe. Before the economic crisis, I always took a tuk-tuk. Lately, tuk-tuks have been a little too expensive because of fuel price hikes in Sri Lanka. So, I started taking a bike taxi to the train station. A Dutch girl interning in my office introduced me to it since, in their country, travelling on bikes and bicycles is very typical, though for Sri Lankans, it is not. When I started taking the bike taxi, all my friends at the office advised me against it. I didn't tell my parents, although I live with them, fearing they would talk me out of using bikes. But it is much cheaper than a tuk-tuk, so it made sense to me to continue with it. At first, it was scary because of the traffic, but soon, I got accustomed to it.

Then, I had a very uncomfortable experience with a bike driver one day. I had worked late that day and left the office around 6.30 p.m. I needed to get some shopping done, so I went to Majestic City Mall. I realized I had stayed longer than intended in the mall, and it was getting late. I hurriedly booked a bike ride using the app. When the guy arrived, he looked at me, smirked and said, 'Not many girls take bike taxis.'

While riding to the train station, he kept asking me personal questions. He asked me where I lived, and I lied and told him I lived in Colombo. Then he became more inquisitive and asked me why I was going to the train station if I lived in Colombo. I lied again and said I would take the train to Galle (a city two hours away in the south).

He asked me my age and marital status, and I lied about everything, making up random stories in panic. I think he saw through them. He disclosed to me that he was divorced from his wife. You might wonder why I put up with him for so long and entertained his questions. My main goal was to keep him engaged just enough until I reached my destination. I was also worried that if I offended him in any way, he would hurt me somehow. So, I kept engaging with him.

Then, on the way, he asked for my mobile number. I hesitated to reply, and he asked me if I was scared. I tried to put up a brave front and said 'no' even though I was very uncomfortable. I told him I would give him my phone number when we reached the station. Then it came. He asked me if I would like to go out with him when I returned from Galle. I told him I was unsure of my plans and could not say yes. He again asked for my phone number when we reached the train station. Since the payment was made online, I did not have to interact with him further, so I ran into the train station.

I usually rate my drivers five stars, even if they are not the best. But for this guy, I gave only one star. I did not even bother to complain because app companies take incidents like this lightly. And they never respond. It would have been a wasted effort anyway.

Behind the Five Stars

The episode 'Nosedive' of *Black Mirror*, the series on Netflix, is set in a dystopian world where people must rate each other after every social interaction. Everyone is terrified of getting lower points because the rating determines one's socio-economic class. It also affects their self-worth, and they go to extreme lengths to increase it. The episode presents a nightmarish future where a single number based on others' judgement becomes a measure of the person's value.

In the gig economy, that future is already here when customers who use app-based services and the workers who deliver them rate each other on their 'performance'. How they assign these numbers can be easily ambushed by factors like one's mood, racial bias, gender, cultural factors, personality types and other excruciatingly subjective criteria. It wouldn't have mattered but for the fact that this silly gamification of assigning a score to an interaction between two human beings affects workers' careers profoundly. It also impacts the customer, albeit to a much lesser extent.

Rating Bias—Drivers

Black Uber drivers in the US know this all too well. If a biased customer rates a Black driver 3 out of 5, this rating feeds into other criteria, and the system pushes him down the pecking order. So, he gets fewer rides than those maintaining a rating of 5. Because he gets fewer rides, he has fewer opportunities to improve his ratings, creating a vicious cycle of discrimination. Furthermore, according to a Yale study published in 2023, platforms can spread the effects of racial discrimination by displaying ratings from biased users to those who otherwise would not discriminate. K. Sudhir, Yale faculty member and co-author of the study, explains how that works, 'When some people discriminate against minorities, future customers follow the same pattern of behaviour because they are convinced that these workers are worse performers. So, even unbiased people cancel them more often and give them lower ratings. And those who are biased feel more justified to cancel more often and give even lower ratings to minorities, producing an amplification effect over time.'[5]

Not everyone has to be a bigot, but even a small number of biased customers can tilt the balance against a non-White worker.

Thomas Liu, an Asian from Hawaii with a slight accent, noticed customers cancelling ride requests after he had accepted the ride and they could view his picture. He also encountered riders asking where he was from in an unfriendly way. He believed customers were rating him low because of his race.[6] In 2015, when his ratings fell to 4.6/5, Uber fired him. In 2020, he filed a federal lawsuit against Uber in San Francisco for racial discrimination based on passenger ratings. The suit aims to represent all minority Uber drivers whose services have been terminated because of poor ratings. It asked the court to order Uber to stop using passenger evaluations when deciding whether to ban drivers from the app.

Rating Bias—Passengers

The rating system magnifies biases not only for drivers but also for passengers. In India and neighbouring countries, we either don't realize we are being rated or ignore it. Shishir Gupta, who works for a Delhi-based policy think tank, learnt this the hard way when he went to Washington, D.C., on a work trip in 2019. Gupta found he wasn't getting cabs fast enough until a black woman driver stopped for him and solved the puzzle by asking him to look at his passenger rating. Sure enough, Gupta found it was an unsavoury 3.9/5, which sent US cab drivers running in the opposite direction. Easy-going by temperament, Gupta had never entered into an altercation with any driver, so he was not quite sure what he did in India for drivers to rate him low. But rating, as any market researcher will tell you, is a cultural thing. While 4/5 could be good enough in India, it sounds like warning bells to drivers in the US.

In 2019, Uber in the US announced that it would boot out passengers who were given low ratings by drivers for bad behaviour such as making racist remarks, drinking, eating messily, etc. But gradually, it became evident that the rating system affects minority passengers disproportionately. White passengers have higher scores than minorities even if the non-Whites didn't exhibit problematic behaviours. A collaborative study between researchers from Stanford, MIT and the University of Washington that involved tracking ride-share data for White and African American customers found that drivers were more likely to cancel on African-American travellers who also had to wait longer to be picked up.[7]

Customers in cabs could also mark a five because of a perception of hostility from the driver since the rating is asked for as soon as payment is made, and the passenger has not even stepped off the vehicle. In the absence of a universal code of what each discrete star stands for, there is room for subjective interpretation, like in Shishir Gupta's case. A passenger who rated a driver 3, thinking it stood for 'acceptable', in his view, was yelled at by the driver and accused of spoiling his livelihood because the company treats five as the default.

The passenger is us, i.e. an irrational being whose motives and moods are unpredictable and subject to a dozen variables that have nothing to do with the cab driver.

One passenger describes this aspect eloquently in a discussion forum on the net: 'I feel like a rating system encourages unintended dimensions to come into play. Some people want to engage in conversation with the driver. Others want absolute silence. It can also vary for passengers and drivers day to-day and trip-to-trip. This could also lead to neurodiverse passengers and drivers receiving low scores inappropriately because of mismatched expectations on the social dimension of the trip. All of this has nothing to do with what the ratings should focus on: did the driver do the job of getting from A to B well (and safely)? Was the passenger respective of the driver's time and space?'[8]

More than a Game

Ratings are far from innocuous numbers to boost customer confidence that the company cares about the quality of service. Behind the game, like a facade of stars or emojis, is the ammunition the company collects from customers to contain, investigate, discipline and reprimand the workers.

On a warm day in August 2023, I was at the Jawahar Kala Kendra in Jaipur. There was a rally of Rajasthan's folk artists, street vendors and gig economy workers. Chief Minister Ashok Gehlot was expected to arrive. Around seventy gig workers were already present, togged out in their company T-shirts. The agenda was to press the CM to implement the welfare measures of the recently passed law in the state.

The other two groups of informal workers at the venue were folk artistes and street vendors who had the same demands. Hundreds of performers had arrived from Jaisalmer, Barmer and Marwar in spectacular costumes, and the view of the people under the pandal was a riot of hues, men in *lehariya pagris* and women in *ghagras*. The artists enacted skits on the sidelines to keep the audience engaged before the CM arrived. Some were *behroopiyas*, dressed up as people from different occupations, including witch doctors.

The gig workers take their seats, and the orange of Swiggy, black of Urban Company and red of Zomato add to the saturation of colour at the venue. Against the background of the music of the dhol and sarangi, I speak to Savita and Saima, salon service providers in Urban Company. Savita's ID has been blocked for months because of a customer complaint and poor rating. On her last client visit, she had warned the lady who had called her for a waxing session that her skin did not seem right for such a procedure. But the client was adamant that she do the job she had been called for.

'It's fine then, I'll do it, and you take the responsibility,' Savita told the customer.

It so happened that the customer's skin started peeling, and she slapped a legal case on Urban Company, who immediately blocked Savita's ID. 'They are always on the customer's side. They heard everything she had to say and didn't even give me a fair hearing. You have to listen to both versions, right?'

Across the border, Ghar Par offers salon services at home in select cities of Pakistan. It follows the same business model as Urban Company in India, i.e. one where service partners must buy the company's proprietary kit and undergo a training period. The orders came into the app every night and had to be fulfilled the next day. Saba Kiran in Islamabad was a beautician with Ghar Par for two years through the pandemic.

'The business didn't slow down really. We used to wear masks and gloves, use sanitizer and do the job. It was working fine,' she says.

'Then why did you quit?'

'Because the clients I served through the app became my regular clients, so I didn't need the company any more,' she admits a little bashfully. 'It saves the 40 per cent commission that Ghar Par used to cut.' She doesn't see herself returning to the platform unless she needs customers again.

But once the recorder was off and Saba became more comfortable, she laid bare the real reason for quitting. She felt that the customer's rating was disproportionately important. Not long ago, her friend, Niza, had gone to a client's house for a waxing job. The hot wax had fallen on the floor, and the wire of the machine in which the wax was heated got burnt. Niza told the client that she could not do the waxing and had no choice but to cancel the booking. The client was furious, gave her a rating of 1 star and complained to Ghar Par that the girl was unprepared, made a mess in her house and was unprofessional. Niza was fired, which made Saba quit too, because the incident brought home the precarity of her employment, where so much rested on the single number the client pressed on her phone. 'Even if there are 100 good comments, one bad comment can change the game completely,' she says, explaining her moment of epiphany.

The waxer–waxed relationship is often complicated even in salons and it is fraught with accusations and suspicion. In the early part of this century, when I lived in Churchgate, I had gone to my neighbourhood Chinese parlour, Lu Lu. A shriek pierced the cosmetic-scented air as I sat flipping through *Elle* and awaited my turn. It came from behind the curtain that separated the waxing area from the haircut and facials one. A second later, it was followed by the sound of what was unmistakably a slap. A woman watching paint dry on her nails jumped to her feet. A teen wearing a face pack swung around in her chair. 'What happened?' *'Kya hua?'* asked various anxious voices as Lu, the owner, rapidly approached the crime scene.

She pushed the curtain and revealed two women in very different moods. One was a woman in her mid-forties whose bosom heaved in rage as she held up her sari to her knees, exposing half-waxed legs and glared at the parlour girl. The parlour girl held a palm to her cheek and stared at the floor in shock and humiliation. As the older lady stormed out, we learnt that the cause for the fracas was wax, which she alleged was overheated and had singed her tender skin. I remember thinking of Julia Roberts, who at that time had sent the Western media into a tizzy by appearing with unshaven underarms for an event in London. Someone's got to do it, I had thought. Make hairy the new smooth.

But as Sabita in Jaipur and Saba's friend in Islamabad recounted, certain services were fraught with risk, whether in a physical salon or home. One wrong move could plummet their rating and change the course of their lives.

Gig jobs are exhausting, wearing down workers physically and emotionally as they are put in unpredictable and sometimes dangerous situations. The transient nature of gig employment instils a sense of insecurity. The persistent fear of losing work or experiencing a drop in income because of a poor rating heightens anxiety and stress levels. Relentless performance pressure to meet benchmarks adversely affects workers' well-being.

The interesting part is that anxiety is felt not only among workers but also among customers, such as some of the women travelling on app-based transport. From Peshawar to Hyderabad to Colombo, there were women who had faced anxious moments in their journeys on ride-hailing cabs. This chapter also blew the myth that only passengers are anxious about these rides. Drivers are just as disturbed, if not more, when they encounter inebriated or rowdy behaviours by passengers of either gender.

Reid Hoffman, who founded LinkedIn, predicted the rise of social media way back in 1997. Hoffman's gaze into the crystal ball of work trends, shows that the 9–5 job is going to be extinct by 2034. More and more people are going to be working not only across multiple companies but also multiple industries, not as traditional employees but by doing two or three gigs. While this translates to more opportunity, at the same time, it ratchets up the anxiety of those doing gigs and, to some extent, those being served by them. The challenge for the future of gig work will be to retain flexibility while restructuring those aspects of the work that increase uncertainty for all the actors involved.[9]

ISOLATION

Me, Myself and I

I met Professor Jayadeva Uyangoda, a distinguished political scientist who retired from teaching at the University of Colombo, in a quaint cafe he had recommended called The English Cake Company. The septuagenarian talked to me, among other things, about the growing tendency to pamper oneself in isolation and equate it to freedom. He termed it evocatively as the 'individualization of pleasure' that technology encourages. Growing individualization has been a fundamental societal shift in the past decades. Studies have reported how the digital age promotes new forms of individualism with self-tracking technologies like Fitbits and meal-monitoring apps, self-presentation in social networks and the very existence of the 'selfie', a quintessential symbol of narcissism if ever there was one.

'What is happening to public space is an outcome of human atomization. No one walks to grocery stores. Coffee shops are no longer places to socialize. People come to cafes to be alone with their laptops. Just look around us!'

Around us were four youngsters discussing office work and a few others sitting alone at different tables, immersed in some gadget. A couple on a date seemed to be enjoying the privacy the off-peak hour provides. The good professor was right. Cafes used to be public spaces where artists, writers, businessmen and philosophers came to discuss, debate and exchange ideas and forge camaraderie. Literary and philosophical movements, such as existentialism and surrealism, were born out of the interactions that took place in Parisian cafes on the left bank of the Seine, so much so that prominent customers of the time, including Jean-Paul Sartre, Simone de Beauvoir, Albert Camus, Ernest Hemingway and Pablo Picasso were called 'Left Bank intellectuals'.

Closer home, in 1936, when the first Indian Coffee House opened in Churchgate, Mumbai, the place was an instant hit, and its success triggered a coffee house boom. At its peak, there were seventy-two outlets across undivided India, including in Karachi's Saddar area. Creative people like M.F. Husain and Rajinder Singh Bedi were regulars at the one in Connaught Place, Delhi, talking away, fuelled by the four anna coffees of the Raj days. The scent of sedition wafted from the discussions there to the powers that be during the Emergency (1975–77), causing the coffee house to be temporarily shut down. Irani cafes, with their characteristic marble-topped tables and blackboard menus, were also spaces of social exchange. Most of the Irani cafes have now been run to the ground and the India Coffee House in Delhi caters mostly to a dwindling number of elderly patrons.

With their expensive coffees, contemporary cafes are elite hubs for those who want to be left alone. As Jayadeva says, 'Isolation is the new symbol of privilege!'

Trading off Family Time

When youngsters in the family order their meals, their timings are usually not aligned with the family dinner time. Anaya, the researcher in Colombo who is habituated to online food ordering, admits that it is invariably late when she gets dinner through Uber Eats or Pick Me. By that time, her parents have usually eaten and possibly slept.

'Then, I just take it to my room and eat,' she says. 'But I feel a little guilty though about not sharing it with them and just eating by myself,' she adds.

I recognized this behaviour from my own home. Whenever my teenage son orders in, that process follows a trajectory separate from regular dinner time. When the entire family plans to get food from a restaurant, they eat together. But when only the children order for themselves, dinner time is split. Since dinner is typically when all family members are around and is a classic setting for conversation and catching up on the day, ordering in becomes a trade-off with family bonding time.

Community Life

Gated communities have always had a grocery store within the complex. They were advertised as such with brochures showcasing 'clubhouse' and 'convenience store' as amenities, along with a swimming pool and play area. Developers sold the feature to show that the complex was self-sufficient, and residents need not step outside for anything. The older generation, like my parents-in-law and others I know of, who are used to living in independent houses, complained that gated communities were too restrictive and sanitized. Since there are only one or two grocery shops in a community, they miss the diversity and choice of the bazaar, bargaining with different vendors and making small talk with the ones they've known for years. Quick commerce has made going to the in-house grocery store redundant and feel like too much effort. Unsurprisingly, the social capital and the sense of community life a citizen experiences through interacting with others has been compromised.

'This morning, I wanted brown bread, but my wife told me not to go, and she called for it from one of the apps on the phone,' says Professor Jayadeva, smiling gently as if the ways of the new world amused him. 'Earlier, I would walk down the street and get it from my grocer, who would fill me in on the neighbourhood gossip like who has died, who has moved out, etc. But a lot of local grocery shops have closed. Only one or two shops are left in my neighbourhood. Instead, you have these Western supermarkets: Cargills, Keils, Laugfs and 7/11. They have a monopoly on groceries in Sri Lanka. It has destroyed neighbourhood socialization,' he says regretfully.

The previous day, I had taken a taxi from Colombo to the town of Chilaw in the north of the capital to visit the Munneshwara Temple, where Rama prayed to Shiva, seeking advice on how to atone for killing Ravana. The nearly three-hour idyllic route from Colombo to Negombo and onward to Chilaw is dotted with surreal scenes of shops selling vegetables, clothes and household items with no customers. The palm-fringed roads are lush with greenery, but the abundance is only outside. Inside the shops, shopkeepers sit bored, staring blankly or looking at their phones. The only places with some activity in this struggling economy are the outlets of supermarket chains that the professor had mentioned. They all had apps, and like any other grocery delivery service, they supplied groceries and food from their in-house restaurants to the customers' doorsteps.

Real-estate ads of luxury condominiums in India promise an isolated, exclusive life with just one apartment on the floor. But isolation extracts a harsh price. Actor Jackie Shroff once made an apt observation in an interview. Until he made it big in the movies, Jackie lived in a chawl in Teen Batti, a lower-class locality within Mumbai's uber-posh Malabar Hills. He said back in the chawl, his mother would immediately know if he'd fallen ill because, with the whole family living in a cramped space, it was impossible to lose track of each other. But when he became a successful star, and the family moved to a bigger house, walls came between them. One morning, Jackie found that his mother had died in her sleep in her room during the night. He was wracked by the thought that maybe she had needed him, and he had been far away in his room.[1]

Martin Heidegger (1889–1976) was a German philosopher widely regarded as one of the most influential figures in twentieth-century philosophy. Heidegger explored the essence of technology and its impact on human existence most famously in an essay titled 'In the Question Concerning Technology'.[2] He was perturbed that the dominance of technology in modern society could lead to a loss of authenticity in human existence. He believed that technology encourages a superficial and alienated mode of being in which individuals become disconnected from themselves, others and the world around them. Heidegger's views were prophetic because the disconnection he feared is unfolding in bizarre ways.

South Korea, perhaps the world's most digitally advanced nation, found a solution for loneliness via technology. In a trend called *meok bang/muckbang* or 'broadcast eating', online hosts called broadcast jockeys began live streaming their evening meals to gawking multitudes. Traditionally, food culture ran deep in South Korea. Eating out was primarily a social activity, and it was rare to eat alone, similar to South Asian culture. But now, with an estimated 25 per cent of Koreans living alone, the loneliness of single Koreans in the hyper-digital environment of their country is reflected in the popularity of muckbang videos.[3] For them, a dinner companion, even if virtual, was better than the misery of eating alone. Though it began in South Korea around 2013–14, muckbang videos became a global rage. It begs the question of how we, as a society, got to a point where an enormous number of people join strangers online for dinner and watch them slurp, chew and munch through copious quantities of food.

Human Computing Interface (HCI) research aims to make technology more user-friendly, intuitive and enjoyable by learning how people interact with computers. Recently, the kitchen has become a focus for HCI research. For instance, a software called 'The Living Cookbook' records people's cooking experiences in an interactive digital medium that others can share and playback later. '. . . the use of technology supports intimacy, communication, education, fun and creativity while cooking.'[4] Another application called 'Not Enough Cooks in the Kitchen' uses video conferencing 'to facilitate collaborative cooking experiences, and to record cooking tips from remote friends and family'.[5] Once again, in glaring irony, technology attempts to solve the problem of loneliness it originally created.

These are cautionary red flags for societies like ours that are becoming eager adopters of technology. The words 'depression' and 'mental health' have crept into common parlance. If technology is going to provide conveniences to manage our fast-paced lives, will we also depend on it to solve the complications it is leading us to, such as isolation? Will talking to machines and falling in love with robots, a possibility portrayed in recent movies, erase our loneliness?

That would be straight out of a dystopian plot on an OTT platform.

Loneliness of the Gig Worker

'The Loneliness of the Long-Distance Runner' is a phrase that originated as the title of a short story written by British author Alan Sillitoe in 1959. It later became the title of a film adaptation. It tells the story of a working-class boy, Smith, in a reform school, whose talent for long-distance running is spotted by the authorities. Though the school sees him as a potential champion in an upcoming cross-country race against a prestigious public school, Smith likes running simply for the sense of freedom it makes him feel. In the climactic race, Smith deliberately loses the race by stopping just short of the finish line, defying the school authorities' expectations. By doing so, he reclaims his autonomy and rebels against the idea of being a pawn to fulfil someone else's agenda.

The story could well have a twenty-first-century update, which could be called 'The Loneliness of the Gig Worker', which shows the interplay between freedom and constraint, independence and isolation, that characterizes an average gig worker's life.

Many workers don't know each other and only meet peers in restaurants and warehouses while picking up an order. Their phones are also always buzzing and so there is no time to stand and chat but just enough to grab and run. When I ask a cabbie who drives for PickMe in Colombo if he meets his peer group, he says: 'If I start today in Dematagoda, and there is another cabbie there with whom I make friends, my phone will buzz, and I may get a hire to

Wattala, and he may get a hire to Dehiwala. After that, we will keep getting hires to different places, and after rotating like that, we'll not meet each other. If we go to a bar or have tea, we might say hello to a fellow worker. But that's it.'

'Atomization of workers' is the term critics of digitalized work use to describe how isolated workers run around in orbits that rarely intersect. As the ILO points out, it is a model that disenfranchises them and stops them from organizing themselves to show their collective strength and put forth their demands or protest against injustice.

Not only are workers disconnected from each other, but they are also disconnected from the company, which is now a faceless entity that communicates only through the app. Recruitment is through the app, as a driving license is uploaded on the app and the phone starts buzzing with orders. Even the kit consisting of the bag and T-shirt is couriered home in many cities.

Navin Konella, the person who had worked for five years in food and grocery delivery and had now shifted to a different industry, tells me that when he started working for the platform, there was a brick-and-mortar office dedicated to hiring agents. 'People would walk in every day, be screened and interviewed. They would check the person's attitude and take a couple of days to verify the documents. Only then an agent's ID would be created. Then someone in the office would personally hand over the kit. But there is very high attrition among agents. More than 40 per cent attrition. Too many people join and then leave, join again. So it was too difficult to hire people face to face,' he adds.

A worker can't talk to anyone except customer care on the telephone helpline. There must be something to it if, across the entire South Asian region, no gig worker I spoke to felt that the telephone helpline appointed by the platform to support workers could help them solve a grievance.

'We complain to Foodpanda, but I've never seen anyone's complaint get resolved through them,' says Nasir in Karachi.

Vikas Kumar, a bike taxi driver, sent me a recording of his interaction with the customer support of his platform and a screenshot from his app, which says 'Reason for Suspension: High Cancellations'. Vikas had suffered an injury that morning when his two-wheeler skidded and bumped against a car. He explained to the lady on the phone that he needed to go to the hospital to bandage his hand, so he could not deliver the food packet. He spoke haltingly, in a deadpan drawl, as if he had no expectations from the person at the other end.

'You can't block my ID. I really did have a problem!' he says repeatedly.

'I am sorry, sir. I can't unblock it. I can't do anything about this. Can I help you with something else?' the lady mouths her textbook spiel in a loop. She could have been a chatbot for her discernment in handling the case. Vikas mutters under his breath and disconnects the call.

There is little trust in this system of disembodied voices, the only human connection to the company. A driver in Delhi alleges that customer care gave his ID to someone they knew and blocked him out. He alleged that since his rating was stellar, that person capitalized on all the work he had put in to build a good reputation and get a lot of business. 'It's the customer support people; they do such things because they can see everyone's details on the system. So they manipulate it.'

I am not sure whether the manipulation he suspected the company's support staff of doing was even technically possible. But that's not important. What is worth noting is the level of distrust a worker can develop when there is no identifiable human on the other side.

'Did you go to the office and complain?' I asked.

'I tried to go to the Gurgaon office but could not enter. They never allow anyone. Then, another driver knew someone in the company, so I met someone there, and finally, my ID was opened. At least I didn't have to pay through my nose. There are a lot of *dalals* (middlemen) who take 2000 or 4000 and get the ID released.'

Silos of Solitude: Chanchal's Story

Gig work for platforms includes not only delivery but a lot of work that happens in the background, unseen by customers or restaurants. These could be people in customer support, design or content creation for the platform's website and app. These lower-end contract workers bear the brunt of a faceless employer just as delivery workers do. Chanchal Jangir is one such person I met in Jaipur.

The night before I was going to leave Jaipur after speaking to several gig workers and attending their protest rally, I was scrolling through LinkedIn in the hotel when I stumbled upon a post that made me stay on the page. It was by Chanchal Jangir, a person I did not know and with whom I had no common connections. Maybe because I was in the same location, the LinkedIn algorithm popped up her post on my feed. The profile picture showed a smiling woman, but the post was sad. Here is a mildly edited version of what she wrote.

> Hi everyone, I rarely post here, but today, I would like to talk about work–life balance. #worklifebalance. I lost my father in May 2022 while I was working from home for Blinkit, but still, I couldn't give him the time, care or attention that I should have. He was there in the next room, but I needed space and silence since my profile required talking to people over phone calls. After two months of thinking, 'Papa will get better; let me focus here on work', he left, and there is now space and silence all around the house.
>
> The same month, Blinkit asked me to leave as my profile was no longer there, so I joined Zomato, and today, after a year of dedicating more than 10.5 working hours a day, the profile is no longer there.
>
> For companies, it's just a profile they no longer need, but it means so much to the person. If I had the job, I could have told my vulnerable mother, 'Papa's gone, but I will care of you.' What does the person get for the time and complete dedication they have given to your company despite feeling broken and lost?

Well, this post will change nothing, but I would like
to add here that give your loved ones the time, care and
attention that they deserve because, in the end, they are
the ones who will be there for you, not the company that
has taken over your life completely.[6]

Reading this evoked all kinds of melancholic memories
about my own harried attempts to balance my work,
growing children and spending time with my father, who I
knew was dying, back in 2009–10. I messaged Chanchal on
LinkedIn and asked if I could discuss her recent professional
and personal troubles.

The next day, a couple of hours before I had to catch
my Shatabdi to Delhi, Chanchal and I meet at Gulabji
Chai Wale, an iconic chai shop in the pink city that has
been there since pre-Independence days. Chanchal is a tall
woman of about twenty-five. We ordered two masala chai
and bun maska.

Chanchal finished college and started working from
2016 onwards as an intern, then as a full-time employee
in various industries like market research, events, electrical
appliances and digital marketing. She got them by
persistently googling for hours and then calling up people
in different companies to offer her candidature.

In 2020, she got a job with Grofers (later Blinkit) as
a 'senior associate of customer delight'. The job involved
answering customer queries by phone, text or email for a
salary of Rs 40,000. She could work from home, but the
job was relentless. As soon as the shift started at 8 a.m.,

queries would start. If it wasn't solved there and then, it would get into a pipeline and the resolution time would increase, inviting questioning from her manager. 'My sick father was in the next room. But since the queries would flow continuously, I could barely take a break to go and sit with him.' It was her mother who managed her father's hospitalization because Chanchal was working. In June 2022, Chanchal's father passed away.

Around this time, her contract with Blinkit ended, and Zomato had bought over Blinkit. She was interviewed for the parent company's 'restaurant delight associate' position. She had to upload images of the restaurant and its dishes on the website and change their logos, prices or menu items, as required. Her reporting authority was a lady in Gurgaon called Manpreet,* with the designation of 'team leader' whom Chanchal never met in person during the one year she spent in Zomato. Around fifteen contract employees scattered around the country formed this 'team', but no one knew each other as they were in different processes. There was no HR person either, as HR was replaced by a platform called Zoho with a 'people management' module. On Zoho, everyone had to communicate everything they would have done to an HR executive, like applying for leave or even complaining against one's reporting officer.

At home, she became the only bread earner of her now diminished family consisting of her mother and a brother in middle school.

About ten months into the job, around March 2023, Chanchal started getting feelers from her unseen manager that her contract would likely be terminated. Eventually, those threats were executed and Chanchal's position, like others in the team, was outsourced to external agencies. Only one person was retained to control the quality of the outsourced vendors. The rest submitted their resignations. On Zoho, of course.

The worst part, says Chanchal, was that they were lied to by the manager and told that their performance was not up to the mark, which had never come up earlier. 'It would have hurt less if they were open and just said, these positions are now being outsourced, instead of making up some stuff about our "hygiene factors" (jargon for adherence to timelines).'

Not wanting to leave without setting the record straight, Chanchal asked for a meeting with her super boss, a man called Ruchir,* to whom her team leader reported. They had a video call, and when Chanchal expressed her views, Ruchir unexpectedly said, 'Why don't you just speak to Manpreet? She's right here.' And to Chanchal's dismay, Manpreet, who had been in the room all along without Chanchal's knowledge, swam into view on the screen.

Chanchal was shocked to see her and at the underhanded act but relieved that she had not bad-mouthed her boss while talking to Ruchir. She told them that if her performance had not been up to the mark, she should have been intimated earlier. Then she requested if their decision to relieve her could be reconsidered as she was the only breadwinner in her family following her father's demise.

'There was silence for a full minute. And then Ruchir mumbled that he is sorry but he can do nothing.'

When her father was ill, Chanchal had been unable to leave her seat to spend time with him for fear of the software that was monitoring her. Then, she could never meet her employers to discuss anything in person because everything was remote and faceless. Now, she had been cheated of an honest exit interview through a sleight-of-hand, which would not have been possible if she had been in the same room. Technology had got the better of Chanchal at every stage.

Though she is grateful for the fact that Grofers gave her several days off in 2022 when her father was undergoing treatment without cutting pay, the fact that ultimately, the company, in its merged avatar, threw her out in an underhanded manner when she needed it the most, was what prompted her to write her anguished post.

Chanchal's father had worked in Dubai all his life, so through her years of growing up, he was an occasional presence in her life. A few years before he passed away, he had wound up his work in the Gulf to spend the rest of his life with his family and friends in his home city. 'I was a little intimidated by him in the initial months when he returned because I didn't really know him. So, he would try to ease things by making jokes and saying silly things.' Just when a bond was beginning to form, tragedy struck unexpectedly, as it typically does.

'I feel bad that I didn't prioritize my father over my work. He was more important, of course, but I thought I should work because it was also important to earn for the family,' says Chanchal, who is certain that she wants to be an organ donor after seeing the helplessness of her own family when her father kept deteriorating because of liver and kidney failure.

As I wrote this a year later, I opened the WhatsApp chat with Chanchal because I wondered what she was doing. Her profile picture shows her as a girl of four or five, being hugged by her father. On LinkedIn, she had put her status as 'Open to Work' and written an appeal asking to be hired.

For centuries, since the Industrial Revolution, the idea of work has meant anchoring oneself to a brick-and mortar building called the 'office' or 'factory'. Even in itinerant salesman jobs, the worker returns to this anchor point to deposit what he picks up or report on the day's bounty. For a blue-collar worker, not having that is disorienting and isolating. The workplace is not a sanitized space where only work is clinically performed and payment collected. It is also a throbbing, living site of emotional exchange among those who inhabit that space. It is where gossip is exchanged about changes of roles or romantic dalliances; information is traded; ideas are debated; personal anxieties are discussed with colleagues who also become confidants; anger is expressed at perceived injustices or treats shared to celebrate promotions. Irrespective of the social class of the worker, the workplace is where the better part of a day is spent amidst other flesh and blood human beings. Such an idea is embedded in the consciousness of the urban labour force of modern societies. Gig work yanks this idea out of the worker's head and replaces it with a concept of being on your own, belonging nowhere and to no one. The sharp departure from the work style that existed for generations creates a level of cognitive dissonance that workers feel but cannot wholly articulate because it is made to seem like this is the brave, new world that they must adapt to.

Ambiguity and a strange dualism characterize the lives of platform workers. It is the first time in the history of work that such a paradox presents itself—of having a peer group but rarely, if ever, meeting them; being part of a company and not knowing the supervisor's name or where the local office is; and being told that they are autonomous but be ordered around by an invisible master.

The Frankfurt School of Sociologists, active in the mid-twentieth century, consisting of scholars such as Max Horkheimer and Herbert Marcuse, highlighted how technology used for mass production and consumption could contribute to alienation and estrangement in modern society. Instead of finding fulfilment and meaning in their work, workers are reduced to mere cogs in a machine and invisibilized, performing repetitive tasks without any sense of autonomy or creativity. They work at a company but not for a company. This alienation from labour leads to feelings of powerlessness, disillusionment, and an erosion of well-being among workers.[7]

A good job is one where a worker is seen and valued. Gail Evans was a janitor in Kodak Eastman in the 1980s. A poor black woman in Rochester, she dreamt of giving her mother a better life by moving to a better neighbourhood. She put herself through college, studying for a degree in information technology, doing night shifts at the Kodak building and attending classes in the daytime. One night, a manager saw her sitting at a computer in the office and asked what she was doing. Evans told her that she was a janitor but studying to be a software engineer. Impressed, the manager asked her to teach software to her team, giving her the break that would eventually bring Evans to C-Suite corner offices in Microsoft, HP and Bank of America.[8] Although Evans may be an uncommon story, it was possible because she had an opportunity to be part of a broader community in Kodak and meet managers face to face.

Not only workers but consumers too are isolated from each other and the seller because an app-based lifestyle does not require human interaction. Anything and everything imaginable can be delivered to one's doorstep, which encourages people to remain sedentary and cocooned. There is no need, and indeed no requirement for small talk with the delivery person who anyway has no time. Research now establishes that isolation is one of the chief contributors to depression, especially in older people. On the contrary, casual conversations with people in the neighbourhood engender a sense of social participation and contribute to mental well-being. As platforms assume centre stage in our lives, it would be prudent to consider how the lack of human contact inherent to the model can be compensated for.

COURAGE

Workers' Awakening

The Finnish platform Wolt, which provides food and retail delivery services in over twenty countries, released a report called 'Algorithmic Transparency Report' in 2022 to address criticisms of non-transparency, a first of its kind in the industry.[1] One of its assurances is that the platform does not use any ranking or rating to determine which courier partner is offered a delivery task, except proximity and the type of vehicle the partner is using.

Platform Labor is a research project funded by the European Research Council that aims to determine how digital platforms are transforming the organization of labour, especially in cities marked by eroding welfare systems. Niels van Doorn, the principal investigator of the project who also teaches at the University of Amsterdam, has many more questions he thinks Wolt needs to answer. At the 2022 'Reshaping Work' conference in Amsterdam, he demanded to know why Wolt has decided to opt for a dynamic pricing system. How much is the base fee per delivery in each market, and how many cents per kilometre do partners get as part of the 'distance fee' in different markets? How often are fee calculations updated, and what new data inputs or metrics are they based on? How come distance is calculated as the crow flies, but the actual distance varies due to city conditions? Why aren't they paid for time spent in the restaurant waiting or for the kilometres travelled to the restaurant, why only to the customer's house?[2]

There aren't many answers to this barrage of questions, which workers in India are just beginning to ask. But there is hope that a few leaders have emerged among gig workers who are mobilizing them and knocking on the doors of the government and the public at large, urging them to hear their side of the digital commerce story.

Leading from the front

Amberpet is one of the oldest suburbs of Hyderabad, adjacent to Osmania University. The locality gets its name from the Sufi saint Hazrat Amber Shah Baba, whose dargah is located there. A local belief is that this was a barren land that miraculously transformed into verdant fruit-growing fields after the saint made this place his final resting place. Today, Amberpet is a dusty, grey area, with metro construction adding to the pollution and a general air of neglect characteristic of the inner localities of Indian cities. I have driven down fifty kilometres to Amberpet to meet Shaikh Salauddin, the National General Secretary of the Indian Association of App-based Transport Workers and founder President of the Telangana Gig and Platform Workers Union.

In the recent past in India, leaders among the gig workers have been herding them together, highlighting their issues to policymakers and pushing for reforms. Salauddin is the tallest among such leaders, who noticed long before anyone else that something was not quite right with a model where the worker was flattened between the customer and the firm.

This was my second meeting with Salauddin. The previous year, Kamala Marius, a geography professor from the University of Bordeaux and I had chatted with him over lunch at the Taj Deccan for a study on gender differences in ride-hailing usage in Hyderabad. She had heard that he was the go-to man for anything to do with the gig economy.

Salauddin is a soft-spoken man who, with his pleasant demeanour, appears like a bank officer rather than an influential union leader. But since our previous meeting, Salauddin's stature has grown manifold. Suddenly, he seemed to be everywhere—on the front flap of the *Times of India* and virtually any article on the gig economy in India. He was being given lavish monikers like 'the most powerful Uber driver in India'.

Despite that, his office is a sparsely furnished room above a mutton shop. A banner announcing a scholarship scheme for children of drivers working for ride-sharing companies is the lone decoration on the walls. He tells me that life has indeed been busy. Some time ago, he was flown into IIT Mumbai by a professor who was researching this topic. A business school was making a documentary on gig workers and wanted to feature him. He had just met with Ashok Gehlot, Chief Minister of Rajasthan, who had a battery of officials to sit in the room and hear Salauddin, although it was 10 p.m. This meeting was an offshoot of an encounter with Rahul Gandhi, where Salauddin had rushed to the suburb of Sanga Reddy on a tip-off that there was a possibility to speak to Gandhi there.

Salauddin's angst is that too many workers' lives are hinging on a few platforms pulling the wool over everyone's eyes, including the government's. 'I am telling the government don't make us so dependent on private players like Ola/Uber/Rapido. What if they wrap up and go? 1,25,000 drivers will be on the streets. So, the government should have its own taxis with digital meters under the Smart City mission. There should be some backup for drivers. At least fifty people are doing PhDs on the gig economy. Every day, I spend one or two hours with someone from XLRI, IIT or some foreign university. Where is all this knowledge going—of PhDs in the transport sector? Why are they not able to innovate and bring something new? For so many years, there has been only Ola's Bhavish Agarwal and Uber!

'Government should cap how many cars and two wheelers can ply. If there isn't enough work, why put up ads to call drivers and leave them sitting in their cars? Ola, Swiggy and Zomato are all eyeing IPOs. For an IPO, the company must show how many workers are employed and how much business is generated. There isn't as much business as they project. *Daant hathi ke dikhane ke alag, chabane ke alag* (an elephant has different sets of teeth for chewing and for display—this adage seeks to highlight the gulf between perception and reality).'

I ask him what these workers would have done had they not been part of the gig economy.

'They would have been farmers or plied the trade that they know—like carpentry. They were getting more money and working *apne marzi mafiq* (according to their convenience)! If you want to earn well in this gig, you can't work when you please; you must be on the grind. These guys can't leave because they are used to city life. They go back only when there is a crisis here. Like in the lockdown, they returned to the village, worked on their field, fixed their houses and returned when things became okay.'

Ashish Arora, who is twenty-eight, was part of the team that pushed for the Rajasthan Gig Workers Act passed in July 2023—helped by Magsaysay Award winner Aruna Roy and activists such as Nikhil Dey and Babu Mathew, the team powered through the landmark act. The act mandates the registration of all gig and platform workers, access to social security schemes, proper mechanisms for grievance redressal and participation in discussions that affect their welfare.

Ashish has been a driver/rider on all the existing platforms. In spite of several personal setbacks, he kept going. He is a grassroots leader who commands respect even from older workers. He cuts through meanderings and rants and focuses on what is relevant in WhatsApp group discussions and in-person meetings.

He speaks to me about the macro picture of inequality between the management and workers. He has created a spreadsheet on his laptop from where he rattles off the numbers.

'See, the website Crunchbase has all these details of tech startups. Uber has raised about 30 billion dollars, Ola—5 billion. Swiggy—3.6 billion dollars, Zomato—4.4 billion. The total of just these four is 43 billion USD. That's how much money they have been funded with. They must have kept 20–30 per cent of this in cash, but they've burnt a chunk of it in trying to capture the market by initially subsidizing rides, paying crazy amounts to drivers initially, etc.'

The other workers gather in the small office room are quiet at the mention of these numbers whose zeros they can't begin to fathom.

'They thought India was their big market after China,' Ashish continues. 'So they wanted to show these numbers to raise their valuations. The truth is that this is an overestimation. The market is not as big as they made it out to be. But they kept hiring drivers and riders through referral programmes. I know someone who made 62 lakh just through referrals! Imagine that the business is only Rs100, but first five, then eight, then ten people are hired for it, and they find that their earnings are decreasing. At the same time, the company chucks out those who complain too much, post on social media, have low ratings . . . So eight out of ten anyway leave. But a fresh set will come through referrals. It's all *dikhane ke liye* (just an eyewash) to show the government that so many people have been employed by them.

'All these companies were selling things cheap to customers and paying workers crazy amounts. Customers got used to that; workers got used to that. But that was an unreal situation they created. Workers became frustrated when goods and wages came to their real value because no one likes incomes to go down after going up. So, what have they ultimately done? Spoilt the market, the economy, the trade and the workers in that trade.'

'Our leader here is doing so much work. When the board gets constituted according to the Act, he should be in it,' pipes in a follower seated next to us.

Ashish brushes these entreaties aside and says, 'Being on the board is constraining. One can do more outside. Anyway, there's not even a salary, and I have huge financial constraints. We are doing all this so that something improves in the future.'

Sangam Tripathy is a bespectacled man of average build in his early sixties, who could be mistaken for an innocuous, retired uncle next door if you bumped into him in the elevator. But after hearing the passion with which he speaks to an audience, one can see that he was a trade union activist for forty years.

After working for years in the International Transport Workers Federation (ITWF), Tripathy was aware that

New York, followed by many other American cities, had witnessed ride-hailing disrupting the metered taxi service by luring drivers with the prospect of freedom and higher earnings. Aware that the bubble would likely burst soon enough, Tripathy and some friends tried to organize the drivers, cautioning them to tread carefully and not rake up unmanageable debt in auto loans. However, it was hard to identify who the Ola /Uber drivers were since they did not wear badges or khaki uniforms, unlike the *kali-peeli* (black and yellow) taxi drivers.

An opportunity presented itself in the middle of 2016 when he heard that some drivers were protesting at the eighteenth-century observatory in central Delhi, Jantar Mantar, which is the city's favourite rallying point. Slowly, Tripathy and a few compatriots started gathering the drivers and encouraging them to join unions, which had more legal representation than associations. These efforts helped create the Indian Federation of App-Based Transport Workers (IFAT), representing over 35,000 app-based drivers and riders in ten cities. 'But 35,000 out of how many millions? The strength is in numbers. More workers need to join unions. The question is how to mobilize them, because they are never together in one place.'

Using tech to beat tech

The most fascinating form of mobilization is the way workers are using technology to beat technology. Social media, particularly WhatsApp, is being deployed to potent effect to rage against platforms, react to perceived injustices, galvanize peer groups and rant at the system. I was included in the WhatsApp group of one section of north India's workers. It gave me a voyeur's view of the agency technology gave workers, enabling them to group themselves and break out of the isolation inherent to their jobs.

'Private cars are becoming Uber cabs, which is eating into our incomes,' says a cautionary forward. Cabs in India require a commercial license as per the law, and private cars plying as cabs are sneaky competitors to gig workers who are as it is grappling with reduced incomes. 'We are paying taxes for running commercial vehicles, and others are turning their private cars into cabs, escaping the tax, obviously with the platform's consent! We must protest such cheap tactics by Uber to grow its business.'

'Let us spread the information about unfair and unilateral blocking of IDs. The government, company and media must take this challenge head on to come up with a solution for this,' writes a worker after sharing the circumstances in which his ID was blocked. A while later, a Google form is shared where workers have to write why their ID was blocked, '. . . so that the decision-makers in the government know what we are dealing with.'

Someone posts a series of communally divisive messages. The administrator later deletes them, urging the workers to stick to topics relating to gig work. Another worker comments that this is the company's way of planting a few people to 'divide and rule' like the British Raj did and urges his comrades to stay strong and alert about such tactics.

Kutumb is a private social network for communities that is built for Indians to share their views in their own language and connect with their community. Among the numerous worker communities using the app, such as farmers, and poultry farmers, are gig workers. Leaders repeatedly urge workers to download the app to bolster their numbers to 'claim our social and economic rights'.

It is days before the Lok Sabha election in India as I write this part of the book, and the news is thick with politicians courting various cohorts and adopting causes fervently to build the vote bank. A video of women gig workers standing on a dais and narrating their worries to a prominent national leader is widely circulated. Facebook pages of Foodpanda Bangladesh and Pathao Bangladesh each have more than 50,000 members.

The way workers are using technology to rally against the tech platforms is similar to a Cherokee story about a native Indian called Sequoyah and his creation of a Cherokee syllabary. Sequoyah was a Cherokee silversmith, trader and man of many talents who lived in the early nineteenth century. In 1813–14, while serving as a warrior of the Cherokee Regiment against a renegade group, Sequoyah witnessed the advantage the white colonists enjoyed because they had an established written language. Unlike the white soldiers, he and his fellow Cherokee warriors could not write letters home, read their military orders or record any thoughts that occurred to them while serving on the waterfront. They had to rely solely on memory in the absence of a script. Sequoyah was determined to create some form of written language for the Cherokees. Despite being illiterate in English, he dedicated years to developing a writing system for the Cherokee language inspired by English, Greek and Hebrew letters. The Cherokees thus adapted and repurposed writing technology to serve their own cultural and linguistic preservation, thereby ensuring the survival of their heritage for future generations.

Sometimes, it is possible to use the very tool that is being used by an authority in power to stand your ground and not get crushed.

Power of protests

The Amazon virtual tour video on YouTube projects a cheery, sunny quality to the warehouse, full of laughing employees pushing trolleys and 'adorable robots' waddling around the floor like the droids from Star Wars. The corporate's UK website has a blog of a warehouse in the south-west UK, with ping-pong tables in the cafeteria and rows of chairs in every hue.

Contrary to the convivial atmosphere of warehouse workers in Amazon's self-promotion videos, European and US workers of Amazon strongly support 'Make Amazon Pay', a movement that is on a mission to rein in the global online retailer. In 2023, the campaign held strikes and protests simultaneously in more than thirty countries from Black Friday—the day after the US Thanksgiving holiday, until Monday. While Amazon workers struck work in Germany, France and Spain,[3] in South Asia on the same day protests were held in cities as diverse as Rishikesh, Agra, Kolhapur and Varanasi in India, along with Dhaka and Colombo.

Apart from Black Friday, Amazon's highest sales occur on Prime Day, a forty-eight-hour window when Amazon Prime customers get exclusive deals on merchandise. While customers are lapping up irresistible deals, thousands of workers are protesting in different corners of the world. In 2018, for instance, workers in Spain and Germany walked off the job, while warehouse employees in Poland participated in a 'work-to-rule' action (i.e. strictly following official rules and hours even if it reduces efficiency).[4]

In July 2024, US Senator Bernie Sanders released a report condemning 'outrageous injury levels' at Amazon during the Prime Day week in 2019, which cited internal Amazon data to show that total injury rate surged to nearly 45 per 100 workers, more than double the industry average.[5]

In all countries, common themes of malcontent workers have been a denial of leave, short breaks, ten-hour workdays, being summarily dismissed, poor conditions in the warehouse, intense performance pressure, the risk of injury and too much control and surveillance.

Manju Goel was at the vanguard of these protests in Delhi. I had read her name in a few newspaper articles about angry Amazon workers. Manju, forty-five, is a single mother of three adult children who all work and stay with her. She had worked in the same warehouse for a year managing 'customer returns'. Growing increasingly frustrated with the harsh conditions in the warehouse,[6] she began to secretly mobilize coworkers from her own and other warehouses in the region.

> We held secret meetings in different places. Then I quit because it was not viable to rebel and work there. So, with the help of an NGO, I helped put together a workers' association. Gradually, more people joined in, and now we have close to 100 workers. Our demands are increased pay from Rs10,000 to 25,000, revised targets that are more reasonable, eight hours of work and overtime if we work for more than that and finally not being continuously monitored by a CCTV camera. To that end, we have held protests in Jantar Mantar.

She shows me photographs of her wearing a mask of Jeff Bezos with red horns.

'We wanted to draw his attention to what is happening to Amazon workers in India,' she says.

I ask her if the protests were effective.

'They will be. Many newspapers covered it. Isn't that how you reached me?'

Marching to the Beat of a Different Drummer

A ring of purple mountains encircles the sprawling campus of Tribhuvan University, Kathmandu. I am there to meet Resham Thapa, an economics professor. Dr Thapa, a small-built man with twinkling brown eyes, arrives on a scooter. 'Do you want good coffee or a great view?' he asks. I opt for the latter, and he asks me to sit pillion. We are off to a restaurant called Kirtipur Hillside, named after one of the four districts into which Kathmandu Valley is divided. It is a small hotel with a rooftop restaurant and a stunning panoramic view of the valley bordered by the Himalayas. In the next two hours, Dr Thapa discusses Nepal's development over warm lemon tea with honey, pakodas and peanut *sedheko* (masala peanuts, though *sedheko* is Nepali for barbeque).

'The gig economy is great for livelihoods. But when you take a macro view, you cannot ignore the fact that it makes it so much easier for money to move across borders,' Dr Thapa remarks. He refers to a scam that shook Nepal around 2018. Rubel Chowdhury, a Bangladeshi national and son-in-law of the powerful Koirala family allegedly ran an international telephone call racket that bypassed government regulatory authorities and caused the state a loss of millions in revenue.[7]

'At that time, technology was much less developed, and even then, we could not keep pace; now, technology is so much more advanced, so much of global capital flows happen, and we don't know who is minting money at our expense.

Thapa is sceptical of the more significant goings-on when huge global capital of invisible investors props up a seemingly homegrown startup aimed at growing the local economy.

Far away from mountainous Nepal, Pradeep Peiris in Colombo feels similarly. Peiris is a professor of political science at Colombo University and author of various books on electoral politics, gender, liberal economy and the democratic discourse in Sri Lanka. He is unimpressed by what apps like PickMe and Uber have offered to his country.

> There may be some surface-level victories like jobs and speed. However, the gig economy is not an innovation because it doesn't carry along everyone in society. Uber will not function in a deep rural area where you need to take a patient to a faraway hospital. So, it doesn't serve society. It only serves the rich who can afford it. For example, in a casino, there are winners and losers at the end of the day, but the owner is the happiest person. Every time you order on an app, the app's owner gets richer. A certain class dominates global networks, accumulating unbelievable amounts that would not have been humanly possible but for the economic system under which technology operates.

Peiris shares that he gets a message every month that $15 has been taken from his account because his teen son subscribed to a music channel. 'Each time I think of how this money is going to someone unknown to us, with no affinity to this country, state or society.'

In the eighteenth century, The British East India company wanted direct control over the weavers who manufactured the silk and cotton that were in great demand worldwide. To this end, the company appointed *gomasthas* who would make the weavers enter into a contract and fix the price of the cloth. The new gomasthas were outsiders, with no long-term social link with the village. They acted arrogantly, marched into villages with sepoys and punished weavers for delays in supplying materials. The weavers lost the liberty they had to bargain for prices and sell to different buyers.

Some sellers view tech platforms with the contempt that the weavers held for gomasthas back then, refusing a model that dictates whom they should sell to and at what price. Challenging the deep pockets of Goliaths of digital commerce and creating a locally funded David is a brave act that a few are pulling off. An example is Namma Yatri, a ride-hailing app that originated in Bangalore. It prides itself on being a direct-to-driver app where the entire payment the customer pays goes 100 per cent to the driver, and no intermediary takes a commission. The whole technology is open source and built on an open mobility platform by a few tech companies in collaboration with Bengaluru's drivers. Having completed over 90 million rides,[8] the driver community in other cities has also welcomed the app and flocked to enlist in it.

Homefoodi is an Indian app-based food delivery service that creates self-employment opportunities for women and a way for customers to avoid the adverse health effects of regularly eating restaurant food. It delivers fresh, homemade meals prepared by local home chefs, almost all of them women, to customers' doorsteps in various cities, offering a range of Indian cuisines and dietary options.

Nepal has numerous homegrown apps for ride-hailing and food and grocery delivery. In ride-hailing alone, about thirty-five apps have emerged in seven years since the concept was introduced to the country by Tootle, an app started by a few Kathmandu boys. Homegrown apps understand local peculiarities. For example, an app called Sajilo Sathi in Nepal gets the fact that the driver will typically suggest going offline to the passenger, which is risky in case of accidents because there is no record of the ride on the app. Sometimes, the passenger could be standing on the road and not have the internet on his phone to book a ride. So, the app has a provision where the rider can note the passenger's name, number and destination and then proceed on the offline ride! Essentially, the app tells the passenger, it's okay if you're not booking the ride through me, but I'll still look out for you. If some mishap happens, at least there is some record of who was going where. I found this story so typical of this part of the globe—accepting that people's behaviours will not be perfect and coming up with an 'adjustment' to make all parties involved in the transaction happy.

Bangladeshi entrepreneur Syed Saif's wife once took a cab ride through an app in Dhaka, and the driver began harassing her through text messages. The incident hit home to Syed as to how challenging mobility was for women in Dhaka, with its dense traffic, poor public transport, conservative social norms and pervasive risk of sexual harassment. He began a bike taxi service called Lily Rides, where the passenger and driver would only be women. He employed girls from lower-income households and trained them to ride motorbikes. The girls were heckled when they practised riding their bikes on the streets, but they stood by his dream. Lily Rides has been featured as a case study in a World Bank report on women-oriented transport. Eventually, Lily Rides shut down during the pandemic as demand dwindled because of travel restrictions. But the girls were deployed to another bespoke service that Syed began soon after.

This app is called Lily Tailors and caters to a need that any South Asian woman will instantly recognize with all her heart—getting the right fit for a kurta or blouse. Ladies' tailors are invariably male. Dhaka's conservative norms make it difficult for a woman to interact with them iteratively, which is often required for a garment to be stitched well. That's where Lily Tailors comes in. A customer chooses the fabric and the design she wants on the app and books a visit. A Lily girl comes home to take measurements and delivers the order to one of a panel of tailors. When the dress is ready, she drops it back to the customer. If something is not all right, the process is repeated until the customer is happy. Lily is evidence of how local apps 'get' their customers and manage to fulfil a real need so that all participants win.

Does Everything Need an App?

Apps may have overtaken the lives of most of the urban middle class. However, small movements and certain groups of people see value in the pre-app lifestyle—slower, calmer, earth-friendly and more connected to the community. Pradeep Peiris is unmoved when I tell him about quick commerce in India, where products arrive before we blink.

'Why is quickness a virtue?' he demands to know. 'Neoliberalism has imparted false values masquerading as virtues. Why do you need to get your groceries in ten minutes? What do we achieve in our lives by rushing about so fast?'

Peiris is not alone. An entire movement called 'Slow Food' developed in 1986 in Rome to protest the appearance of fast-food restaurants and is today a global network of activists protecting local food and traditional cooking. While many supermarkets have done away with personal checkout lanes in favour of automated or self-service checkout, Jumbo, a low-profile supermarket chain in the Netherlands, went the opposite way, bringing back the quaint charm of mom-and-pop stores. It introduced 'chat checkouts'—checkout lanes designed so that customers can chat unhurriedly between themselves and with cashiers. Jumbo discovered that many customers, primarily older people, used these fleeting moments at checkout to connect with another human. It was part of Jumbo's support for the Dutch government's campaign launched in 2019 to fight loneliness.

Does everything need an app? How much technology is enough technology? Some customers and sellers wonder if they got briefly carried away by the glamour of it all. It now seems the non-app version was not so bad after all.

For instance, there is an astonishing amount of discontent among customers in India about ride-hailing apps, as evidenced by surveys, newspaper articles and individual conversations. Booking a cab through an app and getting a new driver each time to reach your house involves giving precise instructions on where to turn and which landmark to look out for. Drivers in the US can locate a house effortlessly because the GPS works perfectly when the roads are in a grid system, and every cookie-cutter house has a neat number on it. Our cities have streets with no names, narrow lanes that don't even appear on a map or a newly constructed building in a suburb with a dirt track as an access road. The driver is bound to rely solely on the GPS because the omnipresent platform notes all deviations from the route. Digital savviness is not uniform among drivers. In Nepal, customers complain that some Pathao drivers cannot understand the GPS instructions correctly. Drivers, disgruntled with the company, engage in counterproductive behaviour with customers, insisting on cash payment and cancelling rides. Cars are dirty and smelly because some drivers sleep in them since they work long hours trying to do as many rides as they can.

Parminder Singh, a corporate honcho from Singapore and enthusiastic poster on X, shared a picture of a ride-hailing cab he took from Delhi airport. The driver's shirt was hanging from behind his seat, and food crumbs were lying on the floor. The post, which I have edited a bit, read: Is this a premier ride? I use this ride-hailing app each time I visit, as I do in many other countries. Each time, the cars are dirtier and more poorly maintained. The deterioration is the steepest in India compared to other countries. I won't blame the cab drivers. People simply respond to the prevailing incentives and quality control standards . . . It's a systemic issue. We need to learn that great companies balance expansion with excellence.'[9]

Meanwhile, local taxi services have upped their game while retaining their old advantages. The cars have been spruced up, for one. In any case, the service is personalized as the small team of drivers know the customers and their usual haunts. The local driver is knowledgeable about shortcuts and is free to follow alternate routes. If you leave something behind by mistake, it can be returned quickly as everyone is close by—the taxi owner, driver and customer. A call or WhatsApp message works just as well as an app.

Leo Fernando began a centralized taxi service in Colombo in 2010–11, five years before Uber and PickMe launched. A week before Christmas 2023, he narrates his entrepreneurial journey in a cafe in Colombo where the carols were a tad too loud, but the coffee aromatic.

He had lived in Singapore for a few years, and on comparing taxi rates there and in his home country, he felt Sri Lankans were severely underserved by their taxi system despite paying nearly the same rates as Singaporeans. So, he explored the market, felt that if he centralized the operations, paid the drivers more and offered a quality ride to customers, he could bring something new to the city's limited transport options. He ploughed his personal savings into creating TLC (Taxi Lanka Caller), setting up a centralized call centre, hiring staff and investing in a Swedish technology that matched demand and supply through a smartphone and tablet given to each driver. Then, an American investor he was banking on pulled out leaving him to steer the ship alone.

'Foreign investors often prioritize companies with proprietary technology, which the company has built in-house rather than back businesses that focus on solving local operational problems with outsourced technology, like I was doing with the Swedish software,' says Fernando.

The drivers were gig workers, with no loyalty to him and no alignment with his mission. Soon, Leo was overwhelmed with operational setbacks as drivers would often abandon the job and either steal or misuse the tablets provided to them for work. Fernando was fighting too many operational and financial battles. After several months, it became evident that the business model was unsustainable and he shut it down.

Now he runs a tourism business with about ten drivers who are employed with his company and take tourists on bespoke trips to see dolphins in Galle or architect Geoffery Bawa's house. 'Since the driver owns the car he has an incentive to look after the vehicle and the customer gets quality service. As cool as it sounds, in a gig arrangement, no one takes responsibility. On a peak day, the driver can call you and ask where you are going. If he doesn't like the answer, he can cancel the trip and leave the customer hanging.'

'Yes, that happens often, at least in India,' I respond.

'Whereas if you have a reliable company, that won't happen. There's more control. Someone is there to take responsibility. Everyone is aligned to the same mission.'

Not just travel but in various domains, small sellers are flourishing using familiar, homely technology such as WhatsApp to connect with customers. No commissions are paid to any intermediary, and no controlling algorithm tells them how much to price their products, where to go and whom to sell to. The message system can aggregate demand and supply, enabling the exchange to happen more amicably than a startup unicorn's app does.

'What is the incremental value of an app?' asks Rama Bijapurkar. She shows me a WhatsApp food group on her phone called SoBo (South Bombay) buzzing with activity. 'You can get a cook for any cuisine to come in and do party cooking. There is a Parsi cook offering to make dhansak. There's a vegan, gluten-free . . . Bengali cook who sends a menu to the group every Friday and asks, what would you like? In another group, there are so many chefs that there's a rule that you can't post within five minutes of the other guy having posted. All this is part of your daily economy.' Bijapurkar believes that small suppliers offering intimacy and bespoke experiences through innovation and small consumers yoked together with small digital transactions are cracking the price, performance and profit model.

Vishaka Rautela is an example of how small sellers are winning on their terms. Vishaka, who has won awards for being among the best home bakers in Hyderabad, crafts exquisite and intricately designed cakes in her kitchen without assistance. Since almost all her clientele are co-residents in her apartment complex, she does not need to list on any delivery app. Whether it's focaccia bread or croissants that she plans to make, she posts a message in the Home Chefs WhatsApp group of the building society. The model nets her about Rs 40,000 to 50,000 a month, and she works on her own time with no compulsion to adhere to any schedule.

Some restaurants are wary of food delivery apps making them lose direct touch with customers. Prahalad Sukhtankar, the owner of the popular eatery Black Sheep Bistro in Panjim, Goa, explained why he keeps online delivery marginal to his enterprise.

> Our product is not a dish; our product is the experience of coming to the restaurant. If you go to Black Sheep Bistro, you're going to a place with a certain ambience, music playing, and a certain vibe. It reminds you of some experience, maybe a memory of going to a European bistro. That emotional connection with the brand, flavourful food, good service, and friendly staff make our product. Now, if I take away all of the elements, pack the food in an aluminium container and send it to you, then you're going to think, why is this place even famous?

'I don't have any control over how the food is being consumed at their home,' he continues. 'Sometimes a customer tells me I ordered your cheesecake through an app a few days ago, and it was a little sour. I cannot even argue with that customer. I'm like, okay, whatever. Because I don't know how she consumed it; maybe she left it out for a long time. But in the restaurant, I go around checking my tables and ask, how was everything? If they say it was not so great, it allows me to apologize sincerely and do something about it right there. Such people become the restaurant's most prominent ambassadors. They tell everybody, "Oh my God, this restaurant is so good." "The owner came, and he apologized." "The manager came and did this for me." With Zomato-Swiggy, I can't own my customers. You don't even know who that guy is or who's eating your food. You've never seen him, and he may never come to your restaurant and see what you are offering.'

Sukhtankar concentrates on his dine-in clients, and his restaurant is on food apps only because the brand must be seen when customers search for it; otherwise, it may seem like it doesn't exist. But not more than 5–6 per cent of his business comes from there, and even that, he says, doesn't make him any money because of all the costs associated with delivery.

In another instance, while walking towards Dona Paula beach one evening, I come upon Jaya's Kitchen, a snacks and chai eatery. I sip their special ginger tea and look at the snacks menu.

'Do you deliver?' I ask Prasad, the owner who used to be a civil engineer but opened this eatery a couple of years ago.

'Yes, we do, Madam . . . but I would request you to please eat here,' Prasad implores me.

He explains that though his reach had increased and about 20 per cent of his sales were through online platforms, he was unhappily sending things in plastic dabbas, which turn cold when the customer eats them. His Nepali helper joins the conversation and relates how the delivery boy had arrived late the previous day because it had been pouring. The onion *bhajias* and *sev puri* a lady had asked for were lifeless and limp when they were finally picked up.

'All this online delivery is a waste. People have just become lazy! Customers should eat fresh food at the restaurant. We have a set of loyal customers who will only eat here. Only the doctors in Manipal Hospital nearby and software engineers who want to work while they eat order our stuff online. I always encourage people to sit here and eat as much as possible. It is cheaper by 30–40 per cent and tastier,' says Prasad animatedly.

This chapter was titled 'Courage' to foreground the stories of those trying to alleviate the oppression, anger and anxieties of delivery workers outlined in previous chapters in the book. Because of the efforts of gig worker associations, civil society and activists, governments in South Asian countries are also slowly coming around to recognize the need for legal protection of gig workers. In India, the Code on Social Security 2020 now includes gig and platform workers. In June 2024, the National Human Rights Commission of India took cognizance of the violation of human rights at Amazon's Manesar warehouse. In Pakistan, proposed legislation called the Islamabad Capital Territory Platform Workers Protection Bill aims to balance platform interests and worker rights.

Platforms, on their part, have been nudged towards fairer work conditions, contracts and pay by 'platform watchdogs' such as Fairwork, which produces annual, country-specific reports on the subject. For instance, the Fairwork ratings of 2023 for India, reports that Urban Company has made a public commitment to ensure that its workers earn at least the local living wage after factoring in work-related costs and to redesign its rating system to remove unjustifiably low ratings.[10]

Courage is on display by enterprises, communities and people with a contrarian view towards the unquestioning submission to technology. Some sellers are thriving in a low-tech way, using simple messaging tools like WhatsApp, retaining the freedom to make their product–price mix. A few entrepreneurs are untouched by the hype and continue to conduct their business as if the app era never happened. Their brave decisions to swim against the current or adapt in unique ways to the digital wave compel us to pause and ask essential questions about our own choices.

LIGHTS, CAMERA, ACTION: REGULATING THE DIGITAL STAGE

In the book *The Sharing Economy: The End of Employment and the Rise of Crowd-Based Capitalism*,[1] Arun Sundararajan, a professor at New York's Stern School of Business, points out an important but easily overlooked fact. Today's digital technologies appear new and yet evoke the familiarity of self-employment and forms of community-based exchange that existed in the past. For example, ride-hailing seems like the old black and yellow cab, but just that, we are using the phone to hail one. Food delivery seems like we replaced calling up a restaurant and placing an order by choosing it on an app. This feature of the platform, of being an improved form of something familiar rather than an entirely new experience, has helped in its widespread adoption. However, Sundararajan points out that it has also lulled governments that these apps are merely the same old wine in shiny new bottles. They have often overlooked the fact that several aspects of the new digital economy defy conventional understanding and need a fresh look at existing regulations. In this chapter, some of those aspects are discussed.

I. Protecting the Small

Delivery workers

While watching *Zwigato*, I expected the film to take a dark or tragic turn in the end. Instead, in the last scene, Manas and his wife sped along on their two-wheeler, laughing in abandon as they raced against a train like they once did in their carefree youth.

In a Zoom conversation with me, the film's writer–director, Nandita Das, shares that she wanted the ending to be hopeful yet rooted in reality, where their struggles remain relentless. And the viewer gets this duality. 'It's not about one dramatic incident,' she says. 'But small acts of indignation, the chipping away of human dignity, the constant living in fear . . . these are more important to me to explore. I feel that to create empathy, we have to first understand the people and the fears they live with. It is about psychological insecurities that don't necessarily have to manifest all the time, but they are still very real emotions of fear and anxiety.'

Arjuna Parakrama taught political science at the eminent University of Peradeniya, Sri Lanka. Despite a bout of asthma, he agreed to come to Java Lounge, Rawatte Road in Colombo, for a chat. A tall, heavyset man with a cane and a grey ponytail appears and, within five minutes of arrival, starts to tell me how he finds the gig economy problematic. I scramble to switch on my recorder, and as the Americano goes cold, I listen to him speak about Sri Lanka and the incongruity of models like PickMe and Uber in the context of a depressed economy.

'These business models are very first world in their conceptualizations. Gig, particularly, is very American. It talks about workers' flexibility, informality and independence,' he remarks dismissively. 'These notions become a way of whitewashing the absence of labour rights and any security and, in fact, the breaking of the law. Sri Lanka has reasonably decent labour laws that ensure pension, gratuity and severance pay. But the gig economy denies workers these safety nets and doesn't give them any access to the labour rights that exist for their protection. Despite Sri Lanka's economy's rocky road in the past few years, people have survived because of strong institutional mechanisms set up earlier.'

As tech-mediated work is only expected to grow with the growth of e-commerce, the motivations, frustrations and expectations of those participating in it at the bottom end of the pyramid need to be taken cognizance of. The regulatory framework in all countries must respond to delivery and warehouse workers' demands pertaining to minimum wages, need for social security, overtime for work done beyond hours stipulated by law and abrupt terminations resulting in loss of livelihoods. Payments to workers must be commensurate with a rise in fuel prices, and the terms transparent.

Things are improving, but not across the board and not fast enough. Fairwork India's 2023 report showed that all predominant platforms operating in India provided safety training and adequate safety equipment to delivery workers; Swiggy institutionalized external audits to check for biases in work allocation systems, while BigBasket, Swiggy, Urban Company, Zepto and Zomato agreed to pay for accident and general health insurance.

Balaji Parthasarathy has been the principal investigator for Fairwork's study ever since it began reporting on Indian platforms in 2019, apart from his regular job as a professor at International Institute of Information Technology (IIIT) Bengaluru. I ask him if the many improvements reported in the study means that someday soon, we may not need a platform watchdog like Fairwork. Parthasarathy is cautious in his response.

'There have definitely been changes in the conditions of gig work on certain digital platforms since Fairwork started studying them in 2019. But Fairwork's thresholds only set a floor and meeting them alone is not enough. Consider, for instance, minimum wage. There is evidence that although more workers are earning the minimum wage after accounting for work-related costs, they are able to do so only after working for long hours which go well beyond the duration of a standard work week. Far fewer earn a living wage which is considered essential for a decent and dignified life. Indeed, we have a long way go to.'

Watchdogs from academia or civil society will be critical as long as workers do not have a voice in determining their work conditions. 'The right to a voice must also be institutionalized in a body that brings together workers, the government and platforms, to jointly shape economic and social policies for platform work,' Parthasarathy opined.

The right to bargain collectively is a fundamental right of workers as recognized by the International Labour Organization (ILO), even for workers classified as 'self-employed'. Bargaining can result in substantial wins for workers. For example, an agreement signed between the food delivery app JustEat and labour unions in Spain in December 2021 rules that a platform must make the parameters on which the algorithms and artificial intelligence systems are based transparent and include a measure of human supervision.

The solutions to most of these issues are not unknown to regulators. Numerous models exist where provisions have been made for informal workers to have a degree of financial security, which can be replicated—for example, the Mathadi boards of Maharashtra. *Mathadi* is a Marathi term for a person carrying a load of material on his head (*matha*) or on his back to stack at a designated place. They are covered by the Mathadi Hamal and Other Manual Workers (Regulation of Employment and Welfare) Act, 1969. The boards constituted under it have helped immensely in their struggle to regulate employment terms, welfare facilities and health and safety measures for unprotected manual workers.

Some platforms have blended the old economy style of managing workers while being a tech-centric company. I spent a few hours at Daraz Kathmandu's main warehouse where the HR head explained how their 'delivery heroes' are paid and how grievances are handled. Daraaz Nepal pays workers a fixed salary apart from allowances for fuel and vehicle maintenance and work-related mobile phone bills, greatly reducing the variability in workers' monthly earnings. Once they are recruited, they undergo a three-day, in-person training where executives teach them how to use the app, send alerts, identify locations, interact with customers and deal with different possible scenarios such as cash on delivery or absence of a customer. Then, on the fourth day, a newbie is attached to a 'buddy' and trails him on the job to learn the ropes. Once a week, workers meet the HR executives to discuss their grievances. This helps take the edge off the sense of abandonment and isolation that gig workers often feel.

Weathering the heat

Sweltering days are becoming more common in South Asia due to climate change compounding the occupational hazards of gig work. With large swathes of India under the grip of heatwaves, food delivery companies have set up rest points and recharge zones. Swiggy established 900 'recharge zones' where food delivery workers can rest, use the washrooms and find water. Zomato made 450 'rest points', which any gig worker can use, irrespective of which company they work for. These shelters have comfortable seating, free drinking water, mobile charging points and washrooms. To address any health/medical emergency, a fifteen-minute ambulance and 24×7 SOS support is on standby.

Not everyone has been proactive though. The Centre for Labour Research, a think tank in Rawalpindi, cited the Indian examples in an angry LinkedIn post in June 2024 and urged Foodpanda and other platforms in Pakistan to act immediately, as hundreds have succumbed to the heat in that country.[2]

Southeast Asia's platform economy is ahead of the curve compared to South Asia, which started years earlier. Grab, a 'super app' of the region offering a range of services, started charging an extra fee from customers when local temperatures hit 35 degrees Celsius in countries like Vietnam, apart from its rainy-weather fee. Food delivery companies in South Asia could do the same to serve as a deterrent to customers or compensate workers who deliver at those times. Grab's app also has a 'fatigue nudge', a safety feature to remind drivers to take a break when driving for long hours, based on the app's reading of the driver's online and offline hours, which provides a gauge of fatigue levels.[3]

While all of this is commendable, it does not truly protect workers from being vulnerable in extreme weather conditions. In the summer of 2024, Zomato tweeted an appeal to customers not to order during afternoons[4] and was met with severe flak on social media by customers and delivery agents who were anxious about their earnings reducing, as lunchtime is peak time for orders. However, the question of delivery workers' vulnerability to dangerous heat levels is a public health concern. It cannot be left to the benevolence of those in air-conditioned offices ordering lunch or to the platforms themselves. The state needs to step in and mandate that food and grocery delivery will not happen between noon and 4 p.m. when the temperature crosses 40 degrees Celsius in a city. Delivering lunch is not an essential service like emergency medicines. Customers can plan and work out alternatives. This is where the litmus test comes in for the company as a 'caring' organization: workers need to be suitably compensated for the loss of business on those afternoons. Climate experts suggest a shift in working hours to avoid the hazardous effects of continuous heat exposure on outdoor workers. Climate projections indicate a hotter and drier future for much of the world. The effect of heat stress on labour productivity is a critical economic impact of climate change, and platforms need to factor that into their business models.

E-Commerce Sellers

Is Amazon a marketplace for other sellers or a seller itself? Being both is a clash of conflicting interests that needs regulators like Competition Commission of India to wake up to. Despite the Competition Commission of India's efforts to curb deep discounts through tightened regulations, small-scale sellers claim that Amazon employs intricate business machinations to circumvent these restrictions. In 2020, over 2000 online merchants filed an antitrust lawsuit against Amazon, India. They accused Amazon of procuring goods in bulk from manufacturers and then selling them at a loss to bulk-buying retailers like Cloudtail, who could, in turn, offer discounts that others could never match up to. Cloudtail (co-owned by Infosys co-founder, N.R. Narayana Murthy) has since shut down because of the furore, but vendors allege that the largesse has just been redistributed to a few others.[5]

'At first everyone wants the small seller, the lone driver, the lone restaurant. But eventually when the model consolidates, the big player is whom the company favours. In transportation, it is the fleet owner who has a number of cars on the platform who benefits. At least one of his cars will pop up when a passenger searches while the lone driver has relatively less of a chance. Likewise, it is the big seller who can spend on promotions who will come up tops on a food delivery platform. On an e-commerce site, if there is a Diwali discount, Amazon would rather work with the seller who is able to partner with it and bear part of the discount,' says Janakiraman, an ex-seller of electric appliances on Amazon.

Digital commerce is designed to favour the big and hence small entities need institutions to look out for them.

Restaurants

Even though food delivery apps give small restaurants a platform to get noticed, the chances of it happening are rare. Usually, the clientele of small restaurants' are locals who know of the place and order through the apps for convenience. As, platforms mainly focus on high volume, well-known restaurants, small restaurants almost never appear in top recommendations and get lost in the listings of the dominant names on the apps.

To offer small sellers an alternative platform, the Indian government has established a platform called ONDC, which stands for Open Network for Digital Commerce. A user on ONDC can compare prices, explore options and place orders from different small- and large-scale vendors. ONDC's goal is to level the playing field so that every seller can access the same marketing tools. A seller's products will be available on all platforms linked to the centralized one, i.e. ONDC, considerably broadening their reach. Though ONDC is yet to catch up, it has the potential to create a more equitable market space that allows businesses of all sizes to thrive. As a sought-after speaker and strategy advisor, Capt. Raghu Raman once said, 'We don't need two or three 5000-crore companies, but thousand 2–3 crore companies.'[6]

In August 2024, when I was nearing the end of writing the manuscript for this book, India's union commerce minister, Piyush Goyal was in the news for advocating a more level-playing-field in the e-commerce sector. 'I am not wishing away e-commerce, it's here to stay,' he said.[7] But he expressed concern that there were 100 million small retailers whose livelihoods were endangered because they could not compete with Amazon and Flipkart. The global giants with deep pockets were able to create algorithms to drive consumer preference and use predatory pricing tactics, that could result in a lot of small businesses getting wiped out, the minister observed.

II. Regulation—Caught Napping!

Despite the enthusiasm for modernity in regulating app-based services, the governments of the past decade have behaved like a boomer in a Gen Z party—clueless and out of step.

The regulatory framework for ride-hailing is still in the grey zone a decade after it emerged as a mobility option in India. Ride-hailing companies are termed 'aggregators' under the Motor Vehicles (Amendment) Bill. The Aggregators Act assigns the responsibility to the states to develop policy guidelines, but these have not kept pace with changing modes of mobility options. Different state governments have had flip-flops about whether personal vehicles can be used as taxis. In one state, drivers need a commercial license, but suddenly they don't. In another state, cab sharing is allowed until it isn't.

Seven years after the introduction of ride-hailing on the streets of Nepal, the government finally decided that ride-sharing was a legal activity on the condition that passengers had to be insured against accidents.[8] In 2022, the global ride-sharing app inDrive entered Kathmandu and rapidly became popular because of its bidding and bargaining model (bargaining being the entire region's favourite pastime). But it does not ensure passengers and hence operates in legal limbo while the government twiddles its thumbs.

Like in India, provincial and federal governments take contradictory positions on whether private vehicles can be used for transporting passengers. Traditional taxi operators have taken to the roads in some provinces, protesting that this anomaly makes ride-sharing illegal. Ride-hailing operators criticize the government for not updating itself about tech-based businesses, which constrains operations for such services. Pathao's head of Global Rides, Yeshu Thakali says he would rather have laws than function in a void. 'We want proper laws. We are trying to lobby in the government to get them made. For the first time, Bagmati province (where Kathmandu is situated) brought out a document with the word "ride-sharing" and a table of taxes to be paid. That's a relief that the word appeared in a government document! But beyond that we still don't know where to register, how to pay those taxes they want us to pay . . .' Despite ride-hailing now being a vita l part of the urban transport system for Nepalis, every now and then, a provincial government, confounded by the complexities of this new business, threatens to close the service.

In Mumbai, I visit a cloud kitchen in Andheri East. There, amidst several buildings in the industrial estate, I enter one that looks like a godown transformed into a busy culinary factory. One man is making Chinese food on a wok at military heat, someone else is kneading pizza dough and a young woman at the far end is blending milkshakes. All of them are preparing dishes that customers have ordered through apps. Outside, delivery boys wait impatiently on their bikes. Though the kitchen looks tidy enough, a finicky vegetarian would have been appalled at the absence of a clear divide between vegetarian and non-vegetarian cooking.

In July 2024, R.V. Karnan, the newly appointed food safety commissioner for Telangana, was labelled 'Singham' by the media after the vigilante cop in the Bollywood movie of the same name, for his crackdown on food safety violations in Hyderabad. In seventy-two days, Karnan's task force inspected 129 restaurants, pubs, eateries, warehouses of quick commerce services and cloud kitchens in Hyderabad and slapped ninety show-cause notices mostly on high-end restaurants and pubs. City residents were shocked to see much-loved and iconic brands such as Paradise Biryani, Shah Ghouse, Pista House and Bahubali Kitchen, which they had blindly trusted get exposed for cockroach infestation, expired food items, synthetic colour and more.[9]

Although cloud kitchens are subject to the same legal requirements of food safety standards that restaurants are, since there is no inflow of customers (and food inspectors like Karnan are the exception not the norm!) there is no pressing need for them to maintain the premises. In a country where hygiene even in reputed restaurants is unreliable, who is checking the growing number of cloud kitchens and ensuring that they operate in sanitary conditions?

'No one is,' says Vir Sanghvi, when I met him in his house to talk about the food landscape in India. 'Cloud kitchens in India are a bit like the Wild West. There isn't much regulation. The typical cloud kitchen services an average of six brands, usually owned by the same person who markets them separately. So, when you order from a pizza place, and the order comes from a cloud kitchen, you have no idea that the guy next to the pizza maker is standing and making butter chicken. Restaurants are classified as Grade 1 eating houses, Grade 2 eating houses, etc., but cloud kitchens are not, so they get away with murder.'

In April 2023, a Redditor in Bengaluru who worked as a part-time food delivery agent posted pictures of a shabby cloud kitchen where he went to pick up an order. 'I literally saw the guy put the momo back to the steamer after it fell on the dirtiest floor I've ever seen,' he wrote in a viral post.[10]

As technological innovation evolves rapidly and various business models emerge, regulatory authorities must get updated on how app-based services work and create frameworks to manage the unique aspects of these businesses that are not covered under existing rules.

III. Sustainability

Ride-Hailing

The variant of ride-hailing prevalent in India and, indeed, in America itself didn't pan out the way Uber originally envisioned it. The idea of a private vehicle offering occasional cab rides whenever the driver felt like it died out along the line. The Uber or Lyft driver in the US is now typically a hardworking immigrant functioning as a full-time cab driver. It is not a software engineer who, while going from Freemont to Sunnyvale, picks up a couple of people headed in the same direction. In South Asia, ride-hailing functions as a single passenger transport as sharing of cabs through services like Uber Pool or Ola Share was stopped because of regulatory restrictions or distancing rules during the pandemic. This makes it just as unsustainable as taking one's private car or any kerbside cab because the fuel consumption and vehicle emissions would be the same. Neither is the congestion on the road reduced because, unlike the early promise of jolly fellows driving towards a common destination, there is one sulky passenger and one disgruntled driver in each vehicle, adding to the traffic.

The pillars of 'shared mobility' and 'sustainability' on which the ride-hailing premise was founded have fallen off. The Union of Concerned Scientists (UCS) is an American non-profit organization founded fifty years ago at MIT. Based on publicly available ride-hailing data for seven major US metropolitan areas, the UCS estimates that a non-pooled ride-hailing trip generates nearly 50 per cent greater emissions than a private car trip in a vehicle of average fuel efficiency.[11]

Supporting earlier studies done in California, comparative analysis across three metro cities in India

(Mumbai, New Delhi and Bangalore) suggests that ride-hailing vehicles contribute significantly to city congestion.[12]

High vehicle emissions and the increase in congestion have been attributed to 'deadheading' and lesser use of public transit by the public, who now have the easier door-to-door transport option.

The rise in vehicles on the road has implications for increased heat, climate change and rising temperatures in the city due to increased vehicle emissions. Local governments of all South Asian cities where ride-hailing cabs ply must extract a commitment from the companies to make a phased shift to EVs, which is estimated to reduce emissions by three times.[13] Strategically designed taxes and fees can also do this to steer ride-hailing fleets to electrify, as several US and European cities have done.[14]

In India, the two leading players, Ola and Uber, have announced a transition to electric vehicles following the launch of an all-electric cabs startup called BluSmart, which has emerged as a formidable competitor in Delhi. Policymakers can accelerate the creation of support mechanisms to help the transition to EV cabs.

Quick Commerce

Quick commerce (Blinkit, Zepto, Swiggy Instamart, Big Basket in India) is a distinct business model with a concise window between order and delivery. As Gen Z took control of the digital environment, the delivery schedule shifted from a one-day delivery window to ten minutes, though others quickly caught onto the luxury. In India, if 100 people buy groceries online, thirteen buy them through quick commerce, i.e. those who deliver within ten to fifteen minutes. Comparatively, in China, only 7 per cent of online grocery buyers choose the quick commerce option, while in Europe, just 3 per cent do.[15]

The model, by construction, is unsustainable because it involves more fuel expense and resulting emissions, as its objective is to encourage more deliveries. If a delivery boy rushes on his bike to deliver bread, then a couple of hours later, he again drives down to the same complex (perhaps to the same person!) with a dozen eggs. The customer is thrilled, of course. However, the carbon footprint is much higher than if the customer were to order the same things through regular e-commerce grocery channels rather than through quick commerce apps. A scheduled delivery enables many items to be packed together and delivered in one trip.

In Nepal, 70 per cent of Pathao's food delivery is done by bicycle. Of course, Pathao's food-delivery workers use bicycles because they don't have the money for a motorbike rather than for environmental considerations. However, using bicycles conflicts with the platform's objective of ensuring maximum deliveries in minimum time. Pathao Nepal is mulling over alliances with finance companies to provide soft loans for bicycle riders who have been with them for two years to buy motorbikes. 'The person on a motorized vehicle earns more than someone on a cycle by covering a wider area quickly,' says Yeshu Thakali.

In India, e-cycles and smart bikes have been piloted for deliveries, but the majority of workers still use conventional motorized two-wheelers. Delivery workers could be the most important occupational group that the country's grand EV plans could target because they are on the road all day, burning fuel and adding to emissions. An affordable green transport solution that does not require the driver to spend much time charging or swapping batteries and is easy on the body can be a win on many fronts. Some writers suggest that quick commerce apps ask customers whether they need their delivery immediately or don't mind getting it later or picking it up themselves. Segmenting customers based on requested delivery speed could help avoid multiple trips and the traffic congestion delivery riders currently cause on the road.

IV. Why Is It Always a 'Delivery Boy'?

According to the World Bank, a mere 25 per cent of South Asia's working-age women were in the labour force in 2021, about half the average among emerging market and developing economies.[16] Gig work could hypothetically be a gateway into the workforce for women because of its low entry barriers, flexible timings that allow women to balance work and family duties and the fact that their earnings get promptly credited into their account, enabling independent access to the money.

And yet, we never say 'delivery girl'. It's always 'delivery boy'. A national survey on gig workers that I was part of, whose report was released coincidentally on Women's Day in 2024[17] confirms that women are conspicuously absent (less than 3 per cent) in gig work in India. Why aren't women getting into these jobs in droves, given the many advantages it presents to them?

Firstly, women have low ownership of personal vehicles. Secondly, even if the car is registered in a woman's name, she often does not know how to drive and the actual usage is by male members of her family. Driving is considered a 'man's job' in most societies, and teaching a girl to drive is viewed as a pointless investment. Taking up a driving-centric job like gig work is almost taboo. I interviewed entrepreneurs running transport operations with only female drivers a few years ago. Whether it was a company in Ghana that hired women to steer trucks or one in New Delhi that recruited girls from slums to become cab drivers, their most significant barrier was the family of the potential driver. Most would do everything possible to prevent women from taking up a driving-based job.

How can platforms help?

Tech companies could begin by having a diversity quota among workers with a stated commitment to hiring a minimum number of women. And then they could be sincere in their intent. In Pakistan, companies like Careem, Bykea and Foodpanda regularly signalled their intention for inclusion through ad campaigns featuring female gig workers, especially around International Women's Day. Rubiya Nadeem, who is forty, began working as a Bykea delivery driver in Lahore in August 2021.[18] Financial circumstances compelled her to take the gig. She soon became a poster girl for the women-friendliness of gig work, featuring in several media articles. Bykea even gave her a brand-new bike. But a year later, in December 2022, Nadeem injured her back, and she had to stop riding.

'I would have liked to be able to opt for package deliveries over customer pickups because men would cancel rides with me when they saw I was a woman, but the algorithm didn't allow me to do that.'

Rubiya's experience holds essential lessons in gender-responsiveness for platforms. If more women are to join gig work, they must have the option to choose tasks that they feel comfortable with or to not go to certain areas deemed unsafe or not work at certain hours. Worldwide, women are primary caregivers at home and juggle multiple responsibilities. Their threat perception in public places is also higher than that of men, as they are easy targets for gender-based violence. The mighty algorithm can be programmed to make it easier for women to participate in the workforce as gig workers.

In addition, companies can address the structural barriers women potentially face by:

- Working with urban local bodies to build women's restrooms where female gig workers can take a break
- Partnering with NGOs to teach more women from low-income families how to drive two-wheelers and cars
- Sponsoring soft loans to buy vehicles

- Mitigating women's risks to personal safety through measures like installing an emergency button in the app that connects to the police control room

V. Leaving No One Behind

India has the world's second-largest internet population at about 800 million users almost all accessing the internet via mobile phones.[19] This is a little more than half of the country's estimated population of 1.4 billion people but is heavily skewed towards urban, below sixty, middle- and upper-income groups. The rest are rural folk, women, especially of lower income groups and senior citizens. They form the bottom of the digital hierarchy, living in the umbra of the digital revolution.

There are two kinds of people here. The first category includes those who do not have access to a device that can connect them to the internet, mainly because they cannot afford it. The second one is far more complex to pin down and will never appear in surveys focusing on how many people access the net. It relates to people who, despite owning a smartphone, computer or laptop, are at sea regarding net navigation. This is because the pace at which daily life has become digitized has been too fast for them to catch up, particularly after the pandemic.

To the unsavvy, technology seems like a formidable jungle. A barrage of OTPs land on the phone. Ads pop up all over the screen of an app. Sometimes, the 'x' to close the ad is on the top right; other times, 'close' is written in minute font at the bottom. A cyber rookie misses that, clicks on the ad, lands somewhere else and panics, not knowing how to return to the original site. Clickbaits abound, making fools of those who once thought they were brilliant.

Rural, older and semi-educated folk are deeply suspicious of technology. Tejpal, our erstwhile chauffeur, who sits at the intersection of these labels, treats the omniscient 'GPS lady' as his bête noire. '*Kahin woh humein bewakoof toh nahi bana rahi*? (Is she trying to fool us?)' he would ask sceptically and feel triumphant on the rare occasion that the map directed us to a dead end.

Functional digital literacy is vital to negotiate an increasingly digitized world. The government must work with private telcos to run campaigns that help digitally diffident folk build familiarity with day-to-day technology through outreach programmes and tech camps. For example, Reliance Jio and the GSMA have rolled out a nationwide Digital Skills Program in India to provide digital access to marginalized low-income groups. Digital payment portals could help through educational videos running in shops to encourage customers to go cashless.

Unsurprisingly, the digital divide is deeply gendered. GSMA's latest data[20] shows that in South Asia, women are now 41 per cent less likely than men to use mobile internet. In some countries like Bangladesh, the gender gap is stark due to pervasive cultural barriers, with women being 55 per cent less likely to use the internet than men. Bangladesh must boost its efforts to increase the proportion of women participating in the digital economy.

More pertinent than exulting about the number of smartphones is to ensure that segments of the population are not left behind, feeling dependent as the march of technology brings about its inevitable change.

VI. Better Jobs than Gig Work!

Apart from the visible jobs, like delivery workers, many jobs have been created on the sidelines of digital commerce. In the course of researching for this book, I have encountered people performing various jobs that happen behind the scenes— photographers who shoot pictures of a restaurant and its bestselling dishes to display in a food delivery app; customer support executives who answer queries not of customers but of restaurants on the phone or online chat; those who help train new sellers about the mysterious ways of Amazon and 'onboard' them. Putting a number to these new jobs is tricky as these are also gigs—piecemeal jobs paid on a per-task basis. Irrespective of the number of jobs created in the gig economy, the crucial question is whether countries can rely on gig work to help employ their rapidly increasing working-age population.

Here's why the short answer is 'No'.

First, governments must ask themselves if this is the best deployment of a young person's ability.

South Asian countries are banking on their youthful advantage to leapfrog into a growth phase in the next decade. According to World Bank estimates, 68 per cent of the collective population of South Asia is under forty years of age compared to 47 per cent in Europe and 52 per cent in North America.[21] If the region's demographic dividend is to be reaped, the potential of the youth must be used in better ways than creating armies of delivery workers. The few surveys of gig workers that have been done in India (e.g., by India's National Centre for Applied Economics and Research (NCAER), the government policy think tank NITI Aayog and the grassroots organization PAIGAM) show that, on average, around 34 per cent have completed their secondary school (Grade 10). Around 25 per cent had studied further and acquired a diploma or University degree.[22] Evidently, there is a skills mismatch where people are overqualified for a job that only needs driving ability. This can lead to growing frustration among youth stuck in gig work due to a lack of options. Such a situation can quickly turn the youthful demographic from an asset to a source of social unrest.

No one dreams of becoming a delivery person. They intend to do it as a stop-gap arrangement, but it drags on because they cannot find other options. To celebrate companies engaged in delivery services as a source of national pride is misguided. Genuine national pride should come from building economic prosperity that engages the youth more productively than using them to drop off packets.

Second, gig work cannot be a long-term occupation for a person because of the nature of the work itself, as demonstrated in previous chapters. The algorithmic management of workers is de-personalizing and isolating.

Each worker is like an atomized unit unto himself, orbiting the trajectories outlined for him, rarely meeting a co-worker. Bodies ache from driving around all day in worsening climatic conditions, long hours without a bathroom break and the mental stress of working endlessly under the tyranny of a deadline form a deadly cocktail hurtling towards burnout in two to five years.

Gig work is also unreliable because most app-based companies are startups yet to become profitable. The business model, the distribution mechanism and the customer proposition are all creatures of the twenty-first century with no precedents to learn from. Ever so often, a company packs up, declaring itself as having run its course. The CEO and managers write emotional posts on LinkedIn about the excellent learning experience but a vast number of workers are furloughed at the bottom of the corporate pyramid. To cite a recent example, in early 2024, Daraz Pakistan, which was bought over by Alibaba in 2018, cut its workforce by 11 per cent.[23] Its Swedish founder, Bjarke Mikkelsen, said to Daraz's employees in a letter that a challenging market environment, wars supply chain disruptions, soaring inflation, higher taxes and fewer government subsidies were among the reasons for the cuts.[24] Gigs could also shrink as automation replaces human beings. Drones are hovering overhead, threatening to replace delivery agents, who will have to look for alternative jobs.

So, what kind of jobs should be created if gig jobs cannot anchor our youth? There aren't any easy answers, but I found the premise of a recent book called *The Last Human Job: The Work of Connecting in a Disconnected World* by Allison J. Pugh,[25] resonating closely with my ideas. In an increasingly automated and disconnected world, Pugh makes a case for work in which human connection is imperative, what she calls 'connective labour'. She asks, 'What happens to human relationships when one side is mechanized?' After five years of research, Pugh found no relationship exists when one half of the encounter is a machine. This has been an observation I rant about often, and it was brought home to me again soon after I read about the book. On the eve of my birthday in 2024, I was jolted out of sleep at 1.46 a.m. by my phone ringing incessantly. I scrambled out of bed to answer it and found that it was an automated call from an app-based domestic service provider. A recorded female voice announced that the servicing of my air conditioner had been rescheduled. Unable to sleep again and groggy the next day, I cancelled the appointment. The following week, I saw an angry post on X written by an airline passenger, complaining that the airline's system had allotted four separate seats in different rows for his two small children, himself and his wife, on the same booking code. The system didn't recognize that the children were under ten and ought to be seated beside their parents.

In both instances, even until a decade ago, a human being would have been at the other end. That person would have called at a decent hour to reschedule the AC service booking. A person at the airline check-in counter would have likely allotted adjacent seats to the family. However, as automation is rapidly replacing jobs that humans used to perform, there is a significant lacuna in customer experience that companies are not noticing in their zeal to adopt technology. Companies need to develop a nuanced view of technology deployment in customer interfaces.

Around the mid-1990s, phone banking and ATMs began to be aggressively pushed by private banks, who found that the transaction cost was much lower in these newer modes than if the customer visited a physical branch. This move demanded a behavioural change from customers, especially retired folk, who were used to visiting the bank not just for money matters but also to socialize with the manager over a cup of tea. Now they had to dial a number, and a disembodied voice would say press 1 for this and 2 for that, and each time, a different stranger would answer. The shift from the old ways made customers angry and perplexed. However, moving from physical outlets to call centres foreshadowed a more significant change. Present-day companies have made it hard for customers to reach any human being at all. Those at the end of the phone line are deeply hidden behind a maze of options that must be tackled with dexterity. It's like a video game; one wrong button pressed, and you are back to level 1.

Any self-respecting consumer goods/services company has an 'online chat' option on its website and mobile app. An annoying bot impersonating a friendly human, pops up if one wants any interaction. It is trained to respond to a fixed set of possible scenarios. Any deviation from them leaves the bot dysfunctional and the customer in despair. Despite these limitations, there is a blind rush to replace any activity previously performed by humans with a faceless tech system. The idea is that machine learning will kick in, and eventually, the bot will be better than a human ever was.

The absence of a human interface is stark not just for customers but also for workers. App-based workers (e.g. food delivery workers or app-based cab drivers) self-recruit through the app merely by uploading a couple of documents, watching training videos, receiving payment information and discovering how they are rated by customers, all on the app. All this was work that HR executives did in the old economy. Now, years pass by without workers meeting a human being in the company. This model is expected to become the norm in the world of work in our AI-led future and can exacerbate the alienation that workers are already facing.

As Pugh says, being seen is in short supply. When someone feels seen and understood, that powerful interaction reverberates in what neuroscientists call 'perceptual crossing'. When there is a need for contextual understanding or a situation where empathy is more important than efficiency, homo sapiens do better than machines. Teaching, therapy, customer service, counselling, coaching and salespeople in showrooms are jobs that depend on connecting with others. These are examples of jobs that require skills such as negotiation, critical thinking, active listening and teamwork. They make workers feel valuable and not as if they are mindless machines.

AI is coming for many of these jobs, but protecting them from getting automated may be wise, at least in labour-surplus regions. Governments must ask if we need 3D printing to replace handmade artisanal products, rendering several small-scale industries with substantial job losses. Perfectly produced machine-made things are no longer exclusive like hand-made goods are. Quick commerce threatens the existence of small shops and businesses in urban neighbourhoods. However, small corner shops are part of the community fabric and serve as nodes of human interaction. It would be a loss to the quality of urban life if new business models like quick commerce erase them.

Indeed, some jobs are better done by machines, such as in factories where workers do eight-hour shifts, welding or forging in blazing summers; robots can improve safety and accuracy in such processes. However, sectors such as retail, care, personal and public services must remain sites where one human being meets another face to face. Discerning which jobs can be automated and which jobs are much better served when there is a human presence, will free up jobs for our youth to move out of gig work into jobs where human abilities can be employed.

VII. We Are All in It Together

Despite the different sizes of the markets for app-based goods and services in India, Pakistan, Nepal, Sri Lanka and

Bangladesh, the challenges, dilemmas and opportunities that platforms present are similar across South Asian countries. Pampered customers exploited workers and influential tech companies are the dramatis personae across the region. A rebalancing of privilege, power and precarity between them will distribute the benefits of digital commerce more uniformly. Institutional mechanisms that can help share knowledge and best practices could help the region collaborate in managing this evolving space.

In the fourth century BCE, the written word was the hot technology of the time. The Greek philosopher Socrates disapproved of this and railed against it to his student Plato. 'This discovery of yours will create forgetfulness in the learners' souls because they will not use their memories,' said Socrates.[26] In 1764, England's textile industry saw the advent of the spinning jenny, which could do the work of eight weavers. Threatened by the cost-saving, wage-stealing machinery introduced in the textile industry, English textile workers, who came to be called Luddites, protested fiercely and secretly destroyed the machines. Since then, 'Luddite' is a description that has been used for anyone opposed to technology.

The fear of new technology is as old as civilization itself. But fear is not the answer to the social and economic failures that technology sometimes brings in its wake. As Martin Heidegger, one of the leading thinkers about technology in the twentieth century, cautioned, helplessly rebelling against technology is just as bad as pushing it mindlessly and being compulsively addicted to it. What we need, instead, is to understand that technology is not merely an instrument to do things efficiently but also something that has the power to define our entire being. Heidegger believed it would be more dangerous than the current problems caused by technology—environmental degradation, consumerism, etc.—if technology solved *all* our problems. Our existence would become less authentic, encouraging a superficial and alienated way of being in which individuals become disconnected from themselves, others and the world around them.[27]

About half a century after Heidegger, there is growing concern about technology going awry. Geoffrey Hinton, one of 2024's Nobel winners for Physics, regarded by many as the 'godfather of artificial intelligence', echoed similar sentiments. Hinton's work on machine learning is the basis for powering many of today's AI-based applications. Immediately after winning the award, Hopfield talked about the significance of technology but also warned of it 'getting out of control'. In 2015, Tristan Harris, a Google engineer, quit the company to cofound the Time Well Spent movement and the Centre for Humane Technology (CHT) to halt the unchecked power of tech firms to profit from 'playing tricks' on people's minds.[28]

In March of 2023, nearly 35,000 AI researchers, technologists, entrepreneurs and concerned citizens signed an open letter from the Future of Life Institute that called for a 'pause' on AI development. The public petition warned dramatically that: 'Advanced AI could represent a profound change in the history of life on Earth, and should be planned for and managed with commensurate care and resources.'[29] The digital platforms discussed in this book have enabled innovation, created jobs, expanded market access for merchants and brought conveniences that could not have been imagined even in the late twentieth century. However, the demand for instant gratification that they fulfil also has high social and economic costs. These must be acknowledged and addressed through policy and institutional actions.

The old gives way to the new, as it always has. 'When old words die out on the tongue, new melodies break forth from the heart, and where old tracks are lost, a new country is revealed with its wonders,' wrote Rabindranath Tagore in his Nobel-winning poem, 'Gitanjali'.[30] We are in the midst of a transformative phase where the way we do the routine things required to conduct our daily lives—eating, buying and commuting—has changed irrevocably. A new, wondrous, tech-driven world has emerged and will only further draw us into its maze. We must now navigate it carefully and dodge those bullets that threaten our essential humanity.

ACKNOWLEDGEMENTS

A book born from conversations with more than a hundred and fifty people over a year and across five countries can only be pulled off if the Universe is kind. So, I owe my foremost gratitude to God and the blessings of departed elders such as my dear father, R. Vasudevan.

Heartfelt thanks to all others listed below:

Karthik Venkatesh, my editor, for believing this is a story whose time has come and for always being a call away and the copy editing and design team in Penguin Random House India.

Dr Meenakshi Gopinath, for being a gentle guiding light at various points in my life.

Dr Rakesh Mohan, Dr Laveesh Bhandari and Shishir Gupta of The Centre for Social Economic Progress (CSEP), New Delhi, for their trust, support and insightful discussions and Aparna Preethan for research assistance.

The International Centre Goa and Dr Pushkar for selecting me as a scholar-in-residence for 2023. The best parts of the book were likely written in the quietude of the ICG.

To all my friends from our neighbouring countries for their warm and generous help in enabling interviews with people there.

Aman Shreshtha and Geetanjali Rai, Gaurav Ghale, Prof. Pitambar Bhandari and his two young students, Anjula Joshi and Sagar Khadka, who conducted excellent fieldwork. Meshach Peiris and Zinara Rathnayake. Ammar Malik, Qurat-ul-Ain, Aliza Khalid, Ihtisham-ul-Haq and Momina Ashraf. A huge thank you for reaching the voices across the borders to me.

My friends Shubra Jyotsana, Snehal Soneji and A. Arumugam for enthusiastically introducing me to those I needed to speak to.

Sashrika Pathak and Rituparna Das for research support.

A.K. Shivakumar for his wise suggestions at various points.

Academics and activists Uma Rani of ILO, Vinoj Abraham and Raviraman in Trivandrum, Robert Rahman Raman and Dharmender Kumar for their insights about labour and gig work.

Sincere thanks to every one of the people, whose conversations with me are featured on these pages, for giving me time and sharing their experiences and viewpoints.

My mother, Vasudha Vasudevan, from whom I seemed to have inherited a penchant for social observations. Thank you Ma for prodding me to write every time I slacked off.

Few people are more difficult to live with than a writer in the throes of writing. So, to my universe at home—my husband Partha and my children Prakriti and Sriniketh—a ton of love and a big thank you for being who you are.

APPENDIX

All values in $ billion		Market Size				
Sector	Time Period	INDIA	NEPAL	BANGLADESH	SRI LANKA	PAKISTAN
FOOD DELIVERY	Current	7.65[1]	0.04	0.16	1.06	1.76
	Projected	24.34[1]	0.06	0.202	1.9	2.40
RIDE-HAILING	Current	0.95[2]	0.075	0.101	0.01	0.27
	Projected	3.76[2]	0.107	0.153	0.013	0.37
QUICK COMMERCE	Current	3.34[3]	0.338	1.46	1.02	0.103
	Projected	9.95[3]	0.599	2.56	1.86	0.18
E-COMMERCE	Current	123[4]	1.32	8	2.61	5.91
	Projected	325[4]	1.86	12.25	3.93	6.71
HOME SERVICES	Current	0.217[6]	NA	NA	NA	NA
	Projected	6.39[5]	NA	NA	NA	NA

Current = 2025
Projected = 2029–30

All values in millions		Number of Workers	Number of Customers				
Market	**Time Period**	**INDIA**	**INDIA**	**NEPAL**	**BANGLADESH**	**SRI LANKA**	**PAKISTAN**
FOOD DELIVERY	Current	7.78	320–340	0.4	7	0.37	59.3
	Projected	258	430–4507	0.5	9.6	0.46	78.9
RIDE-HAILING	Current	NA	268	5.32	31.77	4.24	34.67
	Projected	NA	380	7.01	43.81	4.56	44.36
QUICK COMMERCE	Current	0.59	26	4.9	12.7	1.017	2
	Projected	NA	60	6.7	16.7	1.856	NA
E-COMMERCE	Current	16	220	4	11.9	2.273	10.8
	Projected	NA	500	6	15.9	3.061	13.4
HOME SERVICES	Current	NA	NA	NA	NA	NA	NA

Current = 2025
Projected = 2029–30

References

1   ETTech. 2024. 'Food delivery market size to cross Rs 2 lakh crore by 2030: Bain-Swiggy report.' Economic Times, 3 July. https://economictimes.indiatimes.com/tech/startups/online-food-delivery-market-to-grow-18-on-year-to-rs-2-lakh-crore-by-2030-bain-report/articleshow/111452013.cms?from=mdr.

2   'India Ride-Hailing Market Assessment, By Mode of Booking [Online, Offline], By Offering [Affordable, Premium], By Vehicle Type [Two-Wheeler, Three-Wheeler, Four-Wheeler], By Propulsion Type [Internal Combustion Engine (ICE), Electric], By Region, Opportunities and Forecast, FY2018-FY2032F.' Markets & Data. January 2025. https://www.marketsandata.com/industry-reports/india-ride-hailing-market.

3   ANI. 2025. 'Quick Commerce sale in India surge by 280 per cent over two years: Report.' Economic Times, 28 September. https://economictimes.indiatimes.com/industry/services/retail/quick-commerce-sale-in-india-surge-by-280-per-cent-over-two-years-report/articleshow/113760320.cms?from=mdr.

4   'E-commerce Industry in India.' IBEF. April 2025. https://www.ibef.org/industry/ecommerce#:~:text=opportunity%20by%202030.-,The%20Indian%20e%2Dcommerce%20market%20is%20projected%20to%20grow%20from,(CAGR)%20of%2018.7%25.

5   'How on-demand services are crafting the future of home maintenance.' Financial Express, 3 June 2024. https://www.financialexpress.com/money/how-on-demand-services-are-crafting-the-future-of-home-maintenance-3511137/.

6   'India Online On-demand Home Services Market Size & Outlook.' Horizon Grand View Research. https://www.grandviewresearch.com/horizon/outlook/online-on-demand-home-services-market/india.

7   Pradhan, Dipesh and Aashika Jain. 2024. 'E-Commerce Statistics For India In 2024. ' Forbes, 12 April. https://www.forbes.com/advisor/in/business/ecommerce-statistics/.

8   PTI. 2024. 'Food delivery economy crucial as it generates large-scale employment: Nitin Gadkari.' Economic Times, 17 December. https://economictimes.indiatimes.com/news/india/food-delivery-economy-cruciahttps://economictimes.indiatimes.com/news/india/food-delivery-economy-crucial-as-it-generates-large-scale-employment-nitin-gadkari/articleshow/116395478.cms?from=mdrl-as-it-generates-large-scale-employment-nitin-gadkari/articleshow/116395478.cms?from=mdr.

9   PTI. 2025. 'Q-Commerce to employ 5-5.5 lakh people by next year: Report.' Economic Times, 12 March. https://hr.economictimes.indiatimes.com/news/industry/q-commerce-to-employ-5-5-5-lakh-people-by-next-year-report/118957180.

All other figures from Statista. www.statista.com.

NOTES

WHY AND HOW I WROTE THIS BOOK

1   'Acts & Rules, Act no. 25.' Department of Labour, Government of Rajasthan. https://labour.rajasthan.gov.in/ActsAndRules. aspx.

2   Vasudevan, V., Kumar, D. and Alam, M.M. 2024. 'The RIGHTS Survey.' https://www.janpahal.com/_files/ugd/1cfdd7_ f9ce99577d974faa9ef28c9fceb23761.pdf.

3   Staniland, Paul. 2024. 'Bangladesh is Well-Positioned to build a new political area. Can it seize the moment?' Carnegie Endowment for International Peace,15 October. https:// carnegieendowment.org/emissary/2024/10/bangladesh-hasina-government-politics-what-next?lang=en.

SETTING, CAST AND STORYLINE

1   Aggarwal, R. 2023. 'At 1.1 bn, Amazon records highest ever visits in Great Indian Festival 2023.' *Business Standard*, 9 November. https://www.business-standard.com/industry/ news/at-1-1-bn-amazon-records-highest-ever-visits-in-great-indian-festival-2023-123110900854_1.html.

2   'The Amazon Great Indian Festival 2023 Becomes the Biggest Ever Customer And Seller Celebrations!' Amazon India. https://press.aboutamazon.in/news-releases/news-release-details/amazon-great-indian-festival-2023-becomes-biggest-ever-customer.

3   Amazon Staff. 2023. 'Amazon Great Indian Festival 2023: Here's what people ordered so far.' About Amazon, 9 November. https://www.aboutamazon.in/news/retail/great-indian-festival-2023-stats.

4   Amazon Staff. 2020. 'Thank you India for opening the 'khushiyon ka darwaza' for Bharat.' About Amazon, 11 November. https://www.aboutamazon.in/news/retail/thank-you-india-for-opening-the-khushiyon-ka-darwaza-for-bharat.

5   Ghosh, Parijat, Navneet Chahal, Vishesh Shrivastav and Arushie Mangla. 2023. 'e-Conomy India 2023,' Bain, 6 June. https://www.bain.com/insights/e-conomy-india-2023/, last accessed 27 August 2024.

6   'About Us.' Daraz. https://www.daraz.pk/about-us/?spm=a2a0e.tm80335159.footer_top.9.35e3iYsniYsnds&scm=1003.4.icms-zebra-5029545-6852930.OTHER_6502476577_7722624.

7   2024. 'Quick-commerce and Food Delivery Companies End 2023 on a High.' Moneycontrol, 1 January. https://www.moneycontrol.com/news/technology/quick-commerce-and-food-delivery-companies-end-2023-on-a-high-11981501.html.

8   DH Web Desk. 2023. 'Swiggy surprised! Bengaluru resident orders 62 plates of biryani amid India-Pakistan match.' *Deccan Herald,* 3 September. https://www.deccanherald.com/india/karnataka/bengaluru/swiggy-surprised-bengaluru-resident-orders-62-biryanis-amid-india-pakistan-match-2671071. https://www.deccanherald.com/india/karnataka/bengaluru/swiggy-surprised-bengaluru-resident-orders-62-biryanis-amid-india-pakistan-match-2671071.

9   Srivastav, Udisha. 2025. 'New Year's Eve 2025: Blinkit, Zepto, Swiggy Instamart Hit Record Orders.' *Business Standard*, 1

January. https://www.business-standard.com/industry/news/new-year-s-eve-2025-blinkit-zepto-swiggy-instamart-hit-record-orders-125010100791_1.html.

10 Pai, Sajith, Anurag Pagaria, and Nachhamai Savithiri. 2024. 'Indus Valley Report 2024.' Blume Ventures, 18 March. https://blume.vc/reports/indus-valley-annual-report-2024.

11 Shetty, S. 2022. 'Five things you probably didn't know about Swiggy Instamart.' Swiggy Diaries, 20 October. https://blog.swiggy.com/2022/04/04/five-things-you-probably-didnt-know-about-swiggy-instamart/.

12 Bhattacharya, Ananya. 2022. 'A Status Update on the Uber-Ola War in India.' Quartz, 21 July. https://qz.com/india/1696728/ola-has-a-lead-over-uber-in-indias-ride-hailing-market.

13 PTI. 2024. 'Ride-hailing App Uber Ceases Operations Across Pakistan.' *Economic Times*, 30 April. https://economictimes.indiatimes.com/tech/technology/ride-hailing-app-uber-ceases-operations-across-pakistan/articleshow/109729001.cms?from=mdr.

14 Siddiqui, Zuha, and Durga M. Sengupta. 2024. 'How Careem Went From Pakistan's Ride-hailing Leader to Stuck on the Sidelines.' Rest of World, 5 June. https://restofworld.org/2024/careem-indrive-pakistan/.

15 Imtiaz, S. 2020. 'The Global Business of Glam.' *Marie Claire,* 22 April. https://www.marieclaire.com/career-advice/a32237708/gharpar-beauty-company-pakistan/.

16 'Health Nutrition and Population Statistics.' DataBank (n.d.). https://databank.worldbank.org/source/health-nutrition-and-population-statistics.

17 DPIIT Startup India. 'India Bangladesh Startup Bridge.' Ministry of Commerce and Industry, Govt. of India. https://www.startupindia.gov.in/content/sih/en/international/india_bangladesh_startup_bridge.html.

18 Abdur-Rahim, Syed, and Asim Bokhari. 2019. 'Starting up: Unlocking entrepreneurship in Pakistan.' McKinsey & Co.

https://www.mckinsey.com/~/media/mckinsey/featured%20 insights/middle%20east%20and%20africa/pakistans%20 start%20up%20landscape%20three%20ways%20to%20 energize%20entrepreneurship/starting-up-unlocking-entrepreneurship-in-pakistan.pdf.

19 The World Bank Group. Digital Development Partnership. 2022. 'South Asia's Digital Opportunity. Accelerating Growth, Transforming Lives, pp. 22.' World Bank Group. https:// documents1.worldbank.org/curated/en/099340103292239929/ pdf/P172300097cd82032089610283e77293d89.pdf?_ gl=1*1finzrp*_gcl_au*MTczMTYyODYzMC4xNzI 2ODYyNzkw.

20 Times News Network. 2024. 'Daily Average UPI Payments at New High in April.' *Times of India*, 1 May. https://timesofindia. indiatimes.com/business/india-business/daily-average-upi-payments-at-new-high-in-april/articleshow/109766659.cms.

21 Verma, Sapan. 2024. 'Delivery Boys. Standup Comedy by Sapan Verma.' YouTube, 13 February. https://www.youtube. com/watch?v=1Mrj2jeXA-s.

22 ET Online. 2024. ₹5 Lakh on One Meal? Zomato Shouts Out Bengaluru's Biggest Spender in Highlights; Here're Zomato's 2024 Hi.' *Economic Times*, 27 December. https:// economictimes.indiatimes.com/industry/cons-products/ food/5-lakh-on-one-meal-zomato-shouts-out-bengalurus-biggest-spender-in-highlights-herere-zomatos-2024-highlights/articleshow/116705270.cms?from=mdr.

23 2023. 'Zomato Reveals 'nation's Biggest Foodie', in 2023. Mumbai Man Placed Over 9 Orders Everyday.' Moneycontrol, 25 December. https://www.moneycontrol.com/news/trends/ zomato-reveals-nations-biggest-foodie-in-2023-mumbai-man-placed-over-9-orders-everyday-11953501.html.

24 India Today Tech. 2022. 'Pune man ordered food worth Rs 28 lakh from Zomato in 2022.' *India Today*, 30 December. https://www.indiatoday.in/technology/news/story/

pune-man-orders-food-worth-rs-28-lakh-from-zomato-in-2022-2315527-2022-12-30.

25 Thaler, Richard H., and Cass R. Sunstein. 2008. *Nudge: Improving Decisions about Health, Wealth, and Happiness.* Conneticut: Yale University Press.

26 Poojary, T. 2019. 'Swiggy's tech head on how the foodtech startup is using AI to go beyond food deliveries.' YourStory, 5 September. https://yourstory.com/2019/07/foodtech-startup-swiggy-tech-ai-dale-vaz.

PLEASURE

1 Jackson, Elizabeth. 'History of food delivery and how it's changed.' Thistle. https://www.thistle.co/learn/thistle-thoughts/history-of-food-delivery-and-how-its-changed.

2 Rude, E. 2016. 'What Take-Out Food can teach you about American History.' TIME, 14 April. https://time.com/4291197/take-out-delivery-food-history/.

3 'Waiter.com.' Wikipedia. https://en.wikipedia.org/wiki/Waiter.com.

4 Williams-Grut, O. 2018. 'UBS: Online food delivery could be a $365 billion industry by 2030 - here are the winners and losers from that 'mega trend.'' *Business Insider,* July 2. https://www.businessinsider.in/ubs-online-food-delivery-could-be-a-365-billion-industry-by-2030-here-are-the-winners-and-losers-from-that-mega-trend/articleshow/64830748.cms.

5 Marco, Vita. 2023. Uber Newsroom, 19 October. https://www.uber.com/newsroom/2023-uber-eats-cravings-report/.

6 Borresen, Kelsey. 2024. 'Has 'Little Treat' Culture Gone Too Far? Therapists Have Thoughts.' HuffPost, January 25, 2024. https://www.huffpost.com/entry/little-treat-culture-gone-too-far-therapists_l_65b00b52e4b0d65b024e451d.

7 Kamath, Nikhil. 2023. 'Ep #11 | WTF Goes Into Building a Fashion, Beauty, or Home Brand? Nikhil W/ Kishore,

Raj, and Ananth.' https://www.youtube.com/watch?v=hjiZ11lKCrU.

8   Sajith, Pai, Anurag Pagaria, and Nachhamai Savithiri. 2024. 'Indus Valley Report 2024.' Blume Ventures. https://blume.vc/reports/indus-valley-annual-report-2024.

9   2024. 'India's affluent population is likely to hit 100 million by 2027.' Goldman Sachs, 16 February. https://www.goldmansachs.com/insights/articles/indias-affluent-population-is-likely-to-hit-100-million-by-2027.

10   'The Rise of India's Middle Class.' PRICE. https://price360.in/Executive_Summary_Middle_Class.pdf.

11   Bhatia, A. 2022. 'The Journey since 1947-IV: Eating Out Comes of Age in India.' The India Forum, 20 October. https://www.theindiaforum.in/history/journey-1947-iv-eating-out-comes-age-india.

12   Sharma, R. 2024. '25 top YouTubers in India in 2024.' PageTraffic, 18 January. https://www.pagetraffic.in/blog/top-youtubers-in-india/#:~:text=CarryMinati%20is%20the%20most%20popular%20and%20the%20biggest%20YouTuber%20in%20India.

13   2022. 'Working Time and Work-Life Balance Around the World.' International Labour Organization. https://www.ilo.org/wcmsp5/groups/public/---ed_protect/---protrav/---travail/documents/publication/wcms_864222.pdf.

14   Ibid., p. 2.

15   Sebastian, B. M. 2023. 'NR Narayana Murthy: Why Indians are debating a 70-hour work week.' BBC, 1 November. https://www.bbc.com/news/world-asia-india-67269976.

16   Online, E. 2023. 'Not 70, more like 140: Ola CEO Bhavish Aggarwal adds more fuel to Narayana Murthy debate.' Economic Times, 28 October. https://economictimes.indiatimes.com/news/new-updates/not-70-more-like-140-ola-ceo-bhavish-aggarwal-adds-more-fuel-to-narayana-murthy-debate/articleshow/104773917.cms?from=mdr.

17 2017. 'BRIEFING NOTE ON WORKING TIME REDUCED
    STANDARD WORKWEEK IN THE REPUBLIC OF KOREA.'
    International Labour Organization. Accessed 7 March 2025.
    https://www.ilo.org/es/media/68461/download.

GUILT

1   Hughes, M. 1997. 'Soul, Black Women and Soul Food', in
    C. Counihan and P. Van Esterik (eds.) *Food and Culture: A
    Reader.* New York: Routledge, pp. 277–80.
2   Wilkinson, Crystal, and Clarkson Potter. 2024. *Praise song for
    the Kitchen Ghosts: Stories and Recipes From Five Generations
    of Black Country Cooks*, pp. 230.
3   Gupta, Raghav. 2024. 'Council Post: How AI Is Taking Over
    Our Kitchens.' *Forbes*, July 16. https://www.forbes.com/
    councils/forbestechcouncil/2024/07/16/how-ai-is-taking-over-
    our-kitchens/.
4   Pineda, Elisa et. al. 2024. 'Policy implementation and
    recommended actions to create healthy food environments
    using the Healthy Food Environment Policy Index (Food-EPI):
    a comparative analysis in South Asia.' *The Lancet Regional
    Health - Southeast Asia*, Volume 26, 100428.
5   Palaniappan L., et al. 2018. 'South Asian Cardiovascular Disease
    & Cancer Risk: Genetics & Pathophysiology.' *J Community
    Health* 43(6): 1100–14.
6   'World Obesity Atlas 2023.' World Obesity Federation. https://
    data.worldobesity.org/publications/?cat=19.
7   2022. 'WHO EUROPEAN REGIONAL OBESITY REPORT
    2022. Pp.85.' World Health Organization. https://iris.who.int/
    bitstream/handle/10665/353747/9789289057738-eng.pdf.
8   'The State of Food Security and Nutrition in the World.'
    https://www.fao.org/3/cc3017en/online/state-food-security-
    and-nutrition-2023/urbanization-affects-agrifood-systems.
    html#fig20.

9   2024. 'A Lancet study says half of India's adult population physically unfit.' CNBCTV18, 28 June. https://www.cnbctv18.com/india/healthcare/half-of-india-adult-population-physically-unfit-says-lancet-study-19433843.htm.

10   SheepherderGreedy266. Reddit. https://www.reddit.com/r/gurgaon/comments/1c9c7mf/addicted_to_zomatoswiggy/ Accessed on 24 December 2024.

11   'Infographic | How India ordered on Swiggy and Zomato in 2023.' *Deccan Herald*, 26 December 2023. https://www.deccanherald.com/lifestyle/food-and-drink/how-india-ordered-on-swiggy-zomato-2023-2825386.

12   Cajochen, C. et al. (2011). 'Evening exposure to a light-emitting diodes (LED)-backlit computer screen affects circadian physiology and cognitive performance'. *J. Appl. Physiol.* 110: 1432–38. doi: 10.1152/japplphysiol.00165.2011.

13   Nichter, M. 1986. 'Modes of Food Classification and the Diet Health contingency-A South Indian Case study' in Khare, R.S. and Rao, M.S.A. *Food, Society and Culture: Aspects in South Asian Foods Systems*. N.C.: Carolina Academic Press, pp. 185–222.

14   Cazarin, J., et al. (2023). 'MYC disrupts transcriptional and metabolic circadian oscillations in cancer and promotes enhanced biosynthesis'. *PLoS Genet* 19(8): e1010904. https://doi.org/10.1371/journal.pgen.1010904.

15   Bach, D., and Mann, J.D. 2019. *The Latte Factor: Why You Don't Have to Be Rich to Live Rich*. Atria Books.

16   2024. 'History of Petrol Prices in Pakistan.' Petrol Price in Pakistan, 16 September. https://petrol-priceinpakistan.com/history-of-petrol-prices-in-pakistan/.

17   Shanmugasundaram, M. and A. Tamilarasu. 2023. 'The impact of digital technology, social media, and artificial intelligence on cognitive functions: a review, *Front. Cognit.* 2: 1203077.' Frontiers, 24 November. https://www.frontiersin.org/journals/cognition/articles/10.3389/fcogn.2023.1203077/full.

18   Chen, H., G. Dong, and K. Li. 2023. 'Overview on brain function
     enhancement of Internet addicts through exercise intervention:
     based on reward-execution decision cycle, *Front. Psychiatry* 14:
     1094583. doi: 10.3389/fpsyt.2023.109 4583.' Frontiers.

GRATITUDE

1   2023. 'What Is the Gig Economy, and Who Are Its Workers?'
    Maryville University Online Blog, February 28. https://online.
    maryville.edu/blog/what-is-the-gig-economy/#:~:text=:%20
    With%20origins%20in%20early%2020th,%E2%80%94%20
    filling%20full%2Dtime%20roles.

2   2022. 'India's Booming Gig and Platform Economy:
    Perspectives and Recommendations on the Future of
    Work.' NITI Aayog. https://www.niti.gov.in/sites/default/
    files/2022-06/Policy_Brief_India%27s_Booming_Gig_and_
    Platform_Economy_27062022.pdf.

3   Arya, N. 2023. 'Collecting labour market statistics to study the
    platform economy.' Ideas for India. https://www.ideasforindia.
    in/topics/productivity-innovation/collecting-labour-market-
    statistics-to-study-the-platform-economy.html.

4   Ahmed, I. 2023. 'Pakistan's platform economy.' CLR,14
    September.   https://clr.org.pk/wages-and-income/pakistans-
    platform-   economy/#:~:text=It%20guarantees%20fair%20
    pay%20by,social%20protections%20and%20data%20rights.

5   Datta, N. (2023). 'Working Without Borders: The promise and
    peril of online gig work, In Chapter 2.' World Bank. https://
    documents1.worldbank.org/curated/en/099071923113511279/
    pdf/P17730205fbe2002709043043e4d4f7efee.pdf.

6   PTI. 2020. 'Covid-19 Has Led to 20 Lakh Job Losses in Bus,
    Taxi Sector; More on Anvil: Industry Body.' *Economic Times*,
    21 June. https://economictimes.indiatimes.com/jobs/covid-
    19-has-led-to-20-lakh-job-losses-in-bus-taxi-sector-more-on-
    anvil-industry-body/articleshow/76492675.cms?from=mdr.

7   Ranatunga, D.C. 2009. 'Nugegoda: A glimpse into the past.'
     Sunday Times Book Review, 14 June. https://www.sundaytimes.
     lk/090614/Plus/sundaytimesplus_16.html.

8   2021. 'National family Health Survey (NFHS-5) 2019-21: India:
     Volume I. Mumbai: IIPS.' International Institute for Population
     Sciences (IIPS) and ICF.

9   'World Bank Open Data.' World Bank. https://data.worldbank.
     org/indicator/SL.UEM.TOTL.ZS?locations=NP.

10   Perera, Ayesha. 2023. 'Sri Lanka: Why Is the Country in an
     Economic Crisis?' BBC, 29 March. https://www.bbc.com/news/
     world-61028138.

11   Sood, D.S.V. 2023. 'Headcount at IT firms sees first fall in
     25 years.' Livemint, 29 October. https://www.livemint.com/
     companies/news/headcount-at-it-cos-sees-1st-fall-in-25-
     yrs-11698602455934.html.

12   In the appendix is a table which details the number of rider/
     drivers employed in each platform per country.

ANGER

1   The 'Nirbhaya' case refers to the incident where a twenty-three-
     year-old woman was gangraped in Delhi on 16 December
     2012. This incident sparked nationwide protests. The woman
     had boarded a bus in Delhi's Munirka and was travelling home
     after watching a movie with a friend, when she was assaulted by
     six men including the bus driver while aboard the vehicle. The
     victim succumbed to her injuries on 29 December 2012.

2   2014. 'Uber banned in Delhi over taxi driver 'rape.'' BBC
     News, 8 December. https://www.bbc.com/news/world-asia-
     india-30374070.

3   Dhillon, A. 2018. '"My life is spent in this car': Uber drives its
     Indian workers to despair.' *Guardian,* 4 December. https://
     www.theguardian.com/global-development/2018/dec/04/my-
     life-is-spent-in-this-caruber-drives-indian-workers-to-d.

4   Arora, Varun. 2017. 'Delhi High Court Issues Restraining
    Order On Strike By Ola, Uber Drivers.' VC Circle, 17 April.
    https://www.vccircle.com/delhi-high-court-issues-restraining-
    order-on-strike-by-ola-uber-drivers.

5   DHNS & DHNS. 2024. 'The Saturday Story | I hit the road as
    a food delivery agent. . . Guess how much I made?' *Deccan
    Herald,*14 September. https://www.deccanherald.com/india/
    karnataka/bengaluru/i-hit-the-road-as-a-food-delivery-
    agent-3190457.

6   Vasudevan, V., D. Kumar, and M.M. Alam. 2024. 'The RIGHTS
    Survey.' https://www.janpahal.com/_files/ugd/1cfdd7_
    f9ce99577d974faa9ef28c9fceb23761.pdf.

7   Tallam, N. K. 2021. 'Scheduled Caste man's dreams take flight,
    all thanks to Dalit Bandhu scheme.' *New Indian Express,*
    27 September. https://www.newindianexpress.com/states/
    telangana/2021/Sep/27/scheduled-caste-mans-dreams-take-
    flight-all-thanks-to-dalit-bandhu-scheme-2364175.html.

8   2022. 'Telangana Government to Empower Dalit Community,
    Starts Dalit Bandhu Scheme in State.' ANI News, 9 July. https://
    www.aninews.in/news/national/general-news/telangana-
    government-to-empower-dalit-community-starts-dalit-
    bandhu-scheme-in-state20220709152218/.

9   'Mars Climate Orbiter.' NASA Science. https://science.nasa.
    gov/mission/mars-climate-orbiter/.

10 Davies, H., Simon Goodley, Felicity Lawrence, Paul Lewis,
    and Lisa O'Carroll. 2022. 'Uber broke laws, duped police
    and secretly lobbied governments, leak reveals.' *Guardian,*11
    August. https://www.theguardian.com/news/2022/jul/10/
    uber-files-leak-reveals-global-lobbying-campaign.

FREEDOM

1   Powell, E.A. 1929. The Last Home of Mystery. Garden City, NY:
    Garden City Publishing.

2   William-Grut, O. 2018. 'UBS: Online food delivery could be a $365 billion business by 2030 - here are the winners and losers from that 'mega-trend.'' Business Insider India, 2 July.

3   Hemantmorparia. 12 December 2021. https://www.instagram.com/p/CXYCpq0IRA.

4   Zomato. (2021). Annual Report. https://b.zmtcdn.com/data/file_assets/c61ab5ddd64d7eae77b506b02cc3cc111657860353.pdf; Deepinder, Goyal. 2020. 'Mid Covid-19 Performance Report. Zomato, 10 July. https://blog.zomato.com/performance-report.

5   A family structure common in South Asia where a married son, his wife and children live with his parents in the same house.

6   'Blinkit Lit App.' Blinkit. https://blinkit.com/lit.

7   Siddiqui, Z., Z. Rathnayake and D.M. Sengupta. 2024. 'This cab startup helped 100,000 drivers survive Sri Lanka's economic crisis.' Rest of World, 12 March. https://restofworld.org/2024/sri-lanka-pickme/.

8   Mistry, Rohinton. 1996. *A Fine Balance: A Novel*. United Kingdom: Knopf, p. 131.

9   Roberts, G.D. 2004. *Shantaram*. United Kingdom: Hachette Digital, p. 9.

10 2021. 'KATHMANDU VALLEY METRO PROJECT PROJECT DETAILS [Feasibility Study].' Lead Government Agency Office of the Investment Board and Department of Railways of Ministry of Physical Infrastructure and Transport. https://ibn.gov.np/wp-content/uploads/2020/04/Kathmandu-Valley-Metro-Project.pdf.

11 Kolb, H., et al. 2020. 'Gender-Segregated Transportation in Ride-Hailing: NAVIGATING THE DEBATE.' International Finance Corporation. https://www.ifc.org/content/dam/ifc/doc/mgrt/062020-ifc-gender-segregated-ride-hailing.pdf.

12 2020. 'The World's Women 2020: Trends and Statistics.' United Nations. https://www.un.org/en/desa/world%E2%80%99s-women-2020#:~:text=Presented%20on%20an%20

interactive%20portal,the%20impact%20of%20Covid%2D19.

OPPRESSION

1   Issac M. 2017. 'How Uber deceives authorities worldwide.' *NY Times*, 3 March. https://www.nytimes.com/2017/03/03/technology/uber-greyball-program-evade-authorities.html.

2   2023. 'Central PSUs witness cut in total employment; 2.7 lakh jobs down since 2013.' *Economic Times*, 16 June. https://economictimes.indiatimes.com/jobs/government-jobs/central-psus-witness-cut-in-total-employment-2-7-lakh-jobs-down-since-2013/articleshow/101045509.cms?from=mdr.

3   *'India takes suo motu cognizance of anti-labour practices at one of the warehouses of a multinational company in Haryana's Manesar.'* National Human Rights Commission India.https://nhrc.nic.in/media/press-release/nhrc-india-takes-suo-motu-cognizance-anti-labour-practices-one-warehouses.

4   Brown, A. 2020. 'This Influencer Likened Jeff Bezos' $122 Billion Fortune To Grains Of Rice—And TikTok Ate It Up.' *Forbes*, 5 March. https://www.forbes.com/sites/abrambrown/2020/03/05/this-influencer-likened-jeff-bezos-122-billion-fortune-to-grains-of-rice-and-tik-tok-ate-it-up/.

5   ETtech. 2024. 'Salaries for quick commerce delivery execs higher than food delivery: report.' *Economic Times*, 25 November. https://economictimes.indiatimes.com/tech/technology/salaries-for-quick-commerce-delivery-execs-higher-than-food-delivery-report/articleshow/115659626.cms?from=mdr.

6   Potdukhe, Swapnil. 2024. 'Deep-Dive: Quick Commerce.' JM Financial Institutional Securities Limited.

7   @wa808536. 2024. X (Formerly Twitter). 3 February. https://x.com/wa808536/status/1753693580802343339.

8   2024. 'India probe finds Amazon, Walmart's Flipkart breached antitrust laws.' Reuters, 12 September. https://www.reuters.com/world/india/india-probe-finds-amazon-walmarts-flipkart-breached-antitrust-laws-2024-09-12/.

9   This is a direct quote from a recorded phone interview with Paul Chako (name changed).

10 Seller_v9kW1EwWnBonC. Discussions/ Seller Central/ Amazon.com. (July 2024). https://sellercentral.amazon.com/seller-forums/discussions/t/2a05c42a-94ba-4966-bf63-07b9676c6998. Accessed on 29 December 2024.

11 'The first American factories.' US history Pre Columbian to the new millennium. https://www.ushistory.org/us/25d.asp#:~:text=The%20first%20factory%20in%20the,to%20produce%20spindles%20of%20yarn.

12 Noponen, N., et al. (2023). Taylorism on steroids or enabling autonomy? A systematic review of algorithmic management. Management Review Quarterly. https://doi.org/10.1007/s11301-023-00345-5.

13 Noponen, N., et al. 2024. 'Taylorism on steroids or enabling autonomy? A systematic review of algorithmic management.' Manag Rev Q 74, 1695–1721. https://doi.org/10.1007/s11301-023-00345-5.

14 Chou, Steve. 'The Dangers of Selling on Amazon.' www.mywifequitherjob.com. https://mywifequitherjob.com/the-dangers-of-selling-on-amazon/.

ANXIETY

1   T., Anilkumar. 2021. 'Fast and furious driving by food delivery boys results in road accidents.' New Indian Express, 15 July. https://www.newindianexpress.com/cities/kochi/2021/jul/15/fast-and-furious-driving-by-food-delivery-boys-results-in-road-accidents-2330290.html.

2   Kerr, Dara. 2022. 'More Than 350 Gig Workers Carjacked, 28 Killed, Over the Last Five Years.' The Markup, 28 July. https://themarkup.org/working-for-an-algorithm/2022/07/28/more-than-350-gig-workers-carjacked-28-killed-over-the-last-five-years.

3   Apparasu, S.R. 2023. 'Swiggy delivery boy who jumped off 3rd flood escaping dog attack, dies.' *Hindustan Times,* 16 January. https://www.hindustantimes.com/india-news/swiggy-delivery-boy-who-jumped-off-3rd-flood-escaping-dog-attack-dies-101673870327108.html.

4   Bharathi TV. 2024. 'Hyderabad BN Reddy Nagar Vivek Reddy & Cab Driver incident | BTV [Video].' YouTube, 5 August. https://www.youtube.com/watch?v=NF58V_WTlvc.

5   Murray, S. 2023. 'Ratings systems amplify racial bias on GIG-Economy platforms.' Yale Insights, 14 August. https://insights.som.yale.edu/insights/ratings-systems-amplify-racial-bias-on-gig-economy-platforms.

6   2024. 'Uber beats lawsuit alleging race bias in driver ratings.' Economic Times, 25 June. https://legal.economictimes.indiatimes.com/news/international/uber-beats-lawsuit-alleging-race-bias-in-driver-ratings/111267164.

7   Kubota, Taylor. 2016. 'Researchers from Stanford, MIT and the University of Washington find ride-share drivers discriminate based on race and gender.' Stanford Report, 31 October. https://news.stanford.edu/stories/2016/10/researchers-stanford-mit-university-washington-find-ride-share-drivers-discriminate-based-race-gender.

8   Teeray. 2023. 'The Only Acceptable Rating to Leave an Uber Driver Is 5 Stars | Hacker News.' Y Combinator, 27 June. https://news.ycombinator.com/item?id=36492762.

9   @masculinepath04. 2024. 'Hoffman's past predictions . . .' X (Formerly Twitter). 14 December. https://x.com/masculinepath04/status/1867907724010459357.

ISOLATION

1   2023. 'Jackie Shroff was given a private toilet in his chawl after making it in the movies.' *Indian Express*, 14 October. https://indianexpress.com/article/entertainment/bollywood/jackie-shroff-was-given-a-private-toilet-in-his-chawl-after-making-it-in-the-movies-8653861/.

2   Heidegger, Martin. 1977. 'The Question Concerning Technology.' In Krell, David Farell. *Martin Heidegger: Basic Writings*. New York: Harper & Row, pp. 287–317.

3   Kircaburun, Kagan, et al. 2020. 'The Psychology of Mukbang Watching: A Scoping Review of the Academic and Non-academic Literature.' Springer, 6 January. https://link.springer.com/article/10.1007/s11469-019-00211-0.

4   Terrenghi, Lucia, Hilliges, Otmar & Otmar, Butz, and Andreas. 2007. 'Kitchen stories: Sharing recipes with the Living Cookbook.' *Personal Ubiquitous Comput.* 11. 409-. 10.1007/s00779-006-0079-2.

5   Runa, Jason and Harpring, Julie and Rafiuddin, Moe and Zhu, and Miaoqi. 2010. 'Not Enough Cooks in the Kitchen.'

6   Jangir, Chanchal. LinkedIn. https://www.linkedin.com/posts/chanchal-jangir-2b1656177_worklifebalance-worklifebalance-workingfromhome-activity-7081888090822164481-f6Xj?utm_source=share&utm_medium=member_desktop.

7   Marcuse, Herbert. 2012. *One-Dimensional Man: Studies in the Ideology of Advanced Industrial Society*. Beacon Press.

8   Montag, A. 2017. 'How a janitor went from cleaning floors to the C-suite as a 6-figure tech exec.' CNBC, 22 September. https://www.cnbc.com/2017/09/21/gail-evans-went-from-janitor-to-executive-at-microsoft-and-mercer.html.

COURAGE

1   2022. 'Wolt's Algorithmic Transparency Report.' Wolt. https://assets.ctfassets.net/23u853certza/5G5O7KF

nwzDGWzE1JFwCN/aa06955650eaef4a1e0917a257ade688/
Wolt_Algorithmic_Transparency_Report_2022.pdf.

2   Van Neils, Doorn. 2024. 'On the inadequacy of Wolt's
    algorithmic transparency report and the limits of algorithmic
    management discourse.' Platform Labor, 24 October.
    https://platformlabor.net/blog/on-the-inadequacy-of-
    wolts-algorithmic-transparency-report-and-the-limits-of-
    algorithmic-management-discourse.

3   2023. 'Amazon hit by strikes, protests across Europe during
    Black Friday.' Reuters, 24 November. https://www.reuters.
    com/technology/amazon-protests-europe-target-warehouses-
    lockers-busy-black-friday-2023-11-24/.

4   2022. 'Amazon Prime Day strikes sweep Europe, expose dire
    warehouse working conditions.' UNI Global Union, 7 February.
    https://uniglobalunion.org/news/amazon-prime-day-strikes-
    sweep-europe-expose-dire-warehouse-working-conditions/.

5   2024. 'Bernie Sanders report exposes Amazon's 'outrageous
    injury levels' during Prime Day season.' UNI Global Union, 25
    July. https://uniglobalunion.org/news/bernie-sanders-report/.

6   Raj, Aiswarya. 2024. "'No Way Out of This Place': Life as an
    Amazon Warehouse Worker." *Indian Express*, June 29. https://
    indianexpress.com/article/long-reads/no-way-out-of-this-
    place-life-as-an-amazon-warehouse-worker-9421948/.

7   IANS. 2018. 'Nepal's new 'crown prince' gets a Christmas
    reprieve.' Deccan Herald, 3 May. https://www.deccanherald.
    com/world/nepals-crown-prince-gets-christmas-2538691.

8   'Open Data.' https://nammayatri.in/open?cc=&riders=All&
    rides=All&tl=at. Last accessed on 29 April 2025.

9   Singh, P. 2023. [@parrysingh]. X.com., 28 March. https://x.
    com/parrysingh/status/1814217926590996844.

10 Parthasarathy, Balaji, and Janaki Srinivasan et al. 2023. 'Labour
    Standards in the Indian Platform Economy. Fairworks India
    Ratings.' Fairwork. https://fair.work/wp-content/uploads/
    sites/17/2023/10/Fairwork-India-Ratings-2023-English.pdf.

LIGHTS, CAMERA, ACTION: REGULATING THE DIGITAL STAGE

1   Sundararajan, A. 2016. *The Sharing Economy: The End of Employment and the Rise of Crowd-Based Capitalism.* MIT Press Books, p. 7. https://ideas.repec.org/b/mtp/titles/0262034573.html.

2   Centre for Labour Research. Linkedin. https://www.linkedin.com/posts/clrpakistan_foodpanda-heatwave-swiggy-activity-7212062586035445760-ibgT?utm_source=share&utm_medium=member_desktop.

3   Le, Lam, and Zuha Siddiqui. 2024. 'Catching a break: How gig workers find rest.' Rest of World, 19 March. https://restofworld.org/2024/gig-worker-rest-breaks/.

4   Kambiri, K. 2024. 'Zomato appeals amid heatwave: Don't order in 'peak afternoon'; food delivery executives react.' *Hindustan Times,* 4 June. https://www.hindustantimes.com/htcity/htcity-delhi-junction/zomato-appeals-amid-heatwave-dont-order-in-peak-afternoon-food-delivery-executives-react-101717403348030.html.

5   Kalra, Aditya. 2021. 'Inside Amazon's secret strategy to dodge India e-commerce regulations.' *Economic Times,* 17 February. https://economictimes.indiatimes.com/tech/technology/amazon-documents-reveal-its-secret-strategy-to-dodge-india-regulators/articleshow/81059533.cms?from=mdr.

6   Raman, Raghu. 2018. 'The power of India #unInc: Management secrets from India's.' YouTube, 17 May. https://www.youtube.com/watch?v=yQGaoj9Iwro.

7   2024. 'Growth of e-commerce should be citizen centric: Union Minister Shri Piyush Goyal.' https://pib.gov.in/PressReleasePage.aspx?PRID=2047233.

8   Prasain, Krishana. 2024. 'Ride-hailing guidelines uncertain despite court order.' *Kathmandu Post,* 30 August. https://kathmandupost.com/money/2024/08/30/ride-hailing-

guidelines-uncertain-despite-court-order#:~:text=On%
20February%201%2C%20the%20government,\ride%
2Dhailing%20guidelines%20appear%20nowhere.

9   Gulati, T. 2024. 'Telangana IAS spells Singham-like fear among
    restaurants—fined Paradise, suspended BigBasket.' ThePrint,
    11   July.   https://theprint.in/ground-reports/a-telangana-ias-
    officer-spells-singham-like-fear-among-restaurants-he-fined-
    paradise-suspended-bigbasket/2168810/.

10 Jain, V. 2023. 'Redditor claims unhygienic working condition
    at cloud kitchen.' Hindustan Times, 18 April. https://www.
    hindustantimes.com/trending/redditor-claims-unhygienic-
    working-conditions-at-a-bengaluru-based-cloud-kitchen-see-
    pics-101681791677408.html.

11 Eyring, A., and Union of Concerned Scientists. 'Ride-
    Hailing's Climate Risks.' https://www.ucsusa.org/sites/default/
    files/2020-02/Ride-Hailing%27s-Climate-Risks.pdf.

12 Agarwal, S. 2023. 'The Impact of Ride-Hailing Services on
    Congestion: Evidence from Indian Cities.' Manufacturing &
    Service Operations Management, 25–25(3): 862–83. https://
    www.heinz.cmu.edu/~rtelang/msom.2022.1158-1.pdf.

13 Jenn, A. 2020. 'Emissions benefits of electric vehicles in Uber
    and Lyft ride-hailing services.' Nat Energy 5: 520–25. https://
    doi.org/10.1038/s41560-020-0632-7.

14 Slowik, P., Wappelhorst, S. and N. Lutsey. 2019. 'How can
    taxes and fees on ride-hailing fleets steer them to electrify.'
    International Council on Clean Transportation. https://theicct.
    org/wp-content/uploads/2021/06/EV_TNC_ridehailing_
    wp_20190919.pdf.

15 2023. 'Quick commerce: The burgeoning growth story of
    E-commerce.' India Employer Forum, 25 May. https://
    indiaemployerforum.org/quick-commerce-the-burgeoning-
    growth-story-of-e-commerce/.

16 Raiser, M. 2024. 'South Asia needs more women in the
    workforce.' World Bank Blogs, 16 March. https://blogs.

worldbank.org/en/voices/south-asia-needs-more-women-workforce#:~:text=And%20yet%20their%20participation%20in,and%20developing%20economies%20(EMDEs).

17 Vasudevan. V., M.M. Alam, and Dharmendra Kumar. 2024. 'The RIGHTS Survey – Report on a nationwide survey of platform workers in India.'

18 Siddiqui, Zuha. 2023. 'Why women in Pakistan are quitting gig work.' Rest of the World, 24 August. https://restofworld.org/2023/gig-work-women-in-pakistan-quitting/.

19 Roy, A. 2024. 'How India is using the Internet.' *Economic Times,* 10 March. https://economictimes.indiatimes.com/tech/technology/how-india-is-using-the-internet/articleshow/108354854.cms?from=mdr.

20 Jeffrie, N. 2022. 'The mobile gender gap in South Asia is now widening.' GSMA, 8 December. https://www.gsma.com/solutions-and-impact/connectivity-for-good/mobile-for-development/blog/the-mobile-gender-gap-in-south-asia-is-now-widening/.

21 'Population estimates and projections | DataBank.' World Bank group. https://databank.worldbank.org/source/population-estimates-and-projections/preview/on#.

22 2022. 'India's Booming Gig and Platform Economy: Perspectives and Recommendations on the Future of Work; Socio-economic Impact Assessment of Food Delivery Platform Workers National Council of Applied Economic Research (August 2023).' NITI Aayog. https://www.ncaer.org/wp-content/uploads/2023/08/NCAER_Report_Platform_Workers_August_28_2023.pdf; Mathew, B. 2024. 'Report on Working and Living Conditions of App-based workers in India [Report].' PAIGAM, University of Pennsylvania. https://tgpwu.org/wp-content/uploads/2024/03/Report-Final-Print-1.pdf.

23 Shahid, A.S. 2023. 'Alibaba-backed Asian group Daraz cuts workforce 11%' Reuters, 7 February. https://www.reuters.com/

technology/alibaba-backed-pakistani-e-commerce-platform-daraz-cuts-workforce-by-11-2023-02-07/.

24 2023. 'Daraz CEO Bjarke Mikkelsen's Message to Daraz Employees — Daraz.' Daraz, 6 February. https://daraz.com/newsroom/daraz-ceo-bjarke-mikkelsens-message-to-daraz-employees/.

25 Pugh, A.J. 2024. *The Last Human Job: The Work of Connecting in a Disconnected World.* Princeton University Press.

26 Berry, Chris. 'Plato's influence on literature.' Purdue University College of Liberal Arts. https://www.cla.purdue.edu/academic/english/theory/webring/berryPlato.html.

27 Heidegger, Martin. 1977. 'The Question Concerning Technology.' In Krell, David Farell (ed.) Martin Heidegger: Basic Writings. New York: Harper & Row. pp. 287–317.

28 Piven, Ben. 2019. 'Rebelling Against Attention Economy, Humane Tech Movement Expands.' Al Jazeera, July 25. https://www.aljazeera.com/economy/2019/7/25/rebelling-against-attention-economy-humane-tech-movement-expands.

29 Thomson, Iain D. 2025. 'Heidegger on Technology's Danger and Promise in the Age of AI.' https://doi.org/10.1017/9781009629423.

30 'Gitanjali 37.' Academy of American Poets (1916). Poets.org. https://poets.org/poem/gitanjali-37.

INDEX

Scan QR code to access the
Penguin Random House India website